Empire and Beyond

T0374906

Empire and Beyond

Antonio Negri

Translated by Ed Emery

polity

First published in Italian as *Movimenti nell'Impero* © Raffaello Cortina Editore, 2006.

This English edition © Polity Press, 2008

Polity Press
65 Bridge Street
Cambridge CB2 1UR, UK

Polity Press
350 Main Street
Malden, MA 02148, USA

ISBN-13: 978-0-7456-4047-1
ISBN-13: 978-0-7456-4048-8(pb)

A catalogue record for this book is available from the British Library.

Typeset in 10.5 on 12 pt Plantin
by Servis Filmsetting Ltd, Stockport, Cheshire
Printed and bound in Great Britain by MPG Books Ltd, Bodmin, Cornwall

The publisher has used its best endeavours to ensure that the URLs for external websites referred to in this book are correct and active at the time of going to press. However, the publisher has no responsibility for the websites and can make no guarantee that a site will remain live or that the content is or will remain appropriate.

Every effort has been made to trace all copyright holders, but if any have been inadvertently overlooked the publishers will be pleased to include any necessary credits in any subsequent reprint or edition.

For further information on Polity, visit our website: www.polity.co.uk

Contents

Contents

Preface

I was finally discharged from all juridical proceedings, and from the ties and complications of my state of semi-liberty, on 25 April 2003. I received my passport on 11 June. After twenty-five years (eleven years in prison and fourteen in exile), I was able to start travelling in the world again. In the space of about a year and a half (the period covered by the texts published here), I embarked on several trips around Europe, and I must have travelled the equivalent of around the world twice over. Advancing years and infirmity prevented me from doing more. But I wanted to, and this desire has stayed with me . . . You will see it as you read these pages, which gather together some of the talks I delivered in the course of 2003–4 and give a good sense of my political restlessness during that period. These writings look at 'movements' in Empire. What I talk about here is not (or at least is only incidentally) movements as such; rather, I discuss their articulations and the alternatives they produce, as well as the ordering mechanisms and resistances which inhabit Empire. These passages become landscapes, up and down, here and there . . . Here we have objective movements and subjective behaviours that cannot be set in line. Anyone trying to impose linearity on them would almost always be mistaken. That is not what I am trying to do, nor do I want to lay down rigid causal relationships between movements. What I am trying to do is to react with them in respect of what the historical process proposes . . . In other words, Empire exists. Albeit perhaps only in tendency, but it is there. So how do we move within it? How does one move within a tendency? What can be done and what cannot be done? The year 2003–4 was crucial, 'fateful' to a certain degree. In my series of journeys and in the public meetings which I addressed en route, I tried to put words and events into short-circuit, in order to verify – both among friends and among enemies, and always in the real – the possibility (and occasionally the *potenza*) of constructuing truth. I can say that we are seeing, day by day, the truth of our action, and any theoretical work which does not confront itself continuously with the living and political nature of reality is pointless. In that fateful year, when the planetary clash between the imperial aristocracies manifested itself definitively in Iraq, we had the confirmation of the tendency of Empire to represent itself in plural terms, and hence a hypothesis founded on the construction of a global anti-imperial multitude became a real possibility. These writings are not homogeneous. The speeches published here, in a manageable volume, are not the totality of the work I produced during those years. I have gone through the texts and edited out duplicate material, but the reader may notice repetitions. This is inevitable, I suppose, given that some of the texts were delivered off the cuff. Nevertheless I believe that, however disorderly, these texts give a sense of the development of my critical thinking during the various stages in which they were composed and around the various topics which were addressed, before a variety of publics. These writings gather and deepen the reflections developed in *Empire* and *Multitude*, and in some instances extend them and open new hypotheses. However, in this volume only rarely do I push forward, moving beyond the positions developed in *Empire* and *Multitude*, for the simple reason that those two books already represented a maximum of utopian *potenza* and performative intentionality.

So we can say that this book has a certain orderly disorder. I have sought to organize it around four broad parts, addressing themes of (a) Empire; (b) Europe; (c) post-socialist politics; and (d) political philosophy in imperial postmodernity. Just as *Reflections on Empire* [Polity, 2008] was an attempt to go further into various discussions arising from *Empire* and *Multitude*, this present volume is a stage in the work that leads from *Multitude* to . . . well, we have not yet decided on the title of the third book in this series. However, I do know that we have to move the research forward, on the subjective dimensions of transformation and on the ontological determinations of the revolutionary condition. The topic of revolution is back on the agenda. The crisis of neo-liberalism (and of the repressive forces which it has called into being, including those of Islamic fundamentalism) opens no new reformist perspectives, nor does it offer us sublime horizons which we might eventually reach. After this crisis all we are left with is the desperation of poverty and the tension of love, united with a determination to rebuild the world, in the certainty (which the defeat of neo-liberalism once again reveals) that 'another world is possible'.

So these are, in a sense, travel writings. Hard to know exactly what the journey is and where we are headed. However, this journey is utterly profound – something approaching an anthropological meta-morphosis.

I would like to thank the many friends who have contributed to these voyages and to the discussions and the critical novelty of some of the passages therein. In particular I thank Éric Alliez and Michael Hardt for permission to publish two texts which were jointly written with them.

I also thank the directors of the scientific and cultural institutions, in so many parts of the world, for their great generosity in allowing me to address the meetings in question, and to begin to construct, together with students and militants, a new critical *koine*.

PART ONE
EMPIRE AND BEYOND

1

The Empire and Beyond: Aporias and Contradictions*

Empire is an open tendency. In defining it we use three basic analytical approaches: the first examines the phenomenology of globalization; the second looks at the crisis of the nation–state; and the third traces the transformations in social ontology – that is, in material labour, in productive cooperation and in the consequent constitution of a biopolitical horizon.

When we take the view that Empire is an attempt at a sovereign ordering of economic globalization, our attention is drawn to three central phenomena: the breakdown of the colonial order and the precarity of the postcolonial order; the end of the crisis and the division of the world-wide market brought about by actually existing socialism; and the epic impact of migratory phenomena.

When we examine the crisis of the nation–state, we take the position that the modern constitution of the nation–state, in which the exercise of sovereignty is based on closed territorial spaces and a system of international law built on contractual relationships between nation–states (the 'Westphalian' system), has now gone into major crisis. This crisis affects the most fundamental characteristics of the power of the nation–state, namely military, monetary and cultural sovereignty.

Where we speak of the transformation of social ontology, what we are saying is that the quality of capitalist accumulation comes to be fundamentally altered in the post-Fordist and post-industrial phase by the emergence of immaterial labour (i.e. intellectual, affective, relational and linguistic labour) as a central element in the creation of value.

---

* Talk given at the Faculty of Sociology, University of Frankfurt, 3 October 2003.

When the whole of a society is put to work, the basic source of productivity becomes social cooperation. The real subsumption of society by capital means that the entirety of social life is caught up in capitalist relations: when, in Marxian terms, we see capital as a relationship between exploiters and the exploited, we understand that it is life itself which is being exploited. Capital and the sovereign state present themselves as bio-power; the context in which they act is defined as the biopolitical context; exploitation extends into people's modes of living; and the desire for liberation extends over every aspect of society.

Is Empire (the first question we would like to raise) primarily a political structure, or does the economic dimension predominate in its definition?

In answering this we need to mount a critique of the hypertrophy of the political which late-socialist conceptions (particularly those of 'real socialism', for instance the theory of state monopoly capitalism) have handed down to us. The relationship between the economic structure and the political structure is never in reality linear, but the fact that it is not linear does not mean that there is not a homogeneity in the relationship between the political order and productive command. It is obvious that the dynamics of capital's breaking of the resistances effected by the working class (both at the economic and at the political level), within the cycle of struggles in modernity, is extremely ductile, and these processes of breaking are followed by a rearrangement in the mode of production and in relations between classes; for us this is a confirmation of the interaction between the economic and the political. The same thing happens when we look to the global level, that is, the world-wide restructuring of capitalist development carried out by Empire. The breakings and rearrangements remain fundamentally ductile, and the hierarchies between markets are continuously being reshaped and rebuilt. As I said, any image of Empire which is not mobile and based on tendency ends up being unable to understand the dynamics of the process: this confirms the interaction between the economic and the political.

Now, the structure of the system of Empire is articulated in terms of space and time.

From the spatial point of view it is obvious that any idea of capitalist development and accumulation at the global level which regards the relationship between the centre and the periphery as fixed risks failing to grasp the real dynamics of the process. The centre and the periphery in fact become increasingly intertwined in the process which establishes the global market and Empire. The great transition from modernity to postmodernity, in terms of the way global space is envisioned, consists precisely in a relative flattening out of spatial differences. Instead of a 'centre' (of capitalist ordering), the theory of Empire argues for the existence of a 'non-place' (of formation of command over the global articulations of production). This enables us, among other things, to steer clear of pointless controversies over 'Americanism or anti-Americanism', and instead to make the élites of accumulation and domination, wherever they appear and no matter how they concert their unitary action, engage in the capitalist polemic. At the imperial and global level, on a horizon which (as we have stated) embraces both political direction and economic domination, the dynamics of the system cannot be considered in dialectical terms (where, for instance, the nation–state is periodically called on to function as a limit or proposal in the face of the global market); neither can they simply be thought of in functional terms (functionalism – starting from a dialectical viewpoint which is anyway institutionalized – regards positively movements of resistance broadly defined as anti-systemic): our perspective is that only the antagonistic dynamics is valid on this terrain.

From the temporal point of view – that is, in terms of periodization – the entry into the age of Empire implies processes which are irreversible. These irreversible processes are not to be interpreted within a traditional vision of cyclical development, nor should they be viewed in the light of theories of stages. There no longer exists a possibility of reversing these global dynamics. There may well be different and contradictory phases, generated by partial cycles of struggles, but from now on they can only be interpreted within the unity of the global picture. The non-place is seen in temporal terms, as a period of transition, of exchanges, of struggles. There may well be ruptures in Empire, but they will take place within Empire. The object of contention will be nothing other than imperial command.

When we lay out the issues in these terms, they are bound to be controversial. But controversy is welcome if it develops in global terms, in other words within a perspective of the development of Empire. In the case of Germany, there have been three basic controversies arising out of the publication of *Empire*. The first relates to the quality, or rather the tone, of the analysis: what kind of book is *Empire*? The second relates to the relation between transformations in social ontology and the definition of multitude as the tendential subject of antagonism. The third has to do with the present moment in history – what is the intensity of the historical transition which we are witnessing, how strong is the 'post' in post-Fordism, post-Keynesianism, post-modernism and so on?

Let us take the first question: what kind of book is *Empire*? People ask us whether the function of these theses is prophetic, analytical or critical. I reply that the three cannot be separated and that, when considered together, they lose any apodeictic quality: the critique is perfected in the analysis, and the forecast (without being prophetic) is consolidated on the definition of the historical movement. Actually, the only question that has interested me is this: in such a situation (of transition), in the face of the reality of globalization and considering the strength of class movements in bringing about the crisis and the transition beyond modernity, is it possible to recompose a materialist *telos*, a collective purpose, with a view to creating a revolutionary discourse around which a political subject can be rebuilt? If a 'grand narrative' is necessary to this end (against all the prohibitions and excommunications put up by 'weak postmodernism'), then this enterprise should be accepted. And it has to be accepted for one particular reason: because, in the situation of postmodernity, the subjectivity of labour has become central in the processes of accumulation. This means that any project has to be situated within the movement of class struggle, since the movement of class struggle no longer needs an external vanguard to make it act. So Empire is not a political manifesto but a voice which narrates, from within the class struggle, its new urgencies and gives a first sketch of a postmodern revolution.

From here we can move immediately to the second issue, the relationship between the emergence of immaterial labour and the construction of the concept of multitude. It is clear that the notion of immaterial labour is not simply a redefinition of old-style productive labour but a biopolitical concept of new intensity. Immaterial labour is an amalgam between productive labour and ways of life. It is the multitudinarian ensemble of multiple singularities, of multiple differences, all inserted within a context of life that has become productive. Immaterial labour produces not only goods but also corporeality; it produces not only relations but also cooperation; not only institutions but also, in all probability, revolution. If we do not accept the concept of immaterial labour in these terms (obviously, rather than the not particularly felicitous term 'immaterial' we could choose others), then we fail to understand the intensity of the transition we are living. The concept of immaterial labour has also been subjectively understood as a concept of 'mass intellectuality'. The critical genesis of the concept involved various attempts at analysing the decisive functions of intellectuality in the value creation of productive labour, in the forms in which those functions are being constructed today. However, while that definition is essential, it is not enough to determine the generalization of the new intellectual proletariat, its social figure of rupture, and to give this new class figure a biopolitical dimension. It is therefore necessary to address immaterial labour (and the 'multitude' subject configured within it) beyond the definitions of 'mass-worker', 'socialized worker', 'mass intellectuality' and all the other subject positions of the workerist tradition. The subjective figure of immaterial labour is tendentially biopolitical. It is no longer a figure of discipline but a figure of control; it is no longer a figure, simply, of production, but also of reproduction, communication, relationships, modes of life and so on. It is in taking this assumption as our starting point that the concept of multitude comes to be constructed: no longer as an insurrectionary mass, no longer as an institutional species such as 'people' or 'nation', but as a *potenza* [potentiality] of generation, social and full of life.

But – and here is now a third theme – how do all these concepts represent themselves in a given historical moment, that is, in the here and now? Is this a situation of transition, of crisis – in other words, a revolutionary situation? Is the concept of multitude inserted in an open transition, between materiality and immateriality, between discipline and control, between modernity and postmodernity; or is it constrained within the closed passage of a new capitalist control over life and over the global dimensions of the accumulation processes? Obviously, the answer to this question has to be discursive. We have on the one hand an epochal transition marked by the birth of Empire. In this transition there are struggles between the Empire and the 'counter-empire', but also between the various global aristocracies. Capitalism has still not formed a coherent sovereign capacity at the global level: this is only its tendency. But the tendency is still a moment of crisis, of transition, of consolidations and ruptures. In this situation the relationship of the multitude with Empire is in any event a revolutionary relationship. For there to be insurrection, the modernist concept of revolution required a hegemony and a generalization of a particular class interest. Here, however, we have a contradiction which is articulated indefinitely on the rhythm of the emergence of multiple singularities (and, naturally, on the articulations and times of conflicts within the dominant capitalism). Our research and strategic proposals need to take stock of these variations and contradictions.

2

An Axiomatics for Empire*

Empire is a process of constitution of sovereignty – a new sovereignty – over the global market. We have to say that there is no such thing as a market which does not require regulation, and there is no greater mystification than the notion that the market is capable of self-regulation. When the market becomes global, it requires a regulation which is also global.

If we accept this, then we immediately have the problem of understanding what sovereignty means and what global capitalism means. Now, sovereignty is always a relationship between those who command and those who obey; and capital is also always a relationship, between those who exploit and those who are exploited. Between these two relationships, ever since modern bourgeois power was first constructed, there is a deep homology. Here, however, we prefer to address this question no longer simply from the viewpoint of the dominant categories but from a critical point of view. What does critical mean here? It means seeing the sovereign relation and the capital relation as being not closed but critically open, as relations and balances of power which are periodically modified on the basis of productions of material life – that is, of modes of life – and of figures of subjectivity.

In dealing with these questions we effect a methodological synthesis between the theoretical traditions of Italian workerism and French post-structuralism – a fruitful synthesis, which did not emerge simply from the desks of philosophers but which had both its resonances and its development in the proletarian struggles of the twentieth century. Here the historical method is founded on 'rendering autonomous'

---

* Talk given at the Ministry of Culture, Rio de Janeiro, 30 October 2003.

social movements as subjects; on a conception of historical causality which sees the process of transformation as being always open, both at the micropolitical and at the macropolitical and institutional level. Finally, our historical method will be grounded in a specific periodization which sees in the transformations of society and institutions, both those of sovereignty and those of capital, a continually open alternation between struggles and restructurings, between intensities of conflict and new consolidations.

More specifically: the workerist analysis of the transformation of labour (from the mass worker to the socialized worker, from material labour to immaterial labour) encountered the post-structuralist analysis of French political philosophy, and particularly its notions of bio-power and biopolitics. This means that from the conditions of material production to the production of subjectivity there runs a red thread which locates transformations in the social ontology of labour (immaterial labour and informatic cooperation) in a biopolitical horizon. When we say biopolitical, we mean that the entirety of life is subsumed by capital, that the value creation of capital comes about through the whole of society being set to work, and that therefore all social and life relations are drawn into the relationship of production. At the same time, however, we also say that the contradictions of exploitation become diffused throughout the fabric of society. And finally we say that, when capital subsumes in real terms the productive potential of society, it integrates it into a bio-power which is extended over the whole of society. It is from this moment that the forms of exploitation are transformed, since they are now exercised not only over the material and technological dimensions of production, but also over the intellectual and living dimensions of society's productive subjects. Exploitation has become biopolitical.

Now we need to combine our analysis of this new productive structure with that of the phenomena of globalization, the ending of the South's structural dependency on the North, and the crisis of the nation–state, including – and above all – the crisis of the central nation–states. We need to read these objective dimensions in the light of the postcultural and postcolonial analyses of the phenomena of migration and of the hierarchical reclassification of productive spaces at the global level, and also in the light of the consequences of the crisis of real socialism and of its national and international structures, both subjective and historical. This is the postmodernity within which a new political axiomatics is posed, since all the political and philosophical concepts handed down by modernity are now in crisis: from sovereignty to the nation–state, from citizenship to the working class, from borders to migration, from political subjectivity to massification of struggles, from dependency to Third Worldism and so forth.

This linguistic and conceptual transformation needs now to be set alongside a new dynamic. This dynamic is and will undoubtedly continue to be contradictory in the forms in which it expresses itself, but it is and will certainly continue to be homogeneous and uniform, inasmuch as its space of reference is by now purely and simply global. The processes of globalization are transversal, and thus affect all the realities that constitute the global fabric: Empire as structure and Empire as process both lie under the same blanket.

Thus within the imperial tendency there are to be found new contradictions and new processes of liberation. In the modern European tradition there has been a conflict between two conceptions of modernity and democracy. One, the victorious one, has operated with the notion of the 'autonomy of the political', in other words, the autonomy of sovereignty and the nation–state as a synthesis of bourgeois politics and the economic power of capital. The disasters that this ideological position and this material constitution have brought about are plain to see: from the fratricidal wars at the heart of capitalist development to the spread of colonialism and imperialism over the whole planet. The other conception, forever being defeated but always coming back to life, has been that of 'absolute democracy', that is, a collective demand for 'government by everyone, for everyone', for a life which is organized socially, through the organization of the masses. This alternative conception of democracy has been a living and active force right at the heart of capitalist development. It is the clash of these two conceptions (and of the practices that derived from them) as well as the unceasing protest and revolt of proletarians that have shattered the structure of the modern state. Now, at the worldwide level the imperial tendency is met by, and gradually counterposed by, a tendency which is 'counter-imperial'. Capital is forced by the insistence of proletarian struggles to constitute Empire. Sovereignty and capital were unable to contain struggles within the territorial spaces of their traditional dominion: it is for this reason that the globalization of economic and political relations is now being attempted. What is being revealed here is a situation which is strange, ambiguous and perverse, but nevertheless powerful: capital's ability to survive depends once again on shifting the limits, forms and spaces of struggles, albeit at the same time one also has to endure them and to be constrained by them. From this point of view, Empire can be seen as capitalism running ahead of itself, and this suits the proletariat, because in Empire the dimensions, forms, intensity and consistency of the transformations can come to have a cosmopolitical force – embodied in principles of freedom and equality that apply to all, and in that revolution which is no longer international but global, the dream and desire of every exploited person.

Naturally, among the capitalist élites the perception of this global shift of power goes hand in hand with an awareness of conflict. The dynamics of constituting imperial sovereignty thus goes hand in hand with a dynamics of breaking up and rearranging the mode of production and the new configuration of domination over class relationships globally. The processes of disciplining the national working classes give way to new structures of control, which have to be exercised over the ways of life and the networks of micropowers and – on the other hand – over the transnational, imperial processes of development of the structure of power.

At this point we come up against the very basic problem of how to resist imperial bio-power and how to transform the new global order, acting from within and moving no longer as national working classes and proletariats but as multitudes.

However, before going on to deal with this I want to make another couple of points. The first relates to the form of the system which capital offers us in this imperial phase. It has a precise constitutional figure: it is a 'mixed constitution'. Empire is a combination of sovereignty, aristocracy and democracy. In other words it consists in the structure of forces which are being constituted around these three apexes. The hierarchical structuring of Empire works by articulating three levels of power: first, the American monarchic level, which claims military, monetary and cultural hegemony. Facing that we have an aristocracy which extends its operations, subject to contradictions but effectively, over all the spaces of world-wide production – by this I mean the big capitalist multinationals, based on financial systems which by now have lost any national colouring; there are also the remnants of the large nation–states which work to create alliances in order to partipate effectively in the restructuring of the central command organs of political power in Empire. All this has already created moments of irreversible crisis of international law and has introduced new problematics for sovereign centralization within Empire. All these problems remain open. We have seen a continuous experimentation in the search for an eventual hegemonic imperial form. It is beyond doubt that following 11 September 2001 the US government was attempting a kind of *coup d'état*, to reduce the complexity of the imperial mixed constitution and to bring its command back under the governing structures of the United States. In all probability this operation will not succeed. The problem of the constitutional figure of imperial sovereignty, not so much in its form but more in the material dimension of the relations between the forces which constitute it, is still open and will remain so for a long time to come.

A second consideration, before returning to the concept of multitude and counter-empire. This has to do with the countries of the so-called 'Third World'. In modernity's system of imperialism and colonialism, these were in a subaltern position; they were closed within a structural dependency which put limits on their political and economic systems (not to mention their subjection to colonial anthropology and its disastrous effects). However, this situation has now changed radically. In the postmodern schema of Empire and its tendency, dependency is replaced by interdependence. It is not a gift from God, this interdependence, but a product of struggles: of workers' struggles first of all, but also of the independent cultural insurgencies of the subjected countries, the revolts of indigenous peoples, the desire for 'another modernity' than that imposed by imperialism. It is not God-given, this interdependence; rather, it is the product (contradictory and irreversible) of the development of struggles and of globalization, of the centralization of command and of the hybridization of the colonial and/or capitalist ruling classes, of the universality of capital versus the difference of the multitudes. Here too we measure the great opposition to Empire characteristic of our times. It is also here that a new historical causality has come about: that of anticolonial resistance, of anti-imperialist struggles. The latter have not been defeated (despite the pessimism of some of the accounts that describe them), nor have they been simply recuperated into the dynamics of globalization: they have provoked a global shift of power towards globalization.

The counter-empire is the multitude. We already know what the multitude is not: it is not 'the people', in other words a unity constructed by sovereign command; it is not class, in other words a unity constructed by capitalist exploitation; it is not nation, in other words a unity ideologically constructed by those same powers and directed against enemies in other nations. It is, furthermore, not an undifferentiated mass: rather, the multitude is an ensemble of productive singularities set to work and – as such – productive. It stands against that power which continually seeks to shift the levels of its operation (today, from the national to the global), and against that power which sets up new mythologies in order to create social cohesion and to identify the enemy (today, terrorism).

Against all this, we can begin to describe the multitude as a *potenza* of production, as a statement of singularity and as a force of anthropological metamorphosis. But we shall succeed in doing this only if we see the concept of multitude in terms that are militant and creative. In fact multitude is not only a capacity for production (although it is this, and hegemonically so); it is not only a new way of living (increasingly intellectual and cooperative), although it is this too; above all, it is the production of political subjectivity. The multitude, in the new conditions of existence of the proletariat, is a promise of democracy. Of an absolute democracy, of a government by all and for all. Utopia, some will say. But it is actual experience too – the experience of people engaged in production who can live only in freedom and in the production of truth, the experience of an ensemble of bodies which can offer themselves to life only as cooperative association. Finally, is not every singularity a multitude? Is there not, within every change that happens at the global level, a universal *métissage* which configures new subjectivities?

3
Crucial Transitions in Empire*

I shall begin this talk, which addresses some basic transitions in the political theory of Empire and the multitude, by dealing with three traditional positions in the Marxist conception of class, party and state. These positions are the following: there is no class without party; there is no politics without the state; and the political is always posited as independent from the economic.

Let us examine these statements one at a time, starting with the second – that there is no politics without the state. In the more advanced positions of orthodox Marxism it is assumed that capital constitutes itself as (the organization of a) relationship between exploiters and exploited, between the working class and the employers. However, sovereignty is always conceived of as a forced mediation – on the part of capital – of this relationship. This means that capital is a relationship, but sovereignty and the state are not: they constitute the solution of the capital relationship. Two consequences arise from this. The first is that the working class can represent itself at the institutional level only when it expresses itself through the party, in other words when it itself becomes political. The second is that sovereignty, the state and politics will always have a very high degree of autonomy. The state expresses norms that have no direct (let alone immediate) relationship with the class struggle.

We, on the other hand, maintain that capital and sovereignty have a very close relationship and that, in the present situation, the recognition of the duality of the relationship involved in capital must also include the recognition of the dual nature of the sovereignty

---

* Talk given at the Socialist Youth Federation, University of Vienna, 11 November 2003.

relationship. When capital is forced by struggles into a change (not only structural but also historical and determined – that is, when it is forced to pass from the regime of discipline to that of control), at that same moment the political nature of capital also changes, and thus both the concept and the practice of sovereignty change. This transition, we stress, is not simply structural (in fact capital has never been anything other than a relationship), but determined and effective: it is the outcome of the changes in the balance of forces between capital and class, it is the correlation of the deepening and generalization of class conflict in the transition from the processes of accumulation and valorization based on the factory and industrial labour to the processes of accumulation and valorization based on setting the whole of society to work. The subsumption of society by capital, rather than closing the contradictions of exploitation, actually extends them indefinitely over the entire social terrain.

We have an example of this transformation, which entails essentially the total loss of autonomy of the political, when we analyse the phase in which we live. This is a phase in which the various forces which constitute imperial power inhabit a contradictory interregnum. The processes of change in the capital relation (in all its forms, that is, both intercapitalist and in relation to the class struggle) are immediately reflected in the changes taking place in sovereignty. It was the victory of the subordinated classes around 1968 that shifted the axis of dominion from discipline to control, in other words from the statement of the unilateral power of capital to the recognition of an intrinsic duality in the sovereignty relationship, to be recuperated into forms of government. Already the crisis of 1929, and the ensuing Keynesian techniques of management of economic and political power, had given a glimpse of this new experience. But it is only after 1968 that both the capital relationship and the sovereignty relationship enter into overall crisis. How does this crisis manifest itself, and in what forms does it develop? Here is not the place to reiterate the historical and political reconstruction that we have outlined in *Empire*. It is sufficient to say that workers' struggles, anticolonial struggles, the anti-globalization movements and the movements against 'real Socialism' had a direct impact on the national and international organization of labour. They have created a crisis in the nation–state's ability to discipline labour, to measure the productivity of the workforce, to extend colonial dominion over the classes and the territories it subordinates, and to fix an imperialist hierarchy of exploitation. The struggles of 1968 overturned the economic and political order which modernity had given us. The wages form is de facto transcended.

Sovereignty is no longer one and single; like capital, it too is a relationship or, better, a crisis.

Now let us examine things from a historical point of view, in terms of historical periodization. What was happening? Labour power had revealed itself as an immaterial *potenza*. Labour was presenting itself increasingly as a capacity which was linguistic, intellectual, affective and relational. The mass of subjectivities set to labour presented itself as an ensemble of singularities immersed in social and productive cooperation. This was the birth of the multitude.

We can follow with a certain precision the processes of transformation of labour power at the heart of capitalist development. Between 1848 and 1870, the growth of industrialization was based on the organization of generic labour, of the generic worker: this was the period studied by Marx and Engels. Already after 1870 and until at least 1917, the organization of labour was undergoing changes following the great uprising of the Paris Commune, organizing its internal structure in a new way, with the function of the skilled worker coming to the fore. With the First World War, and as a consequence of the October Revolution, capital reorganizes itself in a first big process of subsumption of social labour: around industry, moulding within industry the rules of valorization and its reproduction. This was the great age of the mass worker – of Taylorism as a technique for organizing labour and as a method of social division of labour. The struggles around 1968 definitively break this period of the organization of labour and society: after 1968 labour becomes increasingly socialized and intellectualized, through the automation of the factories and the informatization of society. It is here that a new figure of worker appears: first the socialized worker and then, without incongruity, the immaterial labour worker.

So this is what happened. Now, in the face of this new reality of labour, capital (having extended exploitation over the whole social terrain) was forced to develop new and immediately efficacious political criteria of control over the whole of society. This initiative modified the realities of production, and at the same time, paradoxically but no less coherently, it also modified the political realities, the nature of sovereignty. Command had to extend over the whole of society, through the modalities it had once employed in the factory. This was a paradoxical process, since it meant that society, having become a factory, re-proposed at the political level the entirety of the contradictions that the factory had known. It is in this phase that the class presents itself as – or rather is transformed into – multitude. Multitude means an ensemble of singularities set to work, singularities who recompose labour within mass intellectuality. Secondly, multitude means the ability to express within ways of life, at the biopolitical level, the totality of the needs and contradictions which at other times had been produced by the factory. The multitude presents itself finally as a constitutive potentiality [*potenza*], in other words as a democratic and constituent potentiality: constitutive because labour power has become the sum of all social productive potentialities; democratic because it contains the values and the capacity of expression of all social subjects. It is here that the crisis of representation, of political representation and capitalist representation, defined in terms of modernity (in other words, as alienation of the *potenza* of the masses), fails.

In order to characterize the multitude as subject, it is therefore necessary to define it not only in terms of its positioning in the production process but also as regards its possible praxis. This applies first of all at the level of the capital relation (which, as I said, is dual, and irreversibly dual, as I believe I have shown). Now, overall, labour power no longer presents itself simply as the motor of development, nor does the working class present itself simply as a counter-power within capital. The multitude is both the one thing and the other; it is constituent *potenza*.

Consequently this new situation, this emergence of the multitude, implies major modifications at the political level of the conceptualization of sovereignty, in both its theory and its practice. The change imposed on the evaluation of the nation–state (a category which until this point was completely annexed to the stages of development of capital) is decisive. In this present transition we have a collapse of the essential characteristics of the nation–state. It no longer has the ability to assert itself in spatial, temporal and cultural terms that are sufficient in themselves. The multitude requires spatial, temporal and cultural structures that are suited for intellectuality and cooperation, for the mobility and flexibility of its own productive behaviours. This is the environment in which globalization imposes itself. Hence we have a crisis of modernity's regulation of the social organization of labour in its entirety (that is, as structured and commanded by the nation–state).

Here we find ourselves again within a transition of the modes of production and of their sovereign organization. The social fabric is thrown into disarray as a result. First, the figure of production, which is not able to isolate itself and to individualize the productive subject. Secondly, the figure of exploitation, which extends across the whole of society and which instals new and newly unsustainable techniques of capitalist appropriation everywhere, and in every biopolitical dimension of the social. The antagonism becomes massive and omniversal.

In determining the present situation, we have defined, in political terms, the transition to globalization, and thus to imperial sovereignty, as a decisive and irreversible tendency. At the same time, we also need to qualify this transition at the political level. We call it an 'interregnum': in other words, the formation and conflict of various powers around the problem of a material redefinition of power (or of sovereignty) around the registering of these transitions. In the interregnum there are major contradictions, not only between the imperial tendency and the counter-imperial tendency produced by the multitude, but also, or above all, at this time, between the individual subjects who are the holders of power. Up until now the answer to these unresolved problems has been the production of war. Empire produces war so as to create order, a new order arising out of the crisis of the nation–state and, above all, out of the antagonism that the multitude determines. In the phase of interregnum, war becomes the fundamental element in the reorganization of political power.

So I think that we have answered the initial questions we posed. It used to be said (and some comrades who still think in terms of Marxism continue to maintain it) that there is no class without party, that there is no politics without the state, and that in any event there is an autonomy of the political in relation to the social and the economic. In this interregnum the movements of the multitude indicate the contrary, namely that there is class, that there is *potenza*, that there is antagonism, and that there is transformation without (or perhaps in spite of) the party. The interregnum shows that the multitude now moves on a terrain no longer characterized by the nation–state and by its mechanisms of representation and domination (namely the neutralization of conflict and the symbolic unification of spirits): the multitude moves differently, to raise the problem of the crisis of capitalism at the global level, and specifically to address the problems of the capitalist transition and of the present imperial interregnum. This is an area where detailed analysis, critique and inquiry need to be developed. If there never was, in real terms, such a thing as the 'autonomy of the political', today, in a situation of Empire, it becomes pure fantasy.

4

Empire and War*

Yesterday many Italian soldiers died in Nassiriya: this was state murder; it was the men of our Italian government who murdered them.

The war in which we are engaged – and against which we are campaigning – is a perverse war. There are several aspects of this war that interest us from the theoretical and political point of view and others which do not. Let us look at the reasons which lead us to say this. The fact remains that we find ourselves in something which is as huge as it is disgusting, which calls for resistance by our spirit in its entirety and altogether.

There is one aspect of this war which does not interest me: the aspect which sees the American oilmen struggling against their former allies and employees, namely the Middle Eastern *condottieri* who have been mercenaries in the service of American power. A second point which does not interest me is the way in which some European capitalists and oilmen are opposed to American capitalists and oilmen because they think, possibly correctly, that this American war is also directed against them. And there is one final aspect of this war which does not interest me, and this is the one which sees American sovereignists attempting an imperial *coup d'état* against their European sovereignist associates.

There is, however, one aspect of this war that concerns me very much, namely the fact that, as previously with the wars in the Balkans, this war is a war of learning and apprenticeship (on the part of the various fractions of imperial power) in the constitution of command

* Talk given at the plenary session of the European Social Forum, Saint-Denis (Paris), 13 November 2003.

over the world. The war in Iraq is only partially still a war. It had originally sought to be an operation of international policing: if it has
ended up being a low intensity war, this has happened because of the
inconsistency of American strategy. What we want to consider here is
therefore the characteristics of this international policing operation.
Here, in the first place, the enemy is identified not as a state but as
figures internal to the organization of Empire: as 'public enemies'. It
is no accident that the Geneva Conventions are held not to apply in
their case. Secondly, in order to adapt to this new policing role, armies
are being transformed in both organization and form. They are
tending to reorganize into small, mobile units, air-transported and
integrated in terms of information-gathering and humanitarian assistance. They are simultaneously traditional soldiers, missionaries and
mercenaries, police and firefighters, sailors and humanitarians.
Thirdly, the aim of this policing war is neither to defeat an enemy nor
to reorganize a given hierarchy of international relationships (that is,
between nation–states) but rather to construct democratic nations –
more or less democratic, but firmly within the imperial order – an
order of things that is continuous, smooth and capitalist.
    It may be low intensity war – but it is very high intensity policing.
It results in deaths (too many) and destroys populations. In some
respects it is like war. Although it presents itself as a restoration of
order, the reality is that it involves a great violence that goes beyond
any relation of cohabitation with and rational understanding of the
other. God willing, this injustice creates resistance. We are with all
those who resist imperial power; we are with all those who struggle
and die in the course of resisting. Are they looking for freedom, these
singularities who are dying? We do not know. At times it seems
improbable. However, for sure they do not want domination. How far
and for how long are we going to fight against power?
    We are not with the European or Middle Eastern sovereignists, nor
are we with the feudal capitalists, be they Middle Eastern or
American. In this situation, therefore, what are we to do? How are we
to respond to war without getting mixed up with all those who, for one
reason or another, express themselves as *potenze* of death and of a new
order which by now is decidedly fascist?
    War against war. That is what our communist tradition teaches us.
This is good. But we live an age which is that of the immaterial
worker, of the anti-globalization movement, of a general refusal, and
of exodus from the liberal democracies. At this point, unavoidably, we
have to posit for ourselves the problem of a radical and active disobedience, the proposal of a diplomacy from below which is globally

cosmopolitan, and the project of a continuously active exercise of political counter-power.

Having said this, the basic problem still remains: in every war the motivations are a combination of state interests and appropriative interests; every war is a continuation of capitalist politics, an additional moment which increasingly becomes its foundation. For our part, we are against war because we are against capitalism. Now, against police war we have to oppose social war. The capitalist acceleration of war on the pretext of order and security has to find itself confronted with a continuous acceleration of our social struggle against the power of capital. So, to active disobedience, to diplomacy from below, to the exercise of political counter-power, there needs to be added, as an essential over-determination, the resumption of social struggle against capitalist exploitation.

This morning some Italian mercenaries died in Nassiriya, misled by the regime's propaganda and their mystified consciousness as waged workers. We are sorry for them, and for their families and friends: but at a moment like this we also cannot forget the murderous responsibility of those who sent them to die.

5

Tendencies and Drives towards the Recomposition of Aristocracy in Empire*

Here I would like to discuss some positions that were elaborated after the WTO summit in Cancún, particularly as regards the situation of the movements in Italy.

The WTO has not succeeded in recomposing what the war in Iraq divided. However, we should not lower our guard. It is obvious that huge tensions were in play at the WTO, centring on the recomposition of a world-wide aristocracy capable of imposing itself as a negotiating partner in relation to the American super-power.

The American and European capitalists have attempted to rebuild a common front, underestimating the political differences and egotisms on all sides and, above all, thinking that they could use this situation of general economic and political crisis as an opportunity to get their hands on the new economic reality of globalization. They were hoping that this would be the launchpad for a capitalist reappropriation of common goods and for a real process of 'refeudalization' of the spaces generated by the 'new commons' of the digital sector. In this perspective, the intention was to constitute an alliance of the world-wide aristocracies (the multinationals in particular), to oppose the unilateralist claims of the United States and the *coup d'état* which the US administration was trying to perpetrate on the world. This strategy failed at the WTO summit, because of the opposition of the developing countries, and above all because of the opposition of the movements throughout the developed western world.

This relative crisis internal to the forces of global capitalism is a positive fact for the movements. In fact, if there were to be a successful

---

* Talk given at the Istituto Universitario di Architettura, University of Venice, 20 January 2004.

imperial recomposition of the capitalist super-powers and of the multinationals, then the spaces for action, counter-power, resistance and movement on the part of the multitudes would be enormously reduced.

Against this positive tendency, however, there is also a negative tendency – namely the recomposition of various brands of social democracy at the world-wide level. On the one hand we have the reformist Blairite spirit, representing global interests and deep alliances with the more dynamic aristocracies of command in the multinationals, and on the other we have the social-democratic spirit, nostalgic for the former realities of world capitalism; both tend towards a recomposition around a programme of state management of exploitation. In central Europe this is now self-evident. In Latin America this process is particularly powerful. In Japan and China it is extremely advanced. 'Bipartisan' constitutional formulae accentuate this process, and representation tends to lead the processes of crisis in the capitalist management of the globalization process back to projects of national capital.

Within the Left in Europe, these processes have been particularly fast-moving. The trade-union and party-political forces which oppose the recomposition of the social democratic élites and the world-wide aristocracies are becoming increasingly isolated.

The contradictions remain open today. However, we need to define them on another terrain, which is not simply that of immediate political confrontation, and not simply that of the identity of a movement of resistance. In posing this problem – that of creating a terrain of confrontation which not only grasps the crisis of the capitalist synthesis but also determines new openings, in order to force the spaces that the crisis is opening for the movements and in order not to be reduced to the passive experiencing of this condition – we need to carry the debate to a new level.

The first thing to be noted is the crisis of models of development. Let us take the definition which Manuel Castells gave in the early 1990s of the models of capitalist development which were opening up in the new phase of the information economy.

1   The first was the Anglo-Saxon model, which saw the informatization of the mode of production as extending over the whole world, further developing the extreme liberalism of American ideology. Today, as we know, this model is in crisis. Its crisis became evident at the moment in which the model revealed, both at the international level and – above all – at the national level, that

it was unable to establish an equilibrium of capitalist development. Unemployment, poverty and the production of insuperable
social dualisms are the characteristic traits of this model: the rich
becoming increasingly richer and the poor (always) becoming
poorer.

2   The Franco-German model, whereby the information economy
    and globalization could be moulded to fit with the regulation
    models of welfare-type societies, is also in crisis. This model held
    for the white sector of American and North American industry,
    for a large part of Europe and for the major economies of the Far
    East. The model is now collapsing under the pressure of the global
    process of production: its relative isolation and its effective auton-
    omy have reached the limits of the drive to privatization and refeu-
    dalization of the commons. The great mechanisms of public
    health, universal retirement and care for the weak in society – in
    short, the general Keynesian hypothesis and the political relation-
    ships involved in the contracting of the social wage – all these no
    longer hold and go into deep crisis.

3   There is also a crisis in the model of the information economy as
    a schema for the organization of diffuse labour. Castells had
    theorized this model on the basis of the Italian experience of
    decentralized production and of the social diffusion of the orga-
    nization of labour. The opening of the big markets in the East, in
    conjunction with the crisis of the socialist system and the Chinese
    dumping of cheap-labour goods on overseas markets, increased
    this mode of production in multitudinarian terms, subjecting it to
    fierce rules of exploitation, and also put it into crisis because of
    the impossibility of controlling the segmented and localized forms
    of its development.

The problem of the movement today is that we have to do more than
simply denounce this crisis. We have to highlight the crisis of the three
models but at the same time we have to find escape routes out of that
crisis. We proceed on the basis of understanding and defining the new
figures of productive labour; we have recognized the hegemony of
immaterial labour and the *potenza* of cooperation. The movements
have to identify the new forms of the organization of labour which this
new subjectivity is proposing. The multitude is not a chaotic mass but
a creative, productive presence of new subjective forces. How can
we create a world without exploitation, based on these new social

realities? It is only if we move from the totality of phenomenological perceptions of the new labour and of the new forms of cooperation, from the new anthropology of subjectivity and from the new quality of the activities operating on the global terrain of production and reproduction of the world – it is only if we take all this as our starting point that we shall succeed in transforming the existing contradictions and in living the end of the pre-constituted models, in ways that are subversive and innovative.

Thus far we have considered positively capital's inability to recompose a unified front, able to embrace simultaneously both the political and the economic and to tie them into a single relationship. We have said that this relative split enables us to find openings for positive initiatives.

However, such a situation also brings about negative consequences, which are often very strong. The fragility of the economic and political framework often pushes state structures into repressive policies and security panics, which become particularly strong (and often effective) when the economic model is in crisis and global political perspectives are confused. In this situation there can be particularly violent forms of repression and/or exclusion against the political groups and social forces which most effectively oppose the capitalist recompositional plan at the level of government and/or economy. When the anti-war struggles are followed by struggles which atttack the new models of organization of labour (or propose alternatives to them) – in other words when struggles are engaged both in a global perspective (peace movements, the movements for Europe and democracy and the like) and against the new economic model (struggles against the capitalist appropriation of the commons, energy and services; struggles against the appropriation of informatic space, and so on) – then the temptation (and often the necessity) of resorting to repressive means can become a central concern of power politics. Repression is actually a very conjunctural state policy: it highlights the moments of transition and/or of crisis of the capitalist system and seeks to present itself as a mechanism of equilibrium within these transitions.

In Italy at the present time, on the institutional surface, we are witnessing very violent conflicts. Underlying these, though, a profound recomposition of the entire capitalist order is taking place. The political forces of both Right and Left are being recomposed around a centrist politics geared to the needs of the employing classes (and caricaturing the liberal pressures operating at the global level). In this situation, which is a kind of European laboratory for the Right and repeats the experiments of Tony Blair for the Left – in this situation, the repressive danger presents itself particularly forcefully, positioning itself on the imbalance between the institutional superstructures and the deep-seated processes of capitalist recomposition.

Now it only remains for us to trace the outlines of a post-socialist programme . . . or at least to make the attempt.

Bearing in mind the points made thus far, it is clear that an effective political action on the part of the movements can only be imagined if it is placed in direct contact with experiences and an imaginary which are post-socialist. In global terms, a post-socialist programme must be created through defending the broadest possible freedom of movement for global labour power. (When Marx declared himself in favour of the policy of liberalizing the grain trade, he was not declaring himself in favour of the freedom of the market but simply against all the constraints that were being imposed on a commodity as essential as grain, as a way of speculating on the reproduction cost of labour power. If today the fundamental commodity, the grain on which the new values of labour power are formed, is mental energy, that is, the biopolitical abilities of immaterial workers, then we have to argue for the most complete mobility of labour power. This is not because we agree with the ecological uprooting of populations or with the renewed colonialist models popular among certain strata of multinational capital. No, we simply want an adjustment to the realities of the global labour force, based as it is on the fact of intellectual labour.)

At the European level, a post-socialist programme needs to be defined in relation to a project for a European constitution founded on citizen income, on a total freedom of networks and on the defence and strengthening of all the elements of the common organization of labour and social reproduction. (Europe is a fundamental terrain for the struggle against the 'refeudalization' of the commons.) The European dimension enables us to develop struggles on these kinds of issues, which will be meaningful in their own terms, and which can also have an effect at the global level. We need only look at what has been happening recently – from the European–American conflict over issues in the Middle East to the splits at Cancún – to understand the extraordinary political impact that these movements can have on Europe. As I said above, we need to be politically alert so as not to permit the recomposition of the political horizon and of the economic horizon at the imperial level: bearing in mind that there exists a capitalist tendency to move towards a unitary recentralization of the system, we need to move to keep the situation open-ended. A post-socialist programme should consist not only of objectives, but also of an appraisal of the power relations operating in global political developments.

A further and far from insignificant question for the movement in Italy is the reopening of struggles over justice. This means on the one hand organizing actively and attentively to defend the movements' rights of self-expression and demonstration; on the other, stopping the present government from operating with impunity and from using demagogy and judicial provocations to destroy people's faith in justice. The present government combines corruption, conflicts of interest, the shameless use of the courts for political ends and an erosion of people's belief in justice (often directed against the magistracy): it is not by defending the magistracy but only by demanding justice for all against the rich and powerful that we can remove this weapon from the hands of the present government.

This point is far from being of secondary importance because, as I said, the repressive impulse can re-emerge in policies of the employing class (Right and Left alike) intent on repressing the movements during a period of intensifying crisis. This battle is also important because we have to start to place some kind of obstacle in the way of the pleasure with which a section of the Italian Left uses the magistracy as a political weapon. This choice has resulted in a neutralization of the programme, a mobilization with mystificatory effects over questions of justice (which of course never addresses poverty and demands for justice for the exploited).

6

Utopias and Resistance in Empire*

When we talk about utopia, people often react cynically and dismissively. Utopia – when it presents itself as a project for an alternative world, whether dreamed or actually enacted, posed within a transcendence which at the same time claims to have some relationship with reality, with its movement, whereas it acts very much at the edges of the real – really is deserving of derision and cynicism. And yet . . . what does it mean to speak about utopia in the globalized and imperial world order of today, in postmodernity, in other words in a world that no longer has an 'outside'? I suggest that it means humble voices speaking about the possible. Thus far in our history we have seen a good few phenomenologies of the possible, but they have all been tragic. To speak of the possible seemed to mean speaking of desperation and offering oneself an experience which was precarious and tragic. Benjamin's *Angelus novus* represents this condition. But we are within a new experience, which is of our times and places us in a new utopian condition; or, rather, makes us face the *potenza* of utopia.

So this gives us a number of areas around which we can problematize the question proposed by this conference on the return of utopias and their effectiveness. The first problem is that of the anthropological mutation of utopia, and of its meaning and function: is this related to the transformations of labour and the new developments in technology? The second problem is the one which looks at utopia in terms of experiences of time. You might call this the speeding-up of utopia, of its experimentation and of the relation it can have with common sense. The third question or problem is that of the opening of utopia

---

* Talk given at the *Transmediale 04: Fly Utopia!* festival in Berlin, 31 January 2004.

to the possible: an old problematic, but one which is still relevant. The fourth problem is that of the relation between utopia and an aleatory conception of the limit: which is another way of saying that utopia presents itself not only as possibility but also as risk.

If these are the symptoms of the way utopia presents itself today, we must ask first what utopia was in the past, in other words we must historicize it. In the readings that have been made of it, there have been at least two conceptions of utopia. That of the Right – which is strongly metaphysical – defines utopia as a nostalgia for paradise, as a remembrance of originary archetypes. From Plato down to Rousseau, we have many examples of this form of thinking, inspired by hope. History also offers another conception of utopia: that of the Left, which is strongly futurist, which presents itself as the overcoming of the *nec plus ultra* (of the Pillars of Hercules) and which experiences utopia as excedence, as the promise of an Eden to come. From the humanism of Dante Alighieri through to utopian socialism, this conception of utopia is a recurrent motif.

This is the history of utopia in modernity: it has moved between these opposing poles. But within modernity there is another current – sometimes hidden and secret, constrained or persecuted – which contests the first two definitions of utopia. Here the utopian non-place (unlike what we have in the philosophical fashions of modernity) is always occupied and renewed. It is poor and human – a hungry belly, a loving belly, a free belly that is excedent in eating, in making, in laughing, acting and hoping. It is the materialism that reaches down from Ruzante and Rabelais through to Bakhtin. This is the line of materialistic utopia.

Now the social utopias are behind us, both those of the Right and those of the Left. Some of them were good – for instance those which had to do with hunger, work, exploitation and the possibity of disorder. Cockaigne, carnival, abundance and liberty, sexual freedom, utopias built around work – all these are within our experience. Not only in individual experiences but also in collective experiences. Real socialism, however, wore out the modern concept of utopia.

But today the concept of utopia is being re-born in an unexpected form, in other words within labour, within labour power. It is re-born because today there can be no production without freedom and cooperation, because there can be no hope without bodies and without the expansion and communication of bodies. Paradoxically, utopia is once again read in terms of the possible. 'Another world is possible.' A huge quantity of *cahiers de doléances* have been presented to the world, and they seem to be realizable; their injunctions are effective.

Is it perhaps because the age we are living in is pre-revolutionary? We do not know. What is certain is that the utopian demand is plausible, therefore possible, therefore realizable – and certainly virtually real. The horizons of desire seem close to the horizons of possibility. This materialistic *dispositif* is linked to the 'high philosophy of modernity', to the current of thought that runs from Machiavelli through Spinoza to Marx. In Machiavelli utopia is born out of indignation and becomes resistance and political programme. In Machiavelli the realist, utopia is programmatic. In Spinoza the utopia is drawn within the process of the passions: it is the *potenza* which moves desire towards love. In Marx utopia is connected with the material conditions of exploitation and is a real force which inserts itself into the dynamics of life, of a new collective *potenza* of freedom.

Thus we have identified a materialist and immanentist utopian dimension which, having traversed modernity in hidden ways, reappears as active and actual in postmodernity. How are we to deal with this experience of real possibility, immersed in a world that has no outside? In other words, how are we to match this experience of utopia with the postmodern world in which we live? Can we begin to think of utopia in terms of a present-day strategy of the possible? What does it mean to put into contact with each other – within immanence – utopia and the material precarity of a possible present and of singularity?

We have here a paradox: that of the multitude put to work. In other words the social figure in which labour produces nowadays manifests itself as a form of social and global activity. Now, this multitude is a process which develops between multiple and common singularities. In producing this definition, our reference is to Foucault and Deleuze, but also to the old distinction between *Kronos* and *Aion*, to the difference between a time that develops towards infinity and a time which intensely rediscovers eternity. It is at this point that our reflection on the multitude, positively understood as a relationship between multiple and common singularities, folds back negatively on the critique of individualism. Individualism presupposes that subjects have a soul, a stable and irreducible substrate. But this conception removes the *potenza* of being able to realize the possible, to allow singularity to live in the common! The utopia of modernity, both the one which is defined in terms of transcendence and the one which functions in transcendental terms, conflicts here with the concept of multitude – with the process of singular events and human activity that is open to the construction of increasing multiplicities and increasing commons. The individualist utopia cannot sustain the experience of the multitude.

Quite the contrary: when we think of the multitude we need to see it as a swarming movement: millions of possible movements open to every possibility, as the freedom of every singularity. But, above all, as the immanent motor of every development, as the possibility of constructing a *telos* beginning from singularities and their encounter. This is the point where the *Fly Utopia!* project connects with our hypothesis: technologies become prostheses of subjects, communication becomes cooperation, and spaces become no longer natural but constructed. Many monsters and giants appear here – the social landscape we are opening up is Rabelaisian.

At this point we should be happy: we have constructed a new scenario for utopia. It represents itself as a new accumulation of desires . . . Another world is possible. But, precisely, representation, the symbol, the new stage-setting, is not enough. Because, if it is the case that there is no longer transcendence but only immanence, then utopia – as the possibility of imagining another world – has to live within immanence and must live as activity. Can we imagine utopia as praxis, as multitudinarian activity? The first reply is affirmative: there is always utopia where there is resistance, and resistance brings us back within this world, and resistance brings us back to the construction of utopia as activity.

When we began talking about Empire we were not thinking of a utopia but of a tendency, a tendential process. Our conception of Empire bears no relation to conceptions such as that of Virgil – the Roman *potenza*, organising its power as a world-wide utopia. On the contrary, in our view Empire, since it is tendentially sovereignist, is opposed to utopia as activity of the singularities of the multitude. When Empire seeks to fix an ordering and normative process on the world market, it reveals itself as an equivocal synthesis between an extreme (capitalist) possibility and an extreme danger (that experienced by the subjected peoples). In effect, Empire presents itself as a promise of liberation and as regulatory war. It tendentially organizes a threat which is matched to the *potenza* of the multitude. And yet this conception of Empire is entirely open: if capitalism wants and needs to construct a world ordered by war, if it needs to exercise constituent power as a derivation of its domination – in that case the multitudes press to open another passage, that of the constituent power of a new century.

The 'no-global' movement has applied itself on this terrain; it has recognized that, with the ending of the communist movement, utopia could be run from below, to constitute a fundamental element of the 'march of freedom'.

In short, if the imperial tendency has shown itself to be a derivation of constituent power and capitalism has had no hesitation in resorting to war in order to guarantee the building of Empire, we also have to remember that there exists a counter-empire, acting in the singularity, capable of every utopian upheaval. The multitudes are pressing to open a constituent era, to exercise constituent power as the basis of what is common. When we look at the 'no-global' movement, we have to recognize that it is moving entirely on this terrain. It has recognized the historical end of the communist world movement, but it is launching a project of constructing an ethics of the revolutionary multitude, that is, of subjectivity and antagonism.

The only true utopia, at this moment, is that of fighting within the time of production and domination, against the capitalist segmentation of temporality: here desire articulates with utopia. Of course we still do not have the possibility of overcoming the ultimate limit, that of death, but the promise of removing the negative from life (this could be a new definition of utopia), this is certainly given among the *potenze* of our living. Utopia today means exodus and metamorphosis: the exodus is in action and metamorphosis is possible. Capital has colonized the world, but in colonizing it it has not neutralized its *potenze*. It is within the world that utopia becomes possible. The breaking of bio-power, that is, of the power that acts to destroy humanity in order to put it at the service of capital and productivity – this utopia is possible. We may have to endure slavery, military violence, the economic–financial world order and racism, but beyond all this, within this enduring , the exodus has found again the *potenza* of utopia. Utopia is not a dream but a possibility. As I said, the horizons of desire and the horizons of possibility are close.

7
Empire and Citizenship*

Let us focus on the proposition that it is no longer labour in the factory that determines social relationships, but the setting to work of society as a whole, and thus the exploitation of all those who are active in society. To say multitude is to say this new social condition of exploitation, but it is also to say the new reality of labour – the construction of social wealth by means of cooperation and intelligence.

The working class has never loved wage labour in the factory. Working in factories was and remains a terrible oppression, an additional burden of suffering and exploitation in life. The transition to post-Fordism has brought an enormous advance for labour and for life: this progress, as happens with all improvements in human life, was imposed by workers' struggles in the 1960s and 1970s, and continues to be imposed. However, the hegemonic function of the working class, in this particular situation, does not exist: it remains a pure ideological fiction. The working class actually destroyed itself through struggles; it imposed on capital this transition to a new phase of domination, and hence it is in some way the cause of both the advantages and the disadvantages of this new phase. This capitalist transition is determined by the fact of the general intellect of society being set to work: from this there follows a general precarization and fragmentation of labour. Whether this is advantageous or disadvantageous for the workers depends solely on the degree of resistance that emerges out of this new situation. Immaterial labour – mobile, flexible and precarious, with its productivity, intelligence and spiritual wealth – is today the subject of production: it is exploited as such, but

* Speech at the Schiffbauhalle, Zürich, 7 March 2004.

it contains within it potentiality, constituent power, the ability to construct a new common for all the workers, which is the cornerstone of a possible utopia, under the banner of the multitude and new desires of freedom.

Differences and singularity are what constructs today's productive subject. There is no value creation without difference and singularity. But how is it possible, starting from difference, to construct a political subject? The feminist movements have already addressed this problem; today we face it on the basis of a generalization of the recognition of difference, extended to the entirety of social productive power. This resumption of the question of the political and the common is nevertheless extremely difficult to propose. However, today there are many elements we can begin to draw upon in order to define a new political form of the proletarian subject: first in negative terms, in destroying the traditional categories of the labour movement; secondly in positive terms, which recompose and reconstruct its communist objectives.

Let us first consider the negative aspects. Class as an undifferentiated concept, along with people and nation as concepts of a transcendental unity imposed by power, is by now archaeological. The people and the nation are a fraud, as globalization has shown. If the concept of nation has been a horrible tragedy, which has allowed the dominant bourgeoisie to mobilize its citizens for labour and for war; if the working class has been conceived of as a mass to be led into developmentalist and capitalist ideas of the historical processes – then let us thank globalization for having shown us the falsity of these concepts. Globalization is a revolutionary process. Dominated precariously by neo-liberal ideologies, it needs instead to be traversed by a revolutionary perspective capable of overturning its forms and objectives, pressing forward the capacity of internationalism and cosmopolitanism to overturn the old world and imagine a new one.

Note this, however: it is not Empire that creates the multitude, it is not globalization that shows it to us; the process of globalization, as I said, was imposed by struggles. Our problem today is not simply that of maintaining an open front of struggles and of recognizing it as being operative everywhere; rather, it is to identify the new forms in which capital moves in its attempt to resist the working-class, proletarian and multitudinarian attack. So what are these new imperial forms of domination?

In the first place, they are the forms that affect the multitude as a set of singularities and as a biopolitical reality (that is, as a global composition of vital interests). The politics of disciplining bodies is the first path taken by capital, at this new level of domination. In order to produce, global capitalism and imperial sovereignty need to control our entire existence. What is in play is entirely biopolitical, and has to do with desires and ways of life. Secondly, the imperial rules for the organization of the world are developed via hierarchizing flows and determinations. On this terrain, global capital and imperial sovereign organization determine borders, criteria for ordering populations, and repressive forms that are increasingly insistent and heavy. It is no accident that imperial war presents itself here as a mode of political intervention.

But, while this deterritorialized Empire is a world traversed by a network of command on the part of the imperial government and of the capitalist aristocracies/multinationals, it is also a conflictual world. More conflictual than the world to which we were accustomed – the world of nation–states and of the industrial working class. Infinite numbers of points of control have broken down, while countless points of contradiction have risen up. Working-class antagonism has become multitudinarian antagonism. The class struggle has been transformed into resistance struggle. A new physiology of the political body (not only the capitalist political body but, above all, the proletarian) has presented itself. The political body of the multitude is invested by the mobility of populations, by emigrations, by the metamorphoses of desires and by aspirations to formal rights. When we look at this globalized world we see how it is traversed by huge quantities of freedom, by the *potenza* of the exploited who resist, by the insubordination of the excluded who make their escape . . . This world has become one. It is traversed by a mobility of the multitudes that has neither blockage nor limit – other than the extreme limit of war.

With this we are not saying that the control of the proletariat within the individual central countries or those of the former Third World has now become ineffectual; we are simply saying that the politics of internal restructuring that extends from the disciplining of bodies to the control of movements and to nation-building by means of war, and which goes from the imposition of democracy to the encouragement of private corruption in the transition between 'totalitarian' and 'democratic' regimes – all this, we are saying, has become a new terrain of struggle, traversed by endemic and often uncontrollable resistances. It is here that we have the measure of the new strength of the movements.

Take what happens in Switzerland. Every year the rulers of the world gather to establish a game-plan for governing the world and for running the global processes of exploitation. If you watch what goes on at Davos you will see that the big financial powers which organize the meeting are measuring themselves against the residual state powers, and above all against the monarchic power of the United States. Davos offers a good representation of the present structure of global power: a kind of Russian doll, with American sovereignty as its outer shell, and inside it the multinationals and the political classes of the capitalist countries. The multitude is kept out of Davos, not with snowballs but with police teargas and weapons of every kind. Davos becomes a kind of spectrum of the composition of Empire, where what is on the agenda is the various levels of control within the system, plus the exercise of war and external policing, against the multitude, and decisions regarding hierarchization (exclusion/inclusion).

A counter-empire exists: it is the multitude, always in motion, and the irreducible multiplicity of subjects. To recompose itself politically, this multitude has to pass through the invention of new forms of representation (which do not reproduce the classic constitutional forms characteristic of the development of capitalism) and of mobilization (which do not reproduce the decrepit forms organized by the leftist parties). We need a new programme, which breaks definitively with the old – with the skeleton of capitalism that the leftist parties still have in their cupboards. But before anythng else, the problem is how to gather the mobility of the multitude into strong and effective political structures. The right of universal citizenship, concretized in forms in which it can be accepted in all countries, is a necessary part of this. Here in Switzerland the problem has been widely discussed; this is a question which needs to be developed, as a precondition for any future programme.

The political phase in which we find ourselves is a difficult one. There is a major debate on American unilateralism and the internationalism of sovereign states. The debate is false: in reality, what is at stake is who is going to govern the Empire: will it be the Americans (qua nation) or the world-wide capitalists, unified in their need to create norms and prescriptions for globalization? We should not confuse the struggle against neo-liberalism with the struggle against Americanism: we have a duty to put forward anti-capitalist positions at every level and at every moment. All this does not mean denying that differences exist, or that each situation of struggle has its specifics. The problem is not to deny these differences in the organization of the struggle but always to foreground anti-capitalist struggle as the principal terrain. We should not allow ourselves to be distracted by the power balance that capitalism effects in its dynamics. Instead, we have to pass through these dynamics in order to recognize the interests of the multitude. In Latin America there are important examples of how these questions are being addressed, where some governments (Brazil and Argentina in particular) are opening themselves to a dialectics with the movements. The anti-capitalist thrust of these movements is a fundamental axis of explanation in comparing the experiences of these world-wide *potenze*. No matter how these experiments end up – they are certainly imperfect, and sometimes equivocal – we have here an initial model of what it might mean to bring out the anti-capitalist and multitudinarian interest as a central element characterizing globalization.

Global citizenship is a key anti-capitalist element. We have to work around this theme, opening up constituent and post-socialist spaces.

8

Living the Imperial Transition – In Order to Struggle*

After the 1970s *Le Monde diplomatique* was fundamental to my development. I remember how important *Le Monde diplomatique* was for us when it arrived in prison and we had a shared reading of it among the political prisoners in the early 1980s. It gave us a way into the great crisis of the 'short century'. It kept open the roads of intelligence and anger. It stopped us from repenting! Compared with those days, has *Le Monde diplomatique* maybe aged somewhat? I don't think so. It is true, however, that today we live in a historical situation which is very different from what went before – we are living a period of capitalist interregnum in which a war is being waged to decide who will govern Empire. Now, in this process of imperial construction, of transformation of the chains of command and of the redefining of social classes, the political vocabulary which we use changes completely. We find ourselves having to work at a renewal of political vocabulary. We need to re-state what power is, and what exploitation is, and we need to spread these understandings. Is *Le Monde diplomatique* still our travelling companion along this road?

The transformation of a political vocabulary is a real process, which will involve the elimination of some of the fundamental political categories of modernity; this process has to take as its starting point the identification of new political subjects in the processes of imperial constitution, and in the formation of new ruling classes within Empire and of multitudes of workers. We see day after day the unfolding of processes which we watch, perplexed, as we ask what has become of our old notions of war and peace, the nation–state and

---

* Speech given at the Palais du Sport, Paris, 8 May 2004, on the occasion of the 50th birthday of *Le Monde diplomatique*.

cosmopolitanism, the United Nations and international law, citizenship and rights, private and public and the like, and what they have now become. In marking out a position within the great historical transition through which we are living, we insist that the passion for political freedom and the love for social equality, the resistance to power and the revolt against poverty, all have to walk together. We know that we are living through a remarkable age of transition. Just as the end of the Renaissance saw the beginning of the Thirty Years War, which went hand in hand with a 'refeudalization' of the countryside, so today, at the end of the great socialist revolution, a 'preventive' war has begun which has as its basis the 'privatization of the commons'. This is a transition which, at the same time as constructing a new political vocabulary, also involves a critique of the past and the definition of a programme for the future. We are ready to go down this path. After Seattle and Genoa, after the Social Forums of Porto Alegre and Mumbai, many of us think that the creation of a post-socialist programme needs to be placed firmly on the political agenda. It seems to me that it would be extremely important if *Le Monde diplomatique* wanted and/or was able to situate its critical role, its hard work as a great humanist newspaper, within this nexus. We are not asking for a new Iskra, but for a strong reference point within the networks of international debate of the multitudes.

Today we see three dangers which, at the level of revolutionary critique, might block our capacity for inventing languages and programming effective actions. The first blockage is extremism. Extremism has to be rejected because today we begin from a situation in which we are the majority: this enables us – indeed obliges us – to develop (alongside our critique) constituent motifs, which can be radically linked to the seeking out of consent. The second blockage is that of the ideology of sovereignty, in other words the illusion that these processes of transformation can still be interpreted via the figure and the terminologies (let alone the procedures and political norms) of the sovereign nation–state. This period of transition is particularly dangerous. It requires of us a ceaseless confrontation with retrograde positions, it strangles us in terms of dubious alliances, it prevents us from creating a relationship with structures of global action of the multitude. The third blockage of discourse is that related to Third Worldism. Here we are not denying the terrible problems that affect the South of the world, nor are we denying the fundamental importance of the problem of poverty. We are simply saying that we act not within dependency but within interdependence. It is precisely within certain countries, which we once characterized as Third-World, that we are beginning to see processes of construction of new and original experiments in permanent revolution. We need to direct our political energies to the construction of these new instruments of constitutional politics, to an open relationship between the actions of the movements and national and global 'governance'.

One final issue is the question of war, as it is imposed on us today, in other words as a biopolitical structure which invests the lives of every one of us. This war exists, and the multitudes are opposed to it. The good news is that the USA is losing the war in Iraq. We are happy that the American multitudes may now become aware of this defeat and we hope that they will be able to transform it into a moment of struggle for their liberation. Without the American proletariat, and American intellectuals, and American music . . . in short, without the American multitudes, permanent revolution is not possible, nor is the free development of that great transformation of life we are living through. The same goes for Europe. We are engaged in a struggle to transform the issue of the European constitution. But we know that there is no alternative to this objective, that there is no hope without a unified Europe. It is inconceivable to think in terms of permanent revolution without Europe's proletariat, its intellectuals, its culture and its multitudes.

9
Resistance and Multitude*

I am here to talk about *Multitude*, which is the follow-up volume to *Empire*. In *Empire* Michael Hardt and I have analysed the structural tendencies of the expansion, restructuring and new efficacy of sovereignty at the global level. In *Multitude* we analyse the emergence of the subject that opposes itself to Empire, which we call counter-empire. We expect that these two volumes will be followed by a third, to be called 'De homine': this will be an analysis of the passions and anthropological metamorphoses which the political subject has traversed in this huge transition from modernity to postmodernity. Anyone who knows the philosophy of modernity, and in particular the thinking of Hobbes, will recognize that the theoretical course we have taken represents the opposite of that of modernity. The moderns, and Hobbes in particular, took as their starting point a renewed metaphysics of man, defined in terms of possessive individualism, which resulted in an ideological view of the transcendence of power, in other words a statement of the necessity of power. Our path, on the other hand, is realistic. We take as our starting point a definition of the new global order, of which we then develop a critique: it is the method of Machiavelli, proceeding from the concrete to its critique . . . and thereby advancing the terms of the possible. In our schema of Empire, in our interpretation of capitalist globalization, opposition is the element which needs to be discovered and uncovered; then we will see how human beings have been modified by this reality, and how resistance can be placed at the centre of an alternative path. Thus we adopt the method of Machiavelli against that of Hobbes, the

---

* Speech delivered at the Antwerp Book Festival, 2 October 2004.

method of Spinoza against that of Descartes, and perhaps also that of Hume against that of Kant. The issue for us is to show how resistance is at the root of every political process, how the subject precedes the sovereign abstraction, and how singularity opposes itself to the abstraction of power.

Multitude is thus a book which presents the problem of the political subject, of its innovation in the present day and, above all, of its production. Already in *Empire* the multitude was defined not as people, not as mass, not as a set of individuals – rather it was defined as a network of singularities, where these singularities, in order not to become reduced to chaos, must recognize themselves in a common that extends between them. This recognition of the common is as much a foundation of multitude as is the recognition that the multitude is made up of singularities. Let us see how things stand today: there is no valorization of capital and no productivity that is not produced by the singular labour-power of the multitude; there is no set of productive forces that is not immediately social, that does not present itself as cooperative, intellectual, relational, affective, and therefore biopolitical. The multitude is not simply an economic concept; it is a concept of class transformed into the forms of the biopolitical. In the transition from Fordism to post-Fordism, the reduction of multitude to working class has fallen apart: the productive multitude lives at the level of social productivity, inasmuch as society in its entirety is set to work. Certainly the subsumption of society by capital is complete; certainly this subsumption is presented in bio-power: but this only means that the totality of the contradictions of exploitation and of the struggle between classes is proposed afresh (no longer simply in the factory but) over the entire social terrain. The new processes of capitalist value-creation, which pass through the recuperation of intellectual labour power, of its intellectuality, of its excedence, reopen at the global level the contradictions that we used to find in the factory and in Taylorized society. The recognition of this reality gives us the image of a society completely traversed by antagonisms and insoluble contradictions: the capitalist recuperation of society has nothing to offer us, but it deepens the contradictions of exploitation, and for us this means a lot. Resistance thus comes to be defined in different ways from those of the past: it becomes increasingly central, because it is not simply resistance to industrial exploitation but resistance to social exploitation; not simply an expression of particular interests (for all that they may be universally recognized in the working class) but the expression of social interests, which are immediately relevant to all workers.

But how are we to recognize, within the socialized multitude, and in resistance to socially diffuse exploitation, a common which can constitute a content of resistance of the exploited subject? This is the question that *Multitude* seeks to answer. That bio-power clashes with the biopolitical could simply represent a situation generically defined, only corresponding to the extension of capitalist power from the factory to society, to the real effectuality of capitalist power over all the dimensions or articulations of the social. We need to show the opposite – in other words, we need to show how the common exists as ontologically prior in the productive expressions of biopolitical resistance. To show this is by no means impossible: indeed, in today's postmodern world this is almost to state the obvious. It is not simply a matter of showing how production today is organized via informatic or immaterial networks of the production of singularity in the social; it is not simply a matter of showing (which is obvious) that the relationship between cooperation and innovation is today the fundamental network of production; it is not even a matter, finally, of arguing that the transformations of labour and the hegemony won within it by immaterial labour are an incredible innovation in the definition of the productive work of the labouring classes. What interests us is to show how all these expressions of the new working class are both productive and innovative (their productive force goes beyond capital's capacity for systemic prefiguration); what is fundamental to emphasize is that this productivity exceeds the measuring capacity of capitalist regulation. Capital no longer succeeds in grasping the productivity of labour power; bio-power is no longer able to hold back biopolitical productivity. The common of the subjects of exploitation therefore has to be understood more as something that capital cannot set its hands on, because this common is innovative and exceeding . . . As well as being, naturally, common – in other words belonging to everyone.

The economic forms of exploitation (that is, the capitalist organization of society) are transformed in these completely new conditions. Global capitalist control (imposed beyond the Fordist discipline which was put into effect in the factory, and thus within national territories, and thus in conditions that were localized), while its project is to achieve a full intensity of domination, collapses in the face of the new common ability for multitudinarian cooperation and innovatory excedence of labour power. Capitalist development is in crisis. This crisis is not easily solvable. It is a crisis in which capital's power of containment and control comes up against a force of resistance which is completely transformed. Here singularity and the innovation of labour power have literally exploded: resistance is no longer that of the factory worker extended to the level of society; it is a completely new resistance, based on the innovation and excedence of productive labour, on an independent cooperation between productive subjects, on an ability to develop constituent potentialities beyond biopolitical domination. Resistance is no longer reactive forms of behaviour but a form of action and production.

Only by studying the processes of capitalist financialization, and by studying them in their global dimensions, can we hope to understand the extreme intensity of the capitalist consciousness of this transition – from the disciplining of labour to monetary control, from the awareness of crisis induced by the innovation and excedence of labour power to a new form of transcendence of domination. It is by means of global financial control that capital seeks to block these revolutionary forces – and this is an enormous challenge!

In this context sovereignty enters the argument. Not simply national but also global sovereignty. How is capital to control the multitude on the measureless terrain of its biopolitical existence when productive labour power presents itself as innovative and excedent? The collapse of every measure of development (and underdevelopment – and even the hierarchization of geographic areas of production at the planetary level), the collapse of every measure of exploitation, creates a crisis of the general political criteria of disciplinary command and also of those of control. The possibility of command requires a measure of exploitation. The much denigrated labour law of value used to provide such a measure. What is the form in which the law of value can be expressed when the ability to define such a measure is not available to capitalist command, and when the very expression of labour power is immediately resistance?

Bio-power has no other alternative, in this situation, than the recourse to force. Permanent war, the central role of preventive war as a form of government, never-ending war correspond to this unmeasured, or rather over-measured, relation between command and obedience, between capital and productivity, between imperial design and multitude. In this context, resistance is no longer simply an economic question or an ethical *dispositif*: it is the very materiality of the new productive subject that is expressed. Resistance, disobedience, refusal are the only force of production that our world knows. Only resistance creates wealth: this is the paradox into which we are forced.

In the present phase of the development of war and peace, of sovereignty and domination, the resistance of the multitude presents itself as a proposition of democracy. Democracy is not a form of government but a mode of participation, a management of the common. In the present phase of the transition from modernity to postmodernity, in which every traditional sovereign relationship is burnt, democracy presents itself with two faces: on the one hand as a means of stopping war and the huge disasters which war provokes, and on the other as the building of a new world order. It is within this relationship – which is continually nourished by opposites (resisting war and exercising constituent power) – that democratic resistance imposes itself.

10
The Monstrous Multitude*

These days the concept of multitude is in the public domain. We use it in our discussions, and it is useful from a political point of view. But it is a difficult concept to manoeuvre. In my talk today I shall seek to penetrate the difficulties of the concept and also to discuss its contradictions; in short, to test it as an outline of a potential reality.

By now there is broad agreement as to what the concept of multitude is not. In the first place, multitude is not working class. Note this carefully: it is *also* a concept of working class – and it is certainly a concept of exploited labour power, but it is more extensive than the concept of working class, because, inasmuch as the whole of society is today dominated – and exploited – by capital, the multitude corresponds to this social dimension of exploitation. The multitude is not the same as the working class because the temporal and spatial dimensions of exploitation have been utterly transformed. The form of labour power which is today hegemonic over the fabric of production is immaterial, intellectual, relational and linguistic labour – and thus a labour power which is flexible both in space and in time. But its most basic quality is that of exceeding the traditional dimensions of capitalist control, both spatial and temporal. In spatial terms, like the labour that feeds it, the multitude is mobile and migrant. The multitude is completely inherent to the biopolitical fabric of production and society; the activity of labour and the exploitation associated with it are to be found in every space of life. The centrality of industry and the general conditions of the regulation of labour power (as capitalism had constructed them) are at an end. Labour presents itself, in its

---

* Speech delivered at the Volksbühne Theatre, Berlin, 6 October 2004.

social submission, as free. The monstrousness of the precariat has to be seen in terms of this transformation of labour, and of the stalemate and blockage of all regulation. Labour power presents itself as ungraspable because its productive *potenza* has rendered ineffectual all the terms of its previous regulation.

The multitude is not an undifferentiated mass – this too is a statement that we now take as normal. It is not mass because it is a network of singularities. But it is also mass, because the multiplicity of productive events and the network of singularities present themselves as a massified common. When immaterial labour presents itself in network form, it is not massified, because it is intellectual, affective, relational and linguistic. But it is common. It is monstrous within this contradiction, monstrous because it is no longer individual labour but cooperative labour, autonomously organized and associated by way of singularity. Capitalist rationality on the other hand can be nothing but individualist.

The multitude is not the people, where by people we understand a chaotic ensemble that only the state is able to recompose. By now this too is stating the obvious. But in this case too the multitude, as a *potenza* of a political subject, is monstrous, because this common labour which sustains it is productive and excedent, innovative and constituent. Multitude is monstrous because it is always constituent.

Monstrous means that all the terms of the labour relation and of society have been caught up in the innovation of the forces of production and therefore present themselves in indeterminate and unqualifiable figurations. Nevertheless, within these modifications and these metamorphoses, labour power and social activity are always present, powerful and hegemonic in the face of every repression or regulation. Resistance itself is monstrous, but it is a resistance which is ontologically irresistible, a new way of living and producing which is tendentially becoming hegemonic.

As regards what the multitude is, we are already largely in agreement (furthermore, in defining what the multitude is not, we have adopted positive and common criteria of definition). In the first place the multitude expresses a biopolitical activity, if we look at it from the point of view of the critique of political economy. What does biopolitical production mean? It means, first of all, resistance to biopower. Today's transformation of capital, at the global level, was brought about by workers' struggles, which eroded and carried to destruction the previous forms of capitalist domination. Capital has developed itself in terms of the real subsumption of society through the perfecting of the function of exploitation; the welfare state represented the highest form of this figure of capitalist subsumption of society. But capitalist subsumption is the response to the invasion that living labour had effected into modern societies (during the short century of proletarian revolutions). The response to the capital's inability to control exploitation within the national space (of the nation–state) was, in the end, capitalist globalization. Living labour also pursues this globalization perspective. The intensity of capitalist domination over the time of life today is matched by, and followed by, the global extension of this domination. How are we to distinguish the working-class insurrection, which imposed the transition from the factory to the biopolitical, from the other effect of this insurrection, which was to introduce the extension of exploitation from local terrains to the global terrain? We see the multitude traversing (in resistant manner) this relation between intensity and extension. The refusal of local command has to be matched by the refusal (or at any rate the continuous destructuring) of global command, of the functions of hierarchy and territorial control that follow from it. Reinventing the freedom of labour is a statement of singularity; it is a claim for productive surplus and political hegemony that has to be developed at the global level. It is a defence of the idea of wealth as the product of resistance. Thus at the biopolitical level we are seeing, in positive terms, the paradoxical claim for the monstrous character of a reappropriation, by immaterial labour power and by the multitude, of the negative qualities of the present condition of the working class: mobility, flexibility, precarity become positive elements of a revolution which is uncontrollable and permanent. This is a monstrous characteristic of the multitude.

But what does the construction of the common mean – within this difficult and extreme relationship that mobility, flexibility and precarity of employment impose on multitude? It means two things. In the first place it means an awareness of the common conditions of labour, that is, of the construction of value, of wealth, as it occurs today. These days, what constitutes the effective network of the processes of production is the cooperation of productive subjects and the innovation of singularities. Workers are not united by ideological elements but by the common form of their exploitation (which is exercised essentially over mass intellectuality but which resounds over every other sector of productive labour), by an effective reality of modes and forms in which labour is obliged to organize and express itself. Workers and peasants, women and men, service workers and industrial workers, they all work – this is the reality – within the same modalities of organization of labour, within a common system of employment and exploitation that has become global.

But defining the coming to awareness of the common condition of exploited labour is not sufficient to enable the conscious construction of the common for the multitude and for the new proletariat. This common awareness will emerge and will impose itself as tendency only when it is ready for the construction of common objects of struggle on the part of the multitude. In the first place against the forms of organization, which are utterly homologous, of private property and public property, in the generalization of the processes of exploitation. To the private and the public are opposed the common and the political demand for the common. In the development of a revolutionary consciousness, this transition is decisive.

Let us be clear here: from the objective, sociological point of view we find that the various different functions of labour (be it in informatics or in research, in peasant labour or in manufacturing, in the services or in the care industries, male or female) are characterized on the same terrain. Intellectual labour unifies exploited labour. At the international level, too, the hierarchies of unequal exchange become increasingly fragile. This does not mean that these hierarchies do not exist – as the processes of global outsourcing have shown – but the situation is unsustainable: the processes of the speeding-up of exchanges and the interdependence of the productive areas are becoming increasingly marked and irresistible. The ultimate limit, however, is introduced by the capitalist management of financialization: an enormous vampire that tends to recuperate and mystify the interests of the workers within the capitalist interest. But to what extent does financialization itself not represent a mystified figure, constructed on the determination of the global common? It is in this framework that the debate on the common will be taken up.

Permit me a brief digression. Within this process we are all poor. In other words, we are all in the hands of a power that reduces us to being children, completely available to global exploitation. But in becoming adults and in experimenting in the forms of cooperation and invention, we begin to discover motifs of love. Without these motifs the world would not exist – I mean the form in which people cooperate, life reproduces itself and sadness or joy is expressed. Now, running through this relationship between poverty and love, there is an element of the common: it is monstrous. It invents, or at least discovers, forms of life that cannot be contained within the relationship of power. The biopolitical fabric is a fulness of desire, a fulness of loving relations. Is this perhaps what constitutes resistance? Is this what renders resistance monstrous in the eyes of capital? Probably yes. We are within this relationship; we ourselves are the monsters of a possible innovation and of a fierce antagonism. Our monstrosity is the sign of the clash which is taking place around whether or not it is possible to impose a measure, a control, a figure on this world.

The construction of the common, if we consider it from the point of view of the organization of labour and society, is a vigorous and active presence, but it is also a mute voice. Only reflection and small (or large) expressions of resistance succeed in revealing it. But there is another moment that we want to stress – the moment when we view this power of construction of the common as a political activity; that is, when we regard it from the viewpoint of the critique of politics. The question which we then ask ourselves is this: what does democracy mean? Now, democracy is not what the history of political thinking offers us, in other words the government of the One by the representatives of the many. Much less is it what Bush is offering us, namely the exportation of the Euro-American constitutional model. When we say 'democracy' we mean an absolute democracy, in other words the government of all by all, the political autonomy of the singularities that recognize themselves in the common. Faced with this proposition, the liberal model of democracy presents itself, and is defined, as corruption: corruption of the singularities, which become reduced to individuals, and corruption of the democratic model, which becomes reduced to representative democracy. Fighting for an absolute democracy is the horizon towards which both the objective perception of the common in the labour processes, and antagonist action – in the common, subjectively reinterpreted as cooperation, innovation and excedence – are deployed. Here it is no longer a matter of saying what the multitude is not, but of practising what the multitude is: a continuous interaction between singularity and the common, between antagonism and constituent project. When we consider democracy in the negative (or only from the point of view of the discovery of the common reality of labour power, or from the perspective of antagonistic *prise de conscience*), we find ourselves up against the final blockages that capitalist bio-power, or Empire, imposes, namely war as the foundation of all political order, war as the basis of every figure of citizenship. War has become the (non-rational) coercive measure of the immeasurable nature of productive labour, of its excedence and, therefore, of the totality of biopolitical resistance to power. Building democracy means, above all, getting rid of these obstacles: declaring war on war, without allowing ourselves to be intimidated; expressing the rights of singularities without allowing ourselves to be distracted by human rights; and building the common, coming to terms with the difficulties of the construction of antagonism. This monstrous character of the multitude, its assertion of excess against measure, is at the heart of the philosophical, anthropological and political reasoning of today's antagonistic world.

11
Multitudo, Utopia Station*

The text of this talk is no longer available. However, on 8 October 2004 there was a long discussion at the Haus der Kunst in Munich, Bavaria, about 'making multitude', that is, about making democracy – in art. The themes were those already outlined in the previous article, 'The Monstrous Multitude', and in the two texts which follow. Here I simply want to recall this debate, because it was held in what had once been the Ehrenhalle *of the* House of Art, *the place where Adolf Hitler had called for the destruction of 'degenerate' art. Hans Ulrich Obrist, Rirkrit Tiravanija and Molly Nesbit had built a wooden* Tower of Time *in this same space, in which a walkway led through various works of art towards the utopia of a new possible world. It was in this dramatic space that the* Utopia Station *discussion took place: on totalitarianism, fascism and globalization, but above all on resistance and the political and subversive management of the possible, today. Within art, and outside art, within fascism and against fascism. This debate in Munich was an exceptional experience of discussion and, perhaps, of resistance.*

* Talk delivered at the Haus der Kunst, Munich, 8 October 2004.

12

Peace and War*

Ernest Hemingway once wrote:
'The world is a fine place, and worth fighting for.'
I agree with the second part.
Se7en

1 War and peace: in its classical–modern form, the conjunction of war and peace preserves the disjunctive value implied in the chiasm of these commonplace notions, showing the impossibility of producing historically and conceptually a positive definition of peace. Peace as disarmament negatively denotes the social state characterized by the absence of war. This is the peace through disarmament of which Raymond Aron speaks in *Peace and War between Nations*: 'It is said that peace reigns when commerce among nations does not entail the military forms of struggle.' Neither essential nor existential, peace does not exclude struggles and conflicts (it demilitarizes them), given that its principle 'is no different from that of wars: instances of peace are based on power' in a world in which the imperative of public security already demands to be considered in its entirety (*totus orbis*). Securitarian in essence, this first secular form of political globalization is indissociable from the war/peace antinomy which submits the 'law of peoples' (*jus gentium*) to the universal perspective of power (*potestas*). Antinomy is the word which Proudhon uses (in *War and Peace: Inquiries into the Principle and the Constitution of the Law of Peoples*, 1861) to explain that 'peace demonstrates and confirms war',

* Text written in collaboration with Éric Alliez and projected in English and German translation at the Frieden Weltwärts Gallery, Vienna, from 4 May to 31 October 2002.

and that 'war in turn is a demand of peace'. Despite the impressive actuality of this formula, Proudhon is here describing what he calls 'the alternative conditions of the life of peoples', subjected to the historical, 'phenomenological' alternating of states of peace and states of war in a world in which the national logic of state centralization implies and explicates the propensity to military combat.

2   Peace and war: in its hyper-modern imperial form, the conjunction between peace and war must be understood in terms of a substitutive value which renders the two terms *absolutely contemporaneous* in view of the reversal of their functions and of their 'classical' relationship. Given that war means the regulation of constituted powers and the constituent form of the new order, peace is merely a deceptive illusion, designed to manage the potential of disorder and its threat, *urbi et orbi*, against the security of the world. Well, everything happens as if, in this world which has neither an outside nor and inside and where 'commerce among nations' throws off the mask of external peace through the world-wide disaggregation of living-together ('internal peace'), peace and war were so tightly intermeshed as to form the two faces of a single fabric projected across the planet. Peace, otherwise known as global war . . . My hypothesis, an observation made by all, has to do with this hybrid identity which throws 'everyone' into a metapolitics where peace appears to be merely the continuation of war by other means. An entirely relative alterity of a policing action continuously exercised over the globalized polis, under the state-of-exception jurisdiction of never-ending war. Peace, one deduces, is a permanent state of exception.

3   At the dawn of modernity, when the paradigms of sovereignty and the nation–state were in gestation, Hobbes relates the history of humanity as a grand narrative of the escape from the state of war of 'all against all', identified as the state of nature. Founded on the dissolution of natural relations and on the alienation of individuals' indefinite desire for power, the political institution of sovereignty invents Law as the principle of itself and thus guarantees civil peace. Peace is paid for at the heavy price of total alienation of freedom in obedience to the sovereign, and is the only compensation for a pact of submission (transfer of power) in which juridical absoluteness (the transfer of right) is the real condition of the body politic. The sovereign is absolute by reason of the obedience of subjects, offering security as the sole benefit; the 'safety of the people' is the condition of reality for sovereign power (the power of the sovereign) to judge 'of

what is reasonable, and of what is to be abolished', to use the formula of *Leviathan*. Leviathan carries in its hands the dagger of justice with which to preserve internal peace, and the sword of war with which it preserves external defence and punishes the rebel, declaring (not *jure imperii* or *dominii*, but *jure belli*) that the enemy within comes under the law of war because 'rebellion is but warre renewed' and sets 'the multitude against the people' (*De cive*). War thus presents itself as the negative condition of peace; it is the *raison d'état* determining voluntary submission to the Master of the Law. There is a need for the omnipresence of war and its representations in order to create an Order which makes a single body out of a dispersed multitude – a body which takes the empty name of People, submitted to the 'absolute power' of the will of one person . . . The modern state is born out of this political representation which supports itself through war, monopolizing, in the name of peace, the logic of accumulation of the power taken away from the 'primitive confusion' of the multitudes. Not for nothing was the Thirty Years War associated with the birth of modern sovereignty: it ends with a peace which imposes the definitive victory of the juridical morality of force over the *politeia* as a 'just' distribution of power (Hobbes perceives Greek justice as a school of sedition). But has anyone ever believed in this peace without justice that crosses the landcapes of slaughter on the back of Mother Courage's cart? Between 1618 and 1648, Germany lost half of its inhabitants . . . The Peace concluded by the modern state is an ideal torn between the theory of the just war (Grotius) and the programme of universal peace to which it is thought appropriate to give the name of Utopia (Thomas More).

4   In the age of self-proclaimed postmodernity, whose planetary image is fixed more by the World Trade Organization than by the United Nations, the distant heir to the projects of perpetual peace, war has become a '*potenza* of order' inasmuch as it is authorized through the 'outdated' character of territorial conquest. Unlike in the classical–modern age, which had known a regulatory notion of peace being achieved through the international community by associating the practices of trade and commerce (*usus commerciorum*) to the sovereign will of states, peace can no longer be expressed, under the obligatory item of *peace research*, except within war and through a logic/logistics of war. Taking the 'state of exception' as its starting point, with a view to replacing international relations of force with a unitary world power, war presents itself as peace-keeping, as a custodian and policeman of peace. The difference from the founding

myth of political modernity reveals itself in the reversal of the relationship between War and Peace. Peace and war. Freed from the secularized utopia of the *Respublica christiana*, peace is no longer the
'solution' of war constructed on a (relative) equilibrium of forces or
on a 'reasoned' (through the cost of war) hegemony – peace is the
procedural condition inherent to the conduct of war founded on the
distinction between friend and enemy. In this context, which we
might call opacification, Schmittian decisionism, which puts the production of sovereignty in motion, now serves Empire. As a final statement of the emptiness of its truth based on the theological analogies
of the reality of the state, the notion of politics has now for its only
purpose merely the creation of a coincidence between sovereignty
and decision in an imperial megalopolitics whose axis causes the
entire world, *totus orbis*, to turn around a sovereign power which
makes the ongoing decisions about the 'situation of exception'. (In
the words of the famous opening phrase of Carl Schmitt's first
Politische Theologie: '*Souverän ist, wer über den Ausnahmezustand
entscheidet*' ['He is sovereign who decides on the state of exception'].
So we shall avoid ironizing or being ironic about the *Axis of Evil* – or
the judgement of God – and simply take into consideration the hyper-
modernity of a situation which marks a complete shift in relation to
the hegemonic model of the *pax romana*, as expressed in the formula
si vis pacem, para bellum ['If you want peace, prepare for war']. It is
no longer a matter of preparing for war in order to achieve peace (the
principle of dissuasion), but of making peace in war as a function of
a continuous destruction (an inversion of the 'progressive' theological scenario of continuous creation), thereby reducing sovereignty to
an imbalance of terror. Does peace therefore become the postmodern name of war? A project to make war in the world perpetual, a
project of perpetual world war?

5   When it deals with war, the literature of modernity always likes to
stage the moment at which the man discovers his loneliness on the
battlefield. Grimmelshausen, Tolstoy, Stendhal, Céline and
Hemingway show this man being – miraculously – neither harmed nor
hurt, stunned by the noise and fury of battle and, even more, by the
fact that the sun and moon continue to shine. The return to peace is
the natural restoration of the sensory presentation of the world, the
aesthetic restoration of the being-within an outside. The question
immediately becomes: can we still approach peace from within, when
postmodernity designates an anaesthesia of life thrown into emptiness, a mourning of our affinity with the spatio-temporal plasma in its

general commodification, and above all the planification of the world as a theatre of operations for a total war that aims at a total peace? How are we to extract ourselves from the squalor of a war whose aim lies in the definitive supremacy of 'global security'? Has peace itself reached its nihilist age, in capitulation to the reign of an equally monstrous 'humanitarianism' of war (as in the formula proposed by Rancière: 'the category of the humanitarian as the double of the *Realpolitik* of States')? Where are we to find peace, if not in a post-war condition in which the civil dissuasion of a post-democracy will have taken over from the 'anti-city strategy' of nuclear dissuasion? Do we have no choice but to await the unexpected, a new monster for sure, in order to free ourselves from the daily misery of this peace and this war, tele-commanded from the towers of the new imperial order? Not knowing how to imagine or describe a battlefield after the massacre robs us of the amazement of being still alive, of feeling oneself alive on the verge of death.

6   'They made a desert and they called it peace', wrote Tacitus. And Thucydides before him. Historians are hyper-realist poets. They are not embarrassed at the thought of force being a lever of historical order. Putting himself at the service of the pure observation of the modalities of politics in its historical reality, Machiavelli scrupulously describes military actions and wars pursued with the aim of imposing an armed peace. Let us be clear: a peace conquered by arms. Arms symbolize the *virtù* of the people, united in the political statement of its (represented) *potenza*. Peace here discovers its transitory value, which only war can 'realize' inasmuch as it is the vector of the general system of power relations whose truth denies every difference except the formal difference between time of peace and time of war. Except at the risk of precipitating quietude into idleness and disorder, which would lead to ruin a state forgetful of the permanence of war, the Prince 'cannot rely on what he has experienced in times of tranquillity'. Because the Prince would thereby succumb to the most dangerous of illusions: the love of peace – when he should instead, together with all his subjects, live peace in the thinking of war. Realism and cynicism here unite in a discourse which identifies war as the condition of truth of every political order. But does Machiavelli's statement, of 'Roman' inspiration, according to which war is creative of order, make sense in a world such as ours, characterized by very little of the 'civic' spirit? Would it not in turn be a simple illusion conveyed by the state of emergency of a communication devoid of being-in-common? The geostrategic reality of the warmongering

illusionism of 'Pentagon-capitalism' – as Virilio calls it – dispenses with all supplementary rhetoric. Now war, peace and barbarism interact within one and the same story, with no other rule than the common sense of the Unworldly. The great pacifisms – whether Christian or communist – taught that war was a sacrifice made in order to build peace: thus one makes war with the thought of, and desire for, peace – 'so as to lead the enemy, by victory, to the advantages of peace' (St Augustine, *Letter 189*, to Boniface). Linked to this 'liberal' idea of peace as the aim of war and of war as a necessary means for peace – 'One must want peace and only make war out of the need [. . .] to achieve peace. So remain peaceful, even when fighting. . .' (*ibidem*) – an idea that is inconceivable except in the reconciled truth (in God or in humanity) of a universal subject – pacifism no longer succeeds in embodying the effectiveness of a project for peace. Peace and war: pacifism can no longer draw its authority from any chronology or teleology capable of leading us from war to a separate peace. No longer able to desire peace, except nostalgically, the resistance to war as a machine constituent of the new order proclaims war against war. Or, better, struggle against war – in the sense in which Deleuze opposes war as the desire for domination founded on the system of judgement ('a judgement of God which makes of destruction something "just"') to the struggle which mobilizes forces against the powers of domination (see 'Pour en finir avec le jugement', in *Critique et clinique*).

7   (What do the 'will to art' and the production of aesthetic acts mean in the context of this global hybridization of war and peace? Where are we to inscribe art, when the new configurations of experience refuse to align themselves on one side or the other? And what do 'war on war' and 'struggle against war' mean for the contemporary artist who is opposed to the poor dramaturgy of thought along the lines of mourning and disenchantment? Very obviously, the aesthetic *potenza* of feeling can only base itself on the expression of indistinction, which constitutes the very violence of the age of the spectacle in the madness of its continuance. So the artist must pass through absolute hybridization, through this immersion in a present where the ruin of the autonomy of art is finally accomplished at the same time as it touches the heteronomy of its vital *potenza*. Inhabiting the sphere of pure means when assuming any singularity whatever, the artist shuns the phantasmagoria of peace and war by beginning to identify the common marks which both of them leave on the bodies of things. Investing this opaque zone of the indiscernible, the artist appropriates

the expropriated regime of politics in a 'war against war' which destroys the system of sensory proofs that belongs to a false social peace. Perhaps the primary reason for the dangerousness of contemporary art lies here: it attacks directly the division of identities which regulates the political effects of the relationship between the utterable and the visible, or between appearance, being and doing. Something that it cannot do in reality, that is, outside of academic mediation, without situating itself in the taking-place of that which it seeks to demonstrate [di-monstrare] in order to reverse – situating itself, and therefore placing us, both within and 'after the passage of life through the ordeal of nihilism' (Giorgio Agamben). This topic, which responds to the hegemonic mediating regime of the image through an expansion of the notion of work of art, reveals what is distinct about artists in their effort to extract the construction of a new possible world from the expression of the unworldly, through a cosmic immersion in the material of sensation. It is characteristic of the contemporary regime of the arts that the experience of the possible as an aesthetic category of the world only creates works through a material removal from the world's collective squalor, and to the degree that the unworkability of the work turns over into a possibility of processual revival for the singularities which are in-common, outside of any representative identity. To expose this position, which no longer allows itself to be represented commonly in the aesthetic anticipation of a communist future, exposing ourselves to the laceration of the sensible through the over-exposure of peace to war – this is the new address of art, which traces its difference in the common machine of an alterity to war no longer able to sustain itself on some remembrance of the being of peace. (The impossibility of thinking the 'fact' of peace as a 'freedom': peace is no longer available except as existence on the 'war front' against the mediating image of the world.)

8   In this world abandoned to the communication of a blind factuality, the artist or the 'non-artist' imposes [im-pone] – for instance, imposes [pone] on the immanence of this world without-either-outside-or-inside – exodus as the only possible creative event:exodus from obedience to the regulation of sayable and visible identities, exile into measurelessness, which is opened up by the deregulation of the a priori forms of war and peace dragging us into struggle. Since exodus, secession and the struggle against war are one sole and single thing which does not lead somewhere other than here, under the condition of an extreme deterritorialization which decides the common telos. The runaway does not flee the spectacle of the market without turning its annihilating power

against the state, which is the administrator of nihilism; he does not
desert war without attacking the semblance of peace in favour of new
common and cooperative spaces. Inverting the messianic dislocation
from the elsewhere to the here in order to construct a new mobility and
a new temporality, exodus is the name of the transmutation of the values
of resistance into the constituent *potenza* of a biopolitics which is otherwise postmodern. To escape, to secede, means to destroy all the transcendent barriers which give meaning to the commanding logic of
political representation, the better to reappropriate 'global' mobility; to
escape while making a constitutive act means to invest in generation and
against corruption, to oppose the cosmopolitan hybridization of the
world of life to the policing hybridization of peace and war. In the exposure to measurelessness that belongs to it, the singularity of art teaches
us that the product of generation is always a 'monster' which implies the
'common' (of bodies, of languages–events and of machines) in a biopolitics of exodus and secession.

9   Struggle against war: peace is no longer a condition of life; peace
has to be reinvented in the exodus from the world without God that
the 'City of men' must enact in order to exit from the unworldly
squalor. In the absence of a peace which can be the *ethos* of the world,
exodus is struggle, guerrilla and creation of peace *ex nihilo*. A peace
which is to be invented as an escape from nihilism, as a global *dispositif* locally creative of meaning, as the de facto meaning of an ecosophy
of the multitudes, making a virtue of the differentiating idea of the
common and of its generations which transform the world. The contrary of an utopia: the open and total dystopia of war against war. A
task that will be long, complex and militant: peace is nothing but an
intuition, just like a work of art; peace, like art, is the capturing of
forces in a becoming which enriches what it gets hold of (the opposite
of a forced pacification: 'A peace without force resembles death', as
Marie-José Mondzain puts it). It follows from this that peace cannot
be conceived without going through the war it is fighting in order to
destroy the misery it feeds on while affirming the life forces, which
build themselves on reserves of violence. Exodus is the opening of this
path, which can lead to the Stoic's 'tranquillity of mind' only by
making a work, a work of peace, out of humanity's traversing of chaos
(an analogy, again, between the work of peace and the work of art that
would not hold up on its own except for the the chaosmos [*sic*] of
forces it implies). Exodus, when there is no longer anything beyond
or elsewhere, in a world without outside. Hence [this is] exodus from
the world as a collective construction of being, [it is] the living labour

of the world and the globalization of living labour launched against the transcendental domination of 'dead labour', when this cannot recompose itself except through war – which is the first precondition (with the police-led establishment of law) and the last stage of the state-form (with the outside-the-law operations of the world-wide sovereign global police). Exodus is the transformation of passions in the *vita activa* of knowledge, when knowledge deploys its generative potential as cooperation, incommensurable to all political thinking of measure and unity and to the transcendental illusion of community. From the point of view of a radical materialism it is not peace, then, but the constituent cooperation of singular multitudes that creates the common existence of the world – in the form of a non-organic community, an operational community which is deterritorialized and deterritorializing, and which we have to think of as ontologically anterior to, and superior to, the transcendental distinction between war and peace, over which sovereign power 'decides'. The test is on the edge of time: it is against this test that the sovereign power 'decides' on the monstrous hybridization of war and peace, marking the definitive identification of sovereignty with the police. The consequence lies on the edge of being: peace is no longer in a position to give the conditions of life to which the name of ethics is tied. Related to the reality of the composition and decomposition of relations, ethics is, quite the opposite, the operational asymmetry of the peace–war situation inasmuch as it is a 'struggle between Self, [. . .] between forces that subjugate or are subjugated, between the powers that express these relationships of force' (Gilles Deleuze), a precipitation of atoms and a struggle of passions, a crystallization of differences in the multitudinarian chaos of singularities and emission of new *potenze* forming constellations which are indissociably affective and productive through the inflection of differences. There is no ethics without this *clinamen* which orients the matter of the common towards exodus as constructivist transitivity of the world. But, in the same way, there is no aesthetics without the decision 'to allow the real connection of existence to appear as the real sense' (Jean-Luc Nancy). It is not impossible to invoke here, in the manner of Félix Guattari, a 'new aesthetic paradigm' which is transversalist and based on social creativity and which reminds us that art is the Vigilambulant, the waking-walker of this process which confronts war (rather than escaping into an illusory peace). The work of art is a vital transmutation of the conditions of death which are commonly imposed, a potentialization of the common in a teleology of liberation which is a creative machination of affections whose intensities are irreducibly singular and plural.

10   Against the negationists of contemporary art: if art is this collective projection which shows that war is impotent in the face of the
singular constructions of the world it intends to break, then contemporary art, in the non-place which is imposed on it (by excess and by
defect) through the 'installations' and the expressive machines it
constructs for itself, must demonstrate that peace can be reinvented
as a biopolitical condition of life, as a common resistance which, in
the multimedia constellation of bodies, unites Eros to the general
intellect of the multitudes.

(Against the negationists again: we have to affirm that the violence of
sensations, the most violent deconstruction of sensation implied in
the 'surface/medium' relationship of this real art, does not provide
reasons for objection to this demonstration.)

13

Art and Culture in the Age of Empire and the Time of Multitudes*

1   The critique of culture is a familiar and recurrent topic. Rightly or wrongly, in relation to our present situation?

When in 1947, at the end of the Second World War, Max Horkheimer and Theodor W. Adorno published their *Dialectic of Enlightenment*, a new critical model was formulated. It was both singular and susceptible to being reproduced, at one and the same time both different and generalizable. Reflecting on the Europe which had just been devastated by fascism – the Europe which they had just left – and on the American society which had received them in their exile, Horkheimer and Adorno examined the tendency of Enlightenment thinking to flip over into its opposite, not only into the explicit barbarities of fascism, but also into the totalitarian enslavement of the masses via the new blandishments of the culture industry. European fascism and American commodification were seen in the same light. From then through till today, that judgement on western culture has gradually been confirmed as Empire has come to be a reality. The conversion of fascism into the commodification of culture has come about seamlessly: it has been diffused all over the planet, and telecommunications have been the basic means of its diffusion. Corruption of the image has now found an extension in the universal prostitution represented by tourism, and in a thousand other insults to good taste. Watch Murdoch's television and you will have the proof that the model of cultural critique offered by Adorno really does spell out the ontology of the new world. The reconversion of this world to fascism,

* Text presented at the Université de tous les savoirs, Beaubourg (Paris), 7 November 2003.

its reconstruction along lines of war, its corruption through degrading images: today all this is progressing exponentially . . . For instance, TV has now become interactive, it produces trash culture and it constructs a public to match; the public in turn demands new trash productions and so we come full circle. The neutering of news and information follows the same laws of the crushing of passions: if romanticism and classicism are both reduced to insignificant signs, then the only thing left for truth is to become the instrument of power or of vulgarity. The Adornian model has now been taken to extremes: what was innovative in its critique of culture at the end of the Second World War today comes to state the obvious. Indignation is no longer possible. Here, therefore, the critique of culture necessarily returns to the fore.

Within – and against – this infernal machine, which globalizes culture at the same moment as it lacerates and perverts its values, there are always dissident spirits ready to rebel. But when the circle of cultural communication is closed and self-contained, the trajectory of the spirit has a need for something else: for a desire of bodies, for the freedom of the multitudes, for the *potenza* of languages. Something, in the horrific abstraction of communication, subjectivizes itself. That something is the soul of the multitude. In the universe of perverted signs someone produces simple signs of truth: look at Basquiat – infantile signs and utopian descriptions . . . If production is linguistic, it is through language that subjectivity is produced. The abstraction of communication becomes the body of singularities. Thus the multitude is born.

2   Television tries to reconstruct the visible world in the image and resemblance of the master and, more generally, of the function of power. It is 'downwardly' interactive – it dominates it, disintegrates it and finally produces it. Wars are recounted in languages that range between the dissimulation of reality and the narration of global fantasies. The documenting of war becomes a video game. However, when the multitude discovers that it exists within a neutralization of life, this whole stage begins to shake and to fall apart. The multitudinarian demystification of the reality of power began in Vietnam. All it took was a few photographers and the odd soldier–philosopher to show how many tears and how much blood had flowed in those trenches. Since that time, people's capacities for demystification and their grasp of the world have become real viruses – viruses which, paradoxically, represent the antidote to the potions which we distil, and which spread with the speed of epidemics. Take the events of

Genoa during the G8 summit of 2001: in vain did the police develop their 'low intensity' war against peaceful demonstrators, accusing them – through the manipulation of the media – of being a bunch of criminals. In vain, because the multitude had many more cameras and video cameras than the police had, and into every home went the image of the policeman responsible for the death of young Carlo Giuliani. The multitude rebelled through its own ability to produce images, rendering rebellious the abstraction of signs. There is no longer the possibility of transforming the world only by interpreting it: the final project of philosophy – as embraced by those communicators whom Adorno would have called fascists – has imploded. As we know – and as a certain bearded old man once said – the only way to interpret the world is to change it.

So if this is the way things are, the dialectics of reason has finally run out. It has been extinguished in the capitalist production of repetitive images ('the end of history') and has been replaced by the new production of desire. Today the abstraction which had been transformed into commodity undoubtedly finds its redemption in this initiative of the multitude. Goodbye Adorno; goodbye to realism and to the repetition of the critical model of modernity: here the critique of culture instals itself on a new terrain, which is precisely that of the multitude, of the postmodern. Perhaps what the multitude produces is no longer utopias but dis-utopias [*disutopie*], that is to say, a capacity for living within them, the possibility of carving out languages from the inside and of facilitating an emergence of the material desire for transformation.

3   The dis-utopia of the multitudes does not live in abstract ways. On the contrary, it is biopolitical. This means that culture is given in forms that are structurally dense and lived. When we speak of the biopolitical, power and violence are considered, so to speak, 'from below', that is, from the point of view opposite to that of bio-power. However, this does not mean that we need to fall back into a dialectics of 'high' and 'low', where the low is opposed to the high and vice versa. The multitude is an ensemble of proliferating singularities capable of expressing new linguistic determinations. The dialectics leads back to the figure of the One: this new dialectics, however, is chaotic – the multitudes are ensembles of atoms which encounter each other along *clinamena* [angles of fall] that are always untimely and exceptional. There is thus no dialectical contradiction between living within the structures of bio-power and the ability freely to traverse these structures in antagonistic ways, qua biopolitical subjects.

Today the only problem that affects us when we look at the new cultural determinations within imperial space is that of grasping the crossings, the events, the innovations which traverse the chaotic ensemble of the multitudes. We have to understand when the biopolitical acquires an advantage over the expression of bio-power. No synthesis, no *Aufhebung* is possible here: we have only oppositions, divergent expressions, multiplicities of linguistic tensions which go in all directions. The transition from modernity to postmodernity is characterized by the lack of measure that postmodernity presents: a lack of measure which marks the end of all the criteria of measure that modern rationalism had proposed and imposed. Measure and instrumental rationality, which impose themselves spontaneously in the golden age of modernity – between humanism and Cartesianism – are expressed in the next phase – from Hegel to Bergson – as the metaphysical synthesis of an ordered world. In short, in the twilight of modernity, this measure and this rationality are applied through the violence of an instrumental rationality, in the manner of Weber and Keynesian planning. But today measure and rationality are at an end. It is not the case that, as Adorno said, after Auschwitz poetry is no longer possible; nor, as Günther Anders said, that all hope died with Hiroshima. Poetry and hope are revived in the postmodern multitudes, losing all homogeneity with what poetry and hope had been in modernity. What is, therefore, the new canon of culture in postmodernity? We do not know, but that is no reason to deny its existence. What we do know is that this great transformation is taking place in life, and that it is in this life that it expresses new figures: figures without measure, a lack of formal measures. Monsters.

4   Thus postmodern innovation is monstrous. This feature of monstrosity has two characteristics: its absence of measure and its boundless ontological becoming. Let us begin, therefore, by discussing the monster in specific terms, in terms of these two characteristics. And let us begin first of all with its ontological becoming. We have already referred to this: the living expressions of our culture are not born in the form of synthetic figures but, on the contrary, in the form of events; they are untimely. Their becoming is within a genealogy of vital elements that constitute a radical innovation and the very form of the lack of measure. Some contemporary philosophers have set off in pursuit of this new expressive force of postmodernity, and they have attempted to characterize it. Already Lacan had pointed to the absence of measure in the new; for Derrida, the productivity of the margins seeks new orders as it disseminates; as for Nancy and

Agamben, we find them picking the flowers that grow in these fields of extreme limit . . . For all these authors there is nothing that characterizes the monstrousness of innovation positively; and yet they all share an acute feeling, an intensity, of ontological exasperation. The more the new forms are unproductive and absent, the more the new forms are a reality and slip over into being. They take the plunge or they sink. They try to breathe in the shifting sands. But what these authors do not perceive is that this material in which they have accepted to immerse themselves is the building clay of other worlds. The ontological dimension does not lead to the edge of nothingness, but on the contrary it nourishes itself on the constitutive dimension of the men who gamble their lives on this impossible margin, recklessly and with no alternative. The ontological dimension does not entrust itself to the power of a capital that is ever-increasingly parasitical, but takes as its developmental starting point the multitudinarian intellectuality of workers who are immaterial, mobile, flexible and precarious. The ontological dimension appears in a series of paradoxes: the becoming woman of work; the joining together of reason and affect at the very heart of production. And one could continue at length in defining the ambivalence and radicality of this ontological condition – a condition which always involves the positioning of the individual who lives this transition from modernity to postmodernity. The monster is born at the heart of this ontological dimension.

But this ontological dimension of innovatory chaos has lack of measure as its second characteristic. The monster is an absence of measure, or rather a new measure. So, in this transition, who will be able to say what is the negative and what is the positive, and the exodus, and the constituent capacity? Between the seventeenth and eighteenth centuries the scientists who were interested in nature applied their curiosity to the search for deformities, and kings collected them in museums of horrors. However, in that very lack of measure there was also a seeking after measure. Horror (and also the sublime) was what brought the soul back to a desire for order. How many three-headed chickens, Siamese twins and hermaphrodites, how many physical deformities and distortions were collected in those museums of anatomical deviation and of the extraordinary! Geoffroy Saint-Hilaire left us historical encyclopedias of anomalies in the organization of nature, and also of the attempts to establish the laws and causes of these monstrosities. A name was given to all this: teratology. But the new postmodern figure of monstrosity is not teratological. It is, simply, life expressing itself differently; it is a hybridization which individual concatenations seek to construct starting from existence as chaos – between the human and the animal; it is the hope and the decision of a life which will be neither ordered hierarchically nor prefigured through measure. Aristotle – and before him a large part of ancient philosophy, which was constructed and imposed as the memory of humanity – says that the origin of being is also its order and its measure: *arche* means both beginning and rule or command. This eugenicism was taken up by a modernity which sought the legitimacy of its tropes in antiquity. In postmodernity, on the contrary, what the monster indicates is the negation of classical and modern eugenicism: this is the exposure of an ontological process which has abandoned the principle of essence. This trajectory, which is ours, may perhaps carry us into dark forests where we might lose our bearings: but we cannot spare ourselves this march in the form of interrogation, this absence of ordered and measured origin. Therein lies the tension that uproots every prejudgement – all prejudgements and all prefigurations; and, beyond prefigurations, every unitary matrix, whether spatial or temporal. And it is here, at the heart of being, that a convulsed creativity opens up . . . Here we are not talking of vanguard genealogies, but of the concrete history of multitudes of singularities. Of anthropological monstrosities. When a forest burns, the ground becomes fertilized. They have burned the forest (and yet it moves); and we become again wild beings, free as the birds. We go to inhabit a new nature.

5   The dimensions of globalization come close to being lack of measure. In any event, the world no longer has an 'outside'. It no longer has an 'outside' and it no longer has precedents. Take cultural anthropology and the way it was formed and developed: the European individual lived at its centre and had two 'outsides': the primitive and the aborigine, also known as the barbarian. An anthropological precedent and a political outside. The European human was the central point towards which all the rest of civilization tended – the market, aesthetic criteria, money, habitat, the *Welt* and the *Umwelt*: history tended towards a monopoly of the European individual; everything which had existed before was primitive, and what the European now dominated was barbarian or aboriginal. But globalization, our present human space, no longer knows limits – or, more exactly, the only limit it has is its external circumference; and once this limit is reached all expressions are forced to turn to the inside. There is a kind of red thread which gives meaning to this huge extension of self-reflection. What we have here is the last Prometheanism, the last universalism of bourgeois culture; yet at the same time it is also the first determina-

tion of the *Gattungswesen* of a liberated humanity. All of history prior to globalization has led us to this limit: it wanted to be the sign of the extension of the domination of western culture, but at the same time it revealed the huge – and sometimes monstrous – effect of a process made up of contradictions and struggles: the genealogy of a subject which expresses itself as uncontrollable but which is there, within those limits. The stage of the world is thus not simply a horizon: it is truly a scenography whose materials – in the manner of the Ballets Russes – become an integral part of the drama. The stage of the world is both limitless and finite; it lives on this monstrous opposition. It is in these terms that the end of history can be predicted, or its complete realization. Every artistic work achieves an aesthetic meaning to the extent that it succeeds in corroborating this paradox (asserting it or denying it). The world has become immense and at the same time minuscule; we find ourselves in a Pascalian situation. But we no longer have a God. Space is smooth and superficial, the immanence of value rests only on the works of men. In this situation, what can it mean to be an artist?

6   What does it mean to make the monster act on the new stage of the world? It means viewing it within a process of anthropological metamorphosis; it means identifying it at the heart of this same muta- tion. As we have seen, this mutation is spatial; but it is also temporal: when bourgeois western civilization has reached the limit of the world, it is in time that the end of history is realized. The spatial synthesis of the 'here' and of the world seeks to absorb the temporal synthesis of the 'now' and of the infinite. The anthropological metamorphosis is played out around these paradoxes. It is in this that postmodernity consists. Here we have a great and monstrous narration . . . Indeed, the flesh of human fortunes cannot be contained in the unity of time and place that the story requires. The flesh does not make itself body. The flesh overflows from the borders of artistic expression onto every border of the global horizon. Enormous passions traverse this impos- sibility of the flesh to make itself body. There was a time – in the course of the great historical span which preceded 1968 – in which this inability of the flesh to make itself body was lived as a utopian opening. This was an artistic utopia: the literary and aesthetic van- guards had to create utopia. The end of the world was brought closer, to the extent that utopia had managed to grasp the extreme possibil- ities of collective practice in constructing the real. But, as in the great early Christian writers, the objective, the masterwork, was the Apocalypse . . . For postmodernity, to be prophetic is no longer a

possibility. Thus we talk about Apocalypse without being prophetic and we speak of vanguards without being utopian: the world has closed in on itself, now the attention is directed globally inwards and the lines of escape are interrupted. We have only the possibility of transforming the world from within. 'Another world is possible' implies an exodus that leads us to ourselves. Every time that we run up against a limit (and this limit has no outside and cannot be gone beyond), we can only look inside ourselves and reconcentrate attention on the *kairos* of the present . . . So what is *kairos*? In Greek culture *kairos* represented the moment at which the arrow was fired: but this was a culture which still conceived of a future, that is, of a temporal relationship between the moment of the firing and the arrival. The arrow fired at the sky could reach the stars. Today the *kairos* is the arrow that strikes full in the heart, it is the arrow that comes back from the limit of stars. *Kairos* is the necessity (but also the possibility) of constructing, starting from oneself, the possibility to transform bodies: not so much to cross-breed them towards the outside, but to construct and hybridize them from the inside. It is the possibility of making politics by leading all the elements of life towards a poetic reconstruction. This constituent project is inherent in the very term 'biopolitical'. If we live in globalization, if we live in a world with unsurpassable limits, a world in which the Copernican revolution has definitively run out, in which Ptolemy and the centrality of *kairos* have become the sole point of reference – if all this is given, then what will it mean to develop the creative and constituent spirit of artistic work? If the only possibility of artistic and ethical action consists in moving internally to being – acting in a biopolitical manner – in such a way as to make action a mutation–transformation of the essence, both spiritual and physical, of the human body; if the structure of the social has become central and the world so small and folded back on itself as to preclude any possibility of making an exodus from this habitat and of formulating utopian illusions based on other *topoi*; then what does it mean to act artistically? It means constructing new being, reflecting global space inwardly – towards the existence of the singularities. Will it mean moving towards the removal of death, and dissolving the internal limits of the global machine? What the monster promises us is precisely this.

7   The multitude is the only subject susceptible of launching this creative challenge to death. The multitude is an ensemble of singularities, but every singularity is in turn an ensemble of multitudes. This concatenation struggles for life within life, and against death. The

multitude's way of being is nothing other than this continuous proliferation of vital experiences which have in common the negation of
death, the radical and definitive refusal of that which arrests the
process of life. The global world as we know it, as Empire delivers it
to us in the political order, is a closed world: it is subject to the entropy
of spatial and temporal exhaustion. But the multitude which acts in
this closed world has learned to transform it, passing through each of
its subjects, through each singularity from which it is composed. Just
when we thought that history was ended, as Foucault says somewhere,
we understood that it was actually renewing itself within ourselves . . .
And this is exactly what happens to us, to us multitudes, to us bodies
of multitude. It is only in our transformation and in a fierce struggle
against death that the action of the multitude opens.

   That, for me, is the meaning of art in the age of Empire and in the
time of multitudes.

14
Marx/Impero-Imperialism*

My impression – ever since the first controversies began to emerge around the concept of Empire – is that the theoretical rejection of the concept of Empire as the new figure of sovereignty within and above the globalization of markets has been not particularly significant. The concept of Empire *in se* is, in some ways, self-evident.

Those who reject the concept of Empire and argue instead for the importance of the old categories of imperialism do so because they reject the idea of Empire politically and think that the condition, figure and presence of the nation–state is essential in order to act. They reject the concept of Empire per se, so to speak; they see it as inadequate to match the urgency of the struggle and organization, which latter seems not to exist outside the constitutional terrain of the modern state. The problem therefore arises at the point where we say that today it is precisely at the level of politics and organization that it is necessary to go beyond the nation–state.

To expand on this brief introduction, I would stress that one of the few critiques that have been directed at Empire per se, in other words from the theoretical point of view (the critique by Bidet, who says that the concept goes beyond, and mystifies, the traditional Marxist relation between the analysis of the structure of capitalist power/exploitation and that of the world system – dependency theory), has been taken on board by us in *Multitude*, although obviously we have altered it in order not to reproduce simply the old figures of imperialism. In fact Bidet's conclusions, where he tends to overvalue the

* Contribution to the plenary session of the *Actuel Marx* Conference, Nanterre (Paris), 30 September 2004.

state's mediation, are unacceptable on the political terrain, in other words on the terrain of Empire per se, as we shall see later. I must therefore defend the concept of Empire and re-launch the political themes (which include and subsume the theoretical themes) presented in the book. In order to do this I would like to begin my analysis by identifying the crisis of the nation–state, not simply for the sake of doing so, but to illustrate the problems which arise in this area, in the constitution of the global market and imperial sovereignty.

1 The first point of crisis can be identified at the level of the critique of political economy. It is in fact starting from the critique of the international organization of labour that the concept of nation–state no longer holds. I am obviously not referring merely to the effects – or rather to the political effectiveness – of the global regime of trade, or to the crisis of the monetary, economic and cultural parameters that had made possible the nation–state's control over development; I am talking about a deeper and more basic dimension, namely the radical transformation in the form of value creation and in the mechanisms of exploitation.

The form of value creation has been modified by the hegemony – tendential but increasingly actual – of immaterial labour (intellectual, relational, linguistic, affective and so on) over and within the production process. The new process of value creation cannot be controlled within spaces that are territorially closed. It is dominated by a mobility of productive factors and forces of production. Moreover, it requires a universal freedom of communication. What is evident here is the urgent need for a new *Tableau Économique*. This will need to construct a new map of the relations and exchanges between fields of production; assure the pre-eminence of social factors over entrepreneurial (or purely industrial) factors; reveal the primacy assumed by financial processes over direct investment; express the massive power potential of the communications industry; present the (by now) irresistible mobilization of the multinational manufacturers of goods and of services and the like. In short, there is a new *Tableau Économique* and it is dominated by the forces which are the bearers of productive general intellect. The *Tableau Économique* of general intellect goes beyond the nation–state.

(And it does not particularly matter if our way of seeing things is accused of interpreting the Marxian thematic too broadly. What interests us is simply that these discourses are, in a continuity of

Marxist method, politically effective, which means historically determined.)

Secondly, the mechanisms of exploitation have been completely transformed today. The law of value (and therefore of surplus value), in the elementary Marxian definition, turns out to be inefficacious (it continues perhaps to be effective only in the marginal sectors of development). Exploitation now configures itself as expropriation of the values of cooperation and productive circulation, as capitalist appropriation of the innovative excedences of immaterial labour in the social organization of labour.

(Around these concepts, I would like to encourage you to revisit Marx's analysis of landed income and of the extraction of surplus value in the transport industry . . . There you will find the basic antecedents of our hypotheses.)

Now, the mechanisms of social exploitation embrace the whole of global space and extend over it. The nation–state is completely ineffectual in the face of this fundamental cell of exploitation and its metastases – which occur immediately at the global level. This means that every form of insubordination, of struggle against wage labour, must be capable – at the same moment at which it is rebelling against exploitation and recognizing its new nature – of calling itself multitude. Because this is the multitude – namely the recognition of the singularity of the new forms of production of value and therefore of the social exploitation that follows from it, and the overcoming of a restricted concept of working class in the organization of revolution. The modern state is the specific political form of capitalist exploitation in the nation–space. This state-based determination is unsustainable in the face of the insubordination against the present form of value-creation and exploitation. To speak of Empire and imperialism without periodizing them is thus really dangerous – in fact, more or less reactionary.

2   The second point regarding the crisis of the nation–state will be identified at the level of the Marxian theory of crises.

In this area too, the space–time of the nation–state is entirely insufficient to identify the present figure of the economic–political crisis. It is obvious that, out of the three types of capitalist crisis (in production and circulation) related by Marx – that deriving from disproportions in production (that is, underproduction and overproduction); that of circulation; and that related to the tendential fall in the rate of profit – certainly the first two, but probably also the third, have been subjected to effective measures of Keynesian and post-Keynesian control: all this has developed increasingly outside the terrain of the nation–state, at the global level. Moreover, the latest crises have definitively exploded the old models of imperialist (and/or colonial) dependency and have increasingly re-framed integration, sometimes presenting it as interdependence. Since the 1930s and the New Deal, crisis has in fact become a crisis controlled (and/or provoked) by an articulated relationship between the structure of exploitation and the global hierarchical system, to take up Bidet's scheme of things.

But it is here that the qualitative modification intervenes. The process of economic regulation of the crisis has passed through increasingly effective and sophisticated techniques (from discipline to control, from Keynesianism to monetarism and so on), but this transition has increasingly driven it and installed it on a biopolitical terrain. So today it is at the biopolitical level that the crisis has to be identified and defined. If disproportions and blockages of circulation are no longer disastrous in their effects and are controlled in advance, if the falling rate of profit is continuously resisted and/or compensated for by an increase in the productivity of labour, then the Marxian approach of identifying the crisis and the proposals of struggle within the crisis needs to be measured against these new dimensions. Here the discussion returns to the earlier point about the reformulation of the theory of exploitation and the reconfiguration of the organization of labour.

Today the crisis presents itself essentially as the difficulty of exercising control over the new social forces of production, both with regard to their *potenza*, which extends to the whole of social life, and with regard to their expression, which is characterized by productive excedence, by the search for political and cultural freedom and by the identification of common values. When production becomes biopolitical, and hence invests every aspect of life – and when power becomes bio-power and hence traverses imperiously (and attempts to configure) all the movements which produce value – then the crisis is defined, from capital's point of view, not only as a greater or lesser marginal blockage of production and/or circulation but as the product of a set of resistances which are born out of the productive activity, always excedent, of the multitudes. Neo-liberalism has failed precisely on this terrain, insofar as it maintained (and in fact accentuated) the old model of control without realizing that the composition of labour power

had been completely altered. The excedence of production
(which has immaterial labour as its technical base and the self-
forming of the multitudes as its political base) cannot be enclosed
within the forms and processes of control which the organizational methods of modern capitalism had constructed, in relation to massified or Fordist labour.

The problem of the modern national state must be seen in the
light of this reality. Imperialism was an expansion of national cap-
italisms, structured by entirely traditional systems of production,
control and sovereignty. When workers' mobility and flexibility,
internal and international migrations and the excedent production of value by the multitudes come into play, the imperialist
projections of the nation–state, if the latter finds itself in difficulty,
are headed for disaster. The polemic of Empire is against the
nation–state, to the extent that the former recognizes a new political–economic fabric (the imperial one, precisely), in which the
class struggle has introduced irreducible elements (excedence,
mobility, new working-class management of production time and
innovation) into the old form of control by the nation–state. Thus
the crisis involves the entire social context. Crisis presents itself as
lack of control over productive and political events, since these can
no longer be controlled: in the biopolitical context, events are in
fact unforeseeable, unexpected relapses, radical insurgencies. On
the question of crisis, Lenin provides us with theoretical advances
which are infinitely more profitable (today, in postmodernity)
than could ever have been offered by the 'ivory tower' economists,
be they Austrian or Soviet. The nation–state and imperialism are
completely disarmed in relation to this *potenza* and unforesee-
ability of the movements of multitude. To develop today a theory
of crisis is to insert the analysis into – and to act within – the parameters of the new *Tableau Économique*. All the main experiences
of economic crisis in the past fifty years have occurred within a
biopolitical complexity of references that has rendered them, each
time increasingly, massively offensive. If we look at imperialism
from a traditional point of view, we see it as a production of dependency. Today, however, 'the production of dependency' is obviously still possible, but this dependency will present itself as a
phenomenon of resistance, immediately within the structures and
dynamics of bio-power, of the imperialist attempts to neutralize
struggles and to invent new cages for them (new nations, for
instance). The theory of imperialism therefore clashes not only
with the quantity of relations and the global connections, but

also with deep structural phenomena, with unwillingness to tolerate exploitation on the part of the multitudes (or of the singularity rendered common).

Behind the concept of imperialism, moreover, and, even more so, behind the concept of colonialism, lie productions of imaginaries that are linked to a kind of economic–political Darwinism, constructed and nourished by the nation–state. The Bush notion of 'nation-building' is (after the nationalist excesses of Nazism) the latest embodiment of this illusion. The fact that the recourse to elements of local identity, and sometimes to nationalism, makes it possible to resist the projects of imperialism does not mean that this resistance should be seen to be the same as in former models of anticolonial and anti-imperialist struggle. In fact, in the present biopolitical structure of resistance, it is the very idea of modernity (as well as that of the nation–state) which is put into question. That another world is possible means that national and imperialist dimensions of the domination project are in crisis. The project of modernity as domination and instrumental rationality of capitalism leaves space for sabotage and for an alternative idea of modernity.

3   From this fragility of the capitalist structure of power, from this non-resolvability of the economic and critical dimensions of the structure of the nation–state (and of the consequent category of imperialism), derives the more important and more determining crisis in the definition of the nation–state and imperialism: the crisis of sovereignty. As we know, the theory of sovereignty connects to a logical principle which identifies the very soul of power and its exercise over a people in the reduction to unity. It is not hard to see that in this context sovereignty could only present itself as a mystical, irrational, decisive element, and this has been the case in the history of western political thought right from the start. This influence has been very profound. However, in Marx's own work the concept of sovereignty, albeit related to the analysis of modes of production, is not treated in this light: there is also in Marx (and in general in all the theories which consider sovereignty in terms of a monopoly of power, or in terms of dictatorship) an underestimation of the metaphysical operation of the reduction to one of the multitude and/or of the whole universe of singularities. Now, what appears obvious at this point of our excursus is that such a *reductio ad unum* of sovereignty is no longer possible. When bio-power subsumes the entire world as its category, or as a

product of transcendental imagination, when it traverses the entire world with *dispositifs* that are more or less immanent and ordinative, then contradiction and crisis extend over the whole biopolitical terrain. Through policies of crisis containment, be they purely budgetary or demographic or, latterly, welfarist, the subsumption of society within capital has occurred, but this has gone hand in hand with the subsumption and transformation of contradictions, refusals and resistances. Instead of consolidating itself, the state of late modernity – the Keynesian and Fordist state – entered into a dynamic which was contradictory and destructive.

It is not accidental that today war is no longer the continuation of politics by other means. War today, in postmodernity, has become the very basis of politics and of any possible governance. This centrality of war is a result both of the crisis of the law of value (thus of the lack of excess in exploitation) and of the new ability that labour power has to produce value in a way that exceeds capitalist–political instrumental knowledge and control. The concept of sovereignty (as fixation and hypostasis of the one) no longer succeeds in enclosing within a sphere of control the multitudinarian dynamics of production. The excedence of labour or the production of self that living labour has by now begun to assert in multitudinarian ways (the only way, furthermore, of creating wealth), while it requalifies the concept of crisis (bringing it within the biopolitical relation), also opens first onto the problem, and then onto a new conceptualization, of the notion of sovereignty. Sovereignty is no longer able to present itself as one; or, rather, only war can impose, destructively, the unitary device. Already in the political theories of the heirs of modernity (Schmitt, Benjamin, Derrida, Agamben) war functions as the sole unitary *dispositif* of sovereignty, and therefore as the only foundation of politics (and, in the biopolitical perspective, of legality itself). The exception has become the rule.

As regards the crisis of the idea of the sovereignty of the nation–state, the crisis which is, so to speak, external to its structure – namely the crisis determined by the impossibility of fixing unilaterally value and the measure of values in exchange, and hence money, the measure of power, and hence the imperialist *dispositif*, the form of communication, and hence the ideological autonomy – there now occurs a very new crisis, internal to and consubstantial with the nation–state: in other words there is a crisis of legitimation that can only be resolved by the over-determination of war. Sovereignty is the *dispositif* of a self-destructive victory – in capital's perspective. But even if this were the case, it is the very idea of sovereignty that has exhausted itself; or rather presents itself as an eternally unresolved duality, a continually explosive tension. We should at this point return to the discussion from the point of view of class analysis, that is, starting from questions about the organization, the programme, and hence the project for revolution. However, this is not the right place to be dealing with such issues. Here we shall simply stress that every imperialism, inasmuch as it is expression and extension of the power of the nation–state, not only falls short when it comes up against the totality of political and geopolitical relationships; not only can it not stand up against the new rules that the system of bio-power begins to propose within Empire; but it also (and especially) goes into crisis as regards its fundamentals. When, in fact, it assumes war as the only force (and concept) that conditions and over-determines every relationship of citizenship, Empire becomes simply a new order which extends over the global market; but also a force which is destructive of the inner relationships of the nation–state. The alternative between imperialisms and Empire is not something that affects only questions related to the global market; above all – or rather first of all – it affects the relations internal to the nation–state, and thus the very rules of citizenship.

Today we are certainly living an interregnum, between the ending of modernity and the opening of postmodernity, between the extinction of the nation–state and the foundation of Empire. A thousand contradictions run through this period and nobody can counterpose nation–state and Empire as if these were figures naturally opposed to each other. In the interregnum capital plays, rather, on the interpenetration of these figures, and it deludes itself that the one will evolve into the other: for capital, the dialectic still functions, and the statement of the nation–state is followed by its negation in the interregnum and then by its necessary sublimation in Empire. But the dialectics is something which concerns only capital. We take the opposite position, which involves gambling on the material tendency of the class struggle, as it is organized within the hegemony of living labour; we must build, within the interregnum, within the time which is left to us, the conditions for the clash at the level of Empire. Here too the multitude turns out to be the fundamental matrix of a new figure of class struggle.

PART TWO
EUROPE: AN OPPORTUNITY FOR STRUGGLE

15
Europe and Empire: Issues and Problems*

The question that interests us is whether a united Europe is possible. In my view Europe is a necessity. By this I mean a Europe which is politically and culturally consolidated and built on a social constitution which preserves its traditional characteristics. I shall return to this question at greater length. For the moment I want to discuss the first statement: Europe is a necessity – for political, economic and social reasons related to the global market, that is, within the perspective of the constitution of Empire. The imperial space has created new conditions of democracy. There is probably no point in trying to specify the precise nature of this democracy. For instance, one might wonder whether, at the world level, the democratic slogan 'one man, one vote' is actually practicable. Or whether a global civil society is realistically possible on the terms which have made use of the phrase 'civil society' in the western world. I really don't think so. An American political scientist, Robert O. Keohane, recently joked that 'one man, one vote' at the global level would mean Chinese dictatorship over the world! As for a global civil society, it does not seem that the various bourgeoisies and/or international capitalist aristocracies agree about the construction of such a thing. Making democracy at the global level actually means something completely different: it means developing a tendency towards freedom and equality which in practical terms, through struggles, can become real: this is the political space that Europe can build. A democratic space for the multitudes. Not a proposal of models but the proposal of a history of

---

* Speech given at the Faculty of Political Sciences, University of Ljubljana, 19 September 2003.

struggles; not the re-proposition of a constitution (not even one based on the European welfare model) but the expression of a democratic conflictuality, often radical and always open, something of which (despite everything) Europe has always been capable.

Europe offers itself first of all as a public space and a democratic politics. These are the terms in which it is located within the development of Empire. It is neither an identity nor an institutional paradigm: what it has to be is a living point of reference, a reality which is expressive of rights and democratic potentials.

Naturally the first problem is how to give homogeneous characteristics to this plan, to the process of building Europe. Will it be possible? Will we succeed in building a political union which is worth the effort? And in building a political subject within it who, in the present state of imperial disorder, is not only predisposed but also capable of supporting this project (or even simply a tendency in this direction, a radical democratic conflictuality which is endemic and pursuable in practical terms)?

The question of the European constitution offers a wide range of alternatives. The first alternative is that of Europe as a common market. In this picture the European Community is seen as a configuration of sovereign nations. In both cases I think that this would lead purely and simply to the configuration of an imperial suborganization. In Empire, and particularly in an Empire under US leadership, homogeneously organized areas of market are highly desirable – in fact they are supported and hierarchized – within the development of imperial command. This is not the Europe that interests us.

A second position is the one that sees the building of the European Community as a superstate, reiterating the juridical–administrative models of modernity. This too is a conception which (albeit powerfully present in the current European debate) does not interest us. The polemic against the nation–state – against that nation–state which in Europe has left millions and millions dead over recent centuries, killed by patriotism – is not for us. The fact that this second alternative is strongly supported does not make it possible. I do not think that I am an optimist for thinking so. The resistances that this constitutional thinking, this statist ideology, determines should not, however, be underestimated: the fact that they are archaeological does not diminish their temptation. The democratic deficit that these ideologies represent is a real danger. But I do not see this as a realistic development in the present situation.

There is a third alternative which is being pursued, and it seems to prevail in the debate about the European constitution. This is the line which argues for the building of a 'constitution without a state', a multi-level association of nations and constitutional orderings. This is a spurious figure in terms of the European constitutional tradition, a weak machine of constituent power: nevertheless we prefer it. We prefer it because this constitutional machine would be obliged to keep conflict open, and to move in legislative and administrative terms within practices of governance that would be difficult to close. We need to consider the present situation as being one of transition: the debate may be unified by European opposition to American unilateralism, but it remains completely open as regards the conflict between the European multinational élites and the multitude of workers. The democratic process, in this case, could remain always open, always guaranteed by a non-conclusion.

It is in this context (within the third of these defined alternatives) that the European constitutional union begins to make sense and presents itself on the world stage with those characteristics of rupture and democratic expression which we see as fundamental. When we reject the first alternative – that of the European Community as a market area – we reject the possibility of defining ourselves as a European people subject to the domination of American imperialism. When we reject the perspective of a European Community constitutionally defined as a super-state, we reject the repetition of a sovereign history which in Europe, and particularly in Europe, has reached its limit as a result of struggles. As regards the third alternative, we think that it is possible to construct in Europe something which is no longer a *demos* but an articulation of political subjects who maintain an openness of European public space, as a product of the democratic mobilization of the multitudes. European political space thus becomes a terrain for the construction of a new political subject, who might destroy the limits which the conceptions and practices of the nation–state had imposed.

Who has an interest in the constitution of a European political subject with the kinds of characteristics I have described? The answer is: those productive forces which have emerged out of the new mode of production. In other words, the immaterial workers who nowadays construct the myriad forms of wealth and who have an interest in mobility, flexibility and the new dynamics of wealth production. The other interested parties are all the citizens who are set to work within the social fabric of the new organization of production, and who are able and willing to experiment with new forms of struggle within the biopolitical context of the new production of wealth and subjectivity. What interests us is the construction of a public space matched to the new characteristics of citizenship.

Europe as a non-place: it seems impossible even to imagine such a thing, and yet this is the only possibility. Not a place of power, of bio-power, but a space for a continuous encounter between multitudinarian forces. Only if Europe becomes the subject of a democratic non-place, if it succeeds in abandoning the archaeological condition of a citizenship subordinated to the nation–state, only then will Europe be able to present itself as a place for the founding and expansive expression of rights linked to a new capacity for living and producing. It is with a certain optimism that we view this situation: in the chain of imperial hierarchy, Europe can operate as the 'weak link' in the constitution of Empire. It can present itself as transversal force, not as *demos* but as multitudinarian *potenza*, against Empire. In the present situation the great danger is that of a structure ordered by Empire under US hegemony and created in its image: this process represents the very negation of democracy. Europe is perhaps the most important of the various continental powers that are organizing resistance to the creation of an imperial model under American leadership.

16

Europe and the United States in Empire*

We are in the midst of a fierce polemic between the United States and Europe. The US is Mars and Europe is Venus. To the Americans it seems that the diminishing of the idea of Europe that had dominated the early part of the twentieth century, as between Fitzgerald and Hemingway, has now run its course. How much longer can it continue? There is a terrible fragility in this 'neo-conservative' polemic against Europe. The fact is that Europe is, and will remain, an unavoidable terrain in the discussion of the political forms underpinning the debate on the imperial constitution. This is because the idea of Empire was not born from any individual person's brain, and particularly not from the brain either of the American or of the European bourgeoisie. Globalization is a process brought about by the ending of the global civil war (1917–89), which had its epicentre in Europe. The global civil war developed between capital and the forces of the workers' movement. Proletarian and working-class resistance (and its transformations in the course of the various phases of capitalist domination) was its central element, the motor of all the transformations: first and foremost, the superseding of the nation–state. The European civil war was won by the forces of the proletariat. It was this victory that gave us, along with the superseding of the nation–state (of all the nation–states), the processes of globalization and search for a new global equilibrium, as well as the new structures of the mode of production and the capitalist organization of labour. Today, in this situation, the bourgeois and capitalist aristocracies and the proletarian multitudes again find themselves coming into conflict, and in any

---

* Talk given at the Faculty of Political Sciences, La Sapienza University, Rome, 4 December 2003.

event they exist within an equilibrium which is unstable. The ending of the Soviet blockage of the world market has given this transition a global intensity and extension. This is the Europe, as a paradigm and ongoing development of class struggles (no matter how they represent themselves – but today this is essentially in multitudinarian form), that stands at the heart of global development.

So the question of relations between Europe and the US needs to be re-addressed in these terms. We are no longer in the situation of the Cold War, where American pressure against the constitution and the construction of a European Community, in whatever form, from 1953 onwards, had been successful. The European aristocracies throughout that period had no choice, given that they were resisting the workers' struggles; they had to rely on the capitalist primacy of the USA for support. It was only when the workers' struggles – at the global level – unhinged the relations of power imposed by the Cold War that the picture completely reopened. On the one hand, the American government is offering a unilateral monarchic option with its project of imperial domination; on the other, the European multi-national aristocracies are trying to build a relative independence and increasingly frequent and effective moments of rupture of the monarchic equilibrium of Empire. It is at this point that the Europe of Maastricht, the Europe of the euro (and of the first attempts at a constitution), succeeds in winning back an independent political space from the American super-power. The pressure of the worker multitudes and the opening of the great anti-globalization processes deepen the contradiction: Europe finds itself located on a terrain of polemical antagonism against American imperial monarchy. Note that here every affirmation of Europe becomes an internal limit of American *potenza*, every statement of Europe becomes both an expression of and a demand for new equilibria in the development of Empire.

This brings us to some general considerations. Europe's determination to resist the American monarchic push (a resistance supported on and developed by the presence of struggles and the organization of the multitude) created a crisis for the unilateral hegemonic pretensions of the US. The unilateral management of the war against terrorism by the US is proving ineffective: for the Americans, a series of setbacks at the monetary and economic level has added to the disasters of war. Secondly, European resistance and the new European presence at the global level support and encourage similar resistances and presences by other continental blocs. American unilateralism begins to be encircled by a series of continental counter-positions (China, India, Latin America, in addition to Europe) which put the US into a difficult position, if not into crisis. It is on this newly emergent terrain that the American attack on European unity also becomes problematic, if not downright bankrupt. The tactics pursued by the American government from 1953 to the 1990s have changed completely: European subjection to American unilateralism is no longer attempted solely at the military level, fundamentally through NATO, but also through a series of political operations internal to the development of the European Union. The Americans encourage the expansion of the community to the east, in the expectation that this might bring about bigger crises; they support British isolationism; they try it on again with the oil and energy war; they trigger the conflict with the euro . . . Can we say that each of these operations has only secondary effects on the processes of European unification? No, we cannot. Nevertheless the situation really has changed.

But from the point of view of the multitudes we do not take all this to be the decisive element. The situation is still very open. It is only the ability of the multitudes to take up the slogan of Europe, its unity, and its new global positioning, which can consolidate the antagonism between Europe and the US. It is clear that this plan cannot be considered in the abstract – if by 'abstract' we mean a non-class-based analysis of power. This proposal will become useful and productive only when the European constitution (which today is heading in decidedly liberal directions) can be redirected into a relation of forces which is open to multitudinarian action. We are not interested in institutions except as public places and spaces of conflict. The European constitution must be shaped to this function of openness, conflict and determined and continuous opposition to capital's predomination both within Europe and globally. But it is clear that embarking on this battle today means immediately involving ourselves at the global level. The structure of Empire is not simply a space but constitutes a unity of power. As we have already said, every statement of Europe is an internal limit (not international, and thus not external) to American power. Therefore affirming Europe and bending its constitution to multitudinarian conflict is a vital step, not only in the defence of proletarian interests but also in the attempt to reconfigure the development of Empire democratically.

17
Europe between Universalism and National Differences: A Possible Europe*

We begin from the premise that the United States does not want the European Union. We then add a second premise: that the crisis of American unilateralism opens spaces for a new European initiative.

We can map a precise historical process. Halfway through the 1990s, the supplier industrial groups operating in the national sector (of the nationalized and public industries) and the trade-union corporations which supported them were still marked by a clear rejection of a political Europe. Halfway through the 1990s we continued to find a lack of enthusiasm among certain strata of European capital, or the European technocratic bourgeoisie, about moving towards the construction of a European Community. Now, in 2004, we see how much the climate has changed. On the one hand the big companies are completely globalized and they have an alternating interest in Europe, sometimes positive, sometimes negative; on the other we have a new European proletariat which seems to have a political interest in Europe: it feels the need to establish cultural and political mediations between the globalization of capitalist command and the localized nature of resistance to it. The new intellectual proletariat is probably the only social subject to have a real interest in Europe.

At this point the question of Europe takes on a different aspect, because it involves basically a re-founding of democracy in the imperial age, the definition of a post-socialist programme and the corresponding construction of a political movement. Europe is the only territorial dimension able to sustain resistance and the rebuilding of a

---

* Speech delivered before the Italian representatives at the European Commission, Rome, 26 February 2004.

political programme of the Left. What interests us, therefore, is the idea of a new federalism, a multi-level federalism capable not only of uniting the European nation–states but also of unifying the new programmes of the proletariat. It is at this level that there has been a complete institutional crisis and a crisis of political representation in Europe.

Europe's creation as a political entity is a necessity for the same reasons that have set in train the present constituent process: the quest for peace between the nations that comprise it, the creation of a common economic space, a common cultural environment, and so on. But the necessity of Europe is powerfully obvious also for other reasons, no longer simply static but dynamic, not historical but political, and of the here and now. The necessity of Europe derives from the need to confront the realities of the global market, that is, from the confrontation with the process of imperial constitution that is being put into effect.

Within Empire, since absolute democracy ('one person, one vote') is unthinkable and the image of a global civil society – when it is not pure mystification or illusion – is also very dubious, it will be necessary to delimit a space which makes possible the expression and democratic decision-making of the multitude, in addition to its political organization. It seems, furthermore, that the present political crisis (provoked by the action of American unilateralism) has further accentuated, at the imperial level, the urgency of new configurations of imperial legitimacy. I mean limits, figures and functions at the level of globality.

For us, the political space of Europe (characterized as it is by a long and singular cultural continuity and a specific constitutional dynamic) seems to provide that necessary delimitation. I do not know whether within this space it is possible to think of a political subject matched to the dimensions of Empire. What is certain, however, is that outside of this space, and without an adequate subject, there will be no possibility of resistance, let alone democracy, in Europe.

If these are the conditions in which we have to move, let us ask: is it possible to build this space? And is it possible to build, within this space, a political subject that can bear comparison with the others in Empire? Or, better, a political subject that can take a stand together with the others in relation to imperial hegemony? Is a political union possible which is worth the effort?

It seems to us that no positive answer can be given to these questions if we accept today's dominant positions in the political debate over Europe. Some of these positions (1) are within the communitarian debate, while others (2) concern the political debate on the union. All the positions we shall examine have been expressed – profusely – during the debate around the Giscard plan. As regards the positions within the communitarian debate, they place themselves between two extreme alternatives:

1a   The European Community as a market area, and the regulation thereof.

1b   The European Community as a confederation of sovereign nation–states.

It is evident that in both instances the European Community is designated as a sub-organization of Empire, in other words as one of the decentred organizations within the imperial pyramid. In this case political union produces neither democracy nor a new subjectivity within Empire.

Some might argue, however, that by taking the 'military determinant' to be more important than the economic determinant one could extract Europe from the subaltern function assigned to it by Empire. But that would be true only on the condition (which is manifestly not the case) that Europe could immediately present itself, as a whole, as a military power. This is not the reality of Europe: at the present time the military determinant is sectional, managed by individual nation–states. Consequently, in emphasizing the military determinant, one ends by excluding Europe from any decisive positioning or role in the imperial ambit. Furthermore, if the emphasis on the military determinant was simply a ploy designed to reaffirm the centrality of the nation–state in the European and international reality, then the effectiveness of this position would fail entirely. Another alternative emerges when one considers the positions involved in the debate about political union:

2a   In this perspective, European political union is considered on the one hand as a juridical–administrative superstate (in short, as an empire within Empire).

2b   In another form, the European Union can also be imagined (as it frequently is in the current debate) as a 'constitution without a state', or as a statal structure characterized by numerous levels of organization, rather than moving from a sovereign centre.

What we have here, in both cases, is a spurious constitutional figure or a weak machine of constituent power. Both figures are characterized by a very heavy democratic deficit. In 2a, the European Union seems to be entrusted to a bureaucratic magistracy which produces institutions as the outcome of a functionalistic dynamics. In 2b, the European Union is surrendered to political–juridical machinations rather like to those that sustained the administration of the Holy Roman Empire, and which can be read as a combination of a Pufendorfian architecture with the reactionary imagination of Romanticism.

According to some jurists, we should place our confidence in the existing legal mechanisms of the European Union. Once set into motion, these could operate as the 'constituent power' of a new European sovereignty. This 'spurious' power could, in the jurists' opinion, be produced both by an internal institutional activity (the European courts) and by the efficacy of the combined subsidiary of the European institutions and confederated states. Bureaucracies inside the community thus become the *deus ex machina* which not only makes up for the constitutional deficit but also prepares for the community's going beyond it. Such hypotheses do not seem credible. In fact they require a kind of constituent governance, difficult to hypothesize in a situation characterized (a) by a basic democratic deficit, (b) by various conflicts among the European élites, and (c) by opposing and/or destructive pressures exercised by the imperial élites (American, Russian, and so on).

In any case, if the political and constituent debate continues in these terms, we may well end up with a European Union . . . But it will not have been worth the effort because, on the side of those governing, it will be completely subordinated to imperial command and, on the side of those governed, it will be locked into a passivity offering options only of revolt, flight or repression.

So, under what other conditions might a political Europe be possible – and, furthermore, a Europe worth the effort?

This will be possible only if the project for a united Europe goes hand in hand with that of a democratic mobilization of the European multitude, and if both projects act with irruptive force at the level of, and within the dimensions of, Empire as a whole. I mean that a political Europe (and one which is worth the effort) is only possible if the European multitude is won to the constitution of political union through the mobilization of powerful social strata (both in the production of commodities and in the expression of values) – of social strata which see political Europe as providing a greater degree of freedom, both here and in the rest of the world.

Perhaps it is worth pointing out here that what should interest those who seek to build a political Europe is not so much the constitution

of a *demos* as the production of a political subject. But to elicit a political subject out of the multitude, and thus to construct a political
Europe which is worth the effort, will not be possible without
divisions, struggles and decisions over values of freedom.

A brief parenthesis at this point: Europe was weary when, halfway
through the twentieth century, after a century of fratricidal wars, the
old cosmopolitical utopia was wheeled out and reformulated into a
political project for European unity. The paradox of this decision was
that it was animated more by strategic necessities in the struggle
against Soviet communism than by a real search for political unity,
economic solidarity and constitutional recomposition. Europe's federalists have long sought to remedy these shortcomings, but they have
always remained prisoners of the pre-established strategic picture. In
particular inasmuch as it excluded the Left and the proletarian masses
from the European project. Thus a class division over-determines the
European project and pre-dates its present actuality. This means that
one cannot construct a European *demos* if one does not excavate this
prehistory and, if necessary, reactivate these deep divisions with a view
– where possible – to overcoming them. In any event one has to take
into account the existence of conflicts (past and present), because
only by so doing will it be possible to articulate in the present an eventual political convergence. The ending of the Cold War in itself
resolves nothing, unless one thinks that in the international conflict of
those times class conflict was somehow not included. On the other
hand, the development of the imperial tendencies in the 1990s risks
accentuating (as we have already been seeing) alternatives to the construction of European unity, as those raised by the nation–states. The
United Kingdom, for instance, has used its role as a privileged ally of
the United States (in both financial and military policy) as a powerful
weapon of Euroscepticism. And meanwhile the other European
powers are watching with suspicion the continental supremacy of
post-reunification Germany and so on. If we want to move beyond
this situation, the debate on Europe, and the recognition of its creation by the people who inhabit it, will have to become open to new
phases of confrontation and to alternative expressions of values,
options and tendencies. Without immersing ourselves in these (sometimes dramatic) demands of life, it will be difficult to make progress
in the debate about Europe . . . National differences thus have to be
assumed as a *terminus a quo* – as the material element which (in
Hegel's words) we must carry to 'evanescence'. We cannot forget the
existence of the so-called nations; on the other hand, while remembering them, we must at the same time be clear in our detestation of

the slaughters that nations have provoked, the colonialisms they have promoted, and the identity-based violence they have fed.

So – who has an interest in a united political Europe? Who is the European subject? The answer is: those populations and those social strata who want to construct an absolute democracy at the level of Empire. Those who propose themselves as counter-empire. In short, those (more or less proletarian) productive strata who necessarily (for reasons dictated by the nature of their productive force) are seeking for:

1 an increasingly universal charter of citizenship and the widest mobility of the citizens, for themselves and for others;
2 guaranteed income, in other words the material possibility, for the multitudes, of having flexibility both in the production of wealth and in the reproduction of life;
3 the common ownership of the means of production – by which I mean the new means of production. If the intellectual worker no longer has the ownership of his instrument of labour, namely his brain, then he is no longer even a proletarian, but only a slave. So what is needed is freedom.

There is a new proletariat which has been created by the new mode of capitalist production. It is a multitude which, in postmodernity, aggregates and recomposes itself in the most varied places of production – in fact, every activity has become a place ever since capital's localization of production became a non-place, from the moment when the Fordist factory became dissolved into post-Fordist society. What we have is the immaterial and precarious proletariat deploying itself through an ongoing and alternative exodus, which, within the framework of globalization, clashes with Empire. Will it be possible to imagine for this proletarian European, as a European line of exodus, a great sovereign *potenza*, a capitalist super-power, a bloc of conservative forces (be they green or yellow, black or red)? Not at all. What is taking shape here is a Europe of intelligent people, of poor people, shifting and mobile, who shatter every aspect of constituted power. Might one see in Europe a Zapatista march of intellectual labour? A Europe of the regions against the Europe of nations, against Europe as imperial province, and so on? And how would it be, finally, if we began to speak of Europe as the revolutionary non-place in Empire?

When we talk like this they call us utopians. But we are simply republicans, inserted in that tradition of thought which runs from Machiavelli and Spinoza through to Marx and finds in the

Enlightenment, through Voltaire and Kant, the republican roots of every cosmopolitical project. Europe was the first (and we promise that it will not be the last) cosmopolitical project.

Let us return to ourselves. It is worth pointing out that the conditions posed here represent a diagram for the constitution of a united Europe which is not only political but also biopolitical. By 'biopolitical' 'I mean that today universal juridical conditions (of citizenship, income, common property) are the precondition, the ontological substrate, of the exercise of liberty. Politics has invested life just as life has invested the political: in the constitution of a united Europe this relationship must be taken as fundamental and irreversible.

Arriving at a provisional conclusion, it seems to me that we need to say that a European subject (and also a European Union worth having) can only be formed by a new and radically democratic European force. The problem of building a united Europe and that of the formation of a new Left are synchronic. Thus the new European subject does not reject globalization, but rather constructs a political Europe as a place from which it becomes possible to speak against globalization within globalization. So this subject is characterized (from within the space of Europe) as a counter-power in relation to capitalist hegemony in Empire.

To refresh the argument, it might be useful here to recall the concept of 'constituent power' and how it might act if we were to imagine Europe as the 'weak link' in the chain of imperial domination, and thus the unitarian constitution of Europe as the product of a 'civil war' within Empire. If we want to ground these hypotheses, we have to assume that imperial command is absolutely not inclined to admit a united Europe (and particularly one that is united on the basis of the new antagonistic social forces) as a 'counter-power' in globalization. This refusal is organized and represented by important fractions of global capital and finds its base in the conservatism of the American Right and in the unique mode of thinking [*pensiero unico*] of world liberalism. American 'unilateralism' is not only 'American' but also capitalist, conservative and reactionary. The great imperial metamorphosis has upset the traditional parameters of political science and public law, and has pushed important fractions of (global) collective capital into a fierce conservatism. This 'unilateralism' represents an attempt to block every movement of the multitudes and to fix an unchanging domination by big capital over Empire. From this point of view, the proposal for a united Europe – a Europe which was capable (because otherwise it could not find itself united) of making spaces for the new social forces that the revolution in the mode of production has created – well, this is something that the masters of Empire, right-wing governments and collective capital do not want. So a hard struggle will have to be fought for these alternative positions, and we are going to have to commit ourselves to a programme of radical transformations. Only in this case can Europe become real – and, in becoming real, present itself as the 'weak link' of imperial constitution and thus as the possibility of a new liberty for the multitudes. And this is where the new European federalism is defined – as an exodus from the nation–state, from the sovereign state, an exodus from the bio-power fetishes of a modernity which has brought about so much oppression and death.

But let us return to the core of our debate and discuss other objections which have emerged recently, particularly following the crisis of the first attempt at creating a European constitution:

- To the objection that the (neo-liberal) capitalist initiative in constructing a sub-imperial Europe is already too far advanced for a response to be possible (and therefore the only possibility is the defence of the nation–state):

- it must be answered that resistance at the national level is no longer possible. The nation–state (even when confederated) is already completely absorbed within the dynamics of Empire . . . Therefore the only possibility is to re-launch struggle within Empire. The call for 'realism' does not mean propaganda for a retreat in Kutusov style, nor the practices of 'Euroscepticism', but an insistence (even belatedly and in situations of defeat . . .) on the construction of global alternatives that can give rise to events of rupture.

- Therefore we say: let us take as our main objective the construction of a new, radically democratic, federalist movement at the European level. En route to the construction of this (and of Europe) we can/must put the imperial non-place under attack, in subversive ways.

- To the objection that Europe is poor, than it lacks raw materials and oil, that its finances and currency are completely subordinated to the world market, and that it doesn't have the bomb or any capacity for deciding on war:

- it must be answered that Europe is rich in invention-power and forms of living. Given its lack of raw materials, the weakness of its financial and monetary institutions and its extreme military impotence, what needs to be promoted is not the reinvention of the *demos* or of some ancient (demotic) solidarity, but a new biopolitical imagination which, in the relationship with the telluric mobility of the workers and the poor and with the mobilization of new intelligences, expresses itself as an exodus from the poverty of the economic and political forms of modernity. Here Balibar's idea of a 'vanishing evanescent Europe', a powerful impotence [*im-potenza potente*], becomes central.

To deepen the points made thus far and to strengthen their con- clusions (a united political Europe should not be so much a new figure of sovereignty, but rather a 'war machine' for the extension of the new fundamental rights of the subjects of Empire), I want to add a few reflections on the European model of social solidarity, on the relation- ship which we find, both in the tradition and in the future, between labour rights law and the European constitution.

In dealing with this I think we should first remember the ambigu- ity of the reference to a European model of social solidarity: this is a model which has its origins in the Bismarckian *Obrigkeitsstaat* and in the crude sociologism of the French Third Republic, and has always has been characterized (in juridical terms) by a subordination (in econ- omic terms) to calculation regarding the reproduction costs of labour power (the deferred wage), and (in political terms) as a function of social peace and the consolidation of state authority – and, further- more, it has often translated into imperialistic or warmongering soli- darity . . . The National Institutes for Social Security financed a major proportion of the wars of the twentieth century. Here what comes to the fore is the biopolitical disciplinary role of the state, which, as we know, ended up in national socialism.

That said, however, we need to add that the European model of welfare and labour law embedded within it slowly took on board the antagonist movements of labour. It was through the struggles of workers that welfare and labour rights in Europe gradually broke free of the corporative, populist, colonialist and imperialist determinations which had previously characterized them. That, then, brought us to a moment, in the 1960s and 1970s, when we deluded ourselves that the European model had freed itself from its initial conditions and that therefore Sinzheimer had won and the ambiguity of the European model of solidarity could now be re-founded in – and also nourish – democracy.

That was not how it turned out . . . From the 1970s onwards the conquests of European welfare came under attack from neo-liberalism, and their outcomes were often neutralized. Methods of repression eliminated forces that had otherwise been irresistible, and obliged them to bow to the over-determination of the global market, now politically recognized as an autonomous power. In addition, European labour law activities were very much disturbed, which in some cases was striking at their most basic presuppositions. Inasmuch as the progress of these activities had been based on conflict, being related to the struggles of workers (a subject who had won constitutional recognition), now not only was this subject (the trade union) attacked in its institutional and representational figure, but the very conditions of its existence were demolished. We use the term post-Fordism to describe the situation in which, for the ontological substrate (the working class) and the political figure (the trade union) of the industrial conflict, the preconditions of their existence no longer applied.

So, within post-Fordism, what does it mean to speak of a European model (a tradition) of social solidarity, when (leaving differences aside and presupposing homogeneity) the very conditions of continuity seem no longer to exist? What does it mean, in the absence of a strong conflictual subject, in the new and definitively established conditions of flexibility and mobility of productive labour, to re-actualize or reinvent the rights of labour on a continental scale? And, in the globalization of markets, what does it mean to bring labour law and European constitution into the same frame? Sometimes I have the impression that what we need is something like Roosevelt at the start of the New Deal: imposing by decree a new trade-union subject in order to allow the creation of a new welfare system. But how can we even begin to think of such a thing today?

There is another point which adds to the difficulties of finding answers to these kinds of question: that of immigration. In a situation of globalized markets, this problem is not an add-on to the problem of the regularization (juridical or political) of indigenous workforces. On the contrary, it is 'consubstantial' to that problem, both as regards the industrial economy (massive availability and virtually 'zero' costs of labour) and as regards budget policy (pensions, social security, education, training, social policy and the like. . .).

Here it would be interesting to address – and perhaps also force – the categories of 'frontier' which Balibar – in his latest writings – now considers to be broader than the 'nation–state'. And anyway to fire point-blank at the present concept of citizenship, which is pitifully limited and constrained compared with the reality of people's lives and their need to work . . .

From this follow two other questions, which are introduced by the problem of immigration, but which are important not only in that light. What is the process by which biopolitical control over the post-Fordist labour force (whether mobile or flexible, native or nomadic) is being configured? And then: how can labour law (at the European level) create an exception (at the global level) against biopolitical control and the imperial hierarchization of labour power?

I end with one final point. Culture and intellectuality have always been a universal in Europe. It is precisely for this reason that the struggle against the subordination of knowledge to power has been so bitter and has continued through long periods of history. Today, when production is based on the mass labour of general intellect, on the brain set to work, the insubordination of intellectual labour towards exploitation could become decisive and could create a lever for universal emancipation.

18

A Thousand European Issues*

To speak of Europe and democracy today, in this political phase of globalization, means developing a critique of American unilateralism. Not only a critique but also an understanding of the present phase in geopolitical terms. American unilateralism – in other words the *coup d'état* over Empire, the 18 Brumaire attempted by George W. Bush, has failed. I am not here to spell out the details of what is happening in Iraq: there, as we know, the strategic project of the Bush administration has come unstuck. However, this defeat of American unilateralism means that the problem of Europe has to be addressed immediately. The fact is that the US has always been against the constitution of a political Europe. In 1953, the defeat of the EDC (European Defence Community) project signalled America's intention to stamp on any possibility of European unity. America's opposition became crystal-clear from 1956 (the moment of the final defeat of European colonialism in the Suez crisis). The periodic reappearance throughout the 1960s of European calls for unity, which were blocked every time, contributed to forming the imperial strategy of the United States. However, finding itself unable to maintain a situation of domination in the face of various European resistances, the United States decided on a radical solution for the European problem. Between 1971 and 1973, the ending of the Bretton Woods agreement resulted in Europe's subordination to the dollar. In 1973 (ironically proclaimed 'The Year of Europe') the oil crisis brought a definitive solution of the problem of Europe for the United States (namely the increased subjection of Europe). As for the history of the

* Speech delivered at the Partito di Rifondazione Comunista Forum, Rome, 21 May 2004.

1970s and 1980s, American dominance in the conduct of the Cold War, combined with Brezhnevism and the Chinese crisis, meant that Europe was forgotten. It was only after 1989, with the end of the Soviet strangulation of the global economy, that the question of relations between Europe and the US was reopened in any real sense. The American imperial project then came up against European resistance. The broad outlines of development were modified: it was within globalization, by now an established fact, that the role of Europe – as an alternative set of values and social tendencies – once again became antagonistic in relation to American imperialism. It was within Empire that the question of Europe again found a specific economic and political location.

During the Iraq War, Europe has been split between the nations favouring war on the one hand and the Europeanist powers opposed to war on the other. Resistance to the war and pro-Europeanism went hand in hand. When Zapatero broke with the American war, he also broke with Spain's pro-American drift in relation to Europe, and with Euroscepticism. The same will be true for Italy.

(In Britain's case the situation is far more complex, involving two problems at once: the immediate problem of Britain's involvement in the war and in the building of Europe, and the long-term question of its privileged relationship with the US. For Eastern Europe, inserted into the EU with strong encouragement from more Atlanticist countries, as part of a plan to weaken the political impact of Europe, new centripetal tendencies are beginning to develop regarding Europe, even if the pro-American and anti-Russian impulses are still there. In any event, Euroscepticism is very much in crisis.)

The question of Europe thus presents itself, in the first place, as an issue of pacifism. The form and the times in which Europe is being constructed politically correspond, in a homogeneous way, to an instance of peace. We cannot afford to be absent from this terrain. It is obvious that all this has to be said with caution and hedged about with reservations . . . But it nevertheless needs to be said, and forcefully. The Europe gamble has to be taken. The crisis of American unilateralism necessitates a broad and complex appraisal of global alignments; it establishes for the first time since the end of the Second World War the possibility of a polycentric scheme of things; it shows the ending of the Soviet Union to have been not only an end to the throttling of the global market but also a moment of proliferation of continental powers: the US, Russia, Europe, China, India, Latin America . . . It is within this new scenario that global peace is determined, in the polycentric interplay of the continental powers.

Obviously we cannot absent ourselves from Europe, within the specific timings and forms in which it is proposed to us, when we take account of the current situation. Accepting Europe as it is today is the precondition for being able to talk politics in relation to questions of globalization and peace. From this point of view we have to wish for a politically united Europe. But if this turns out not to be possible, then we are going to have to move on what is basically a multi-speed terrain, keeping in the forefront the question of peace and the defeat of unilateralism . . . and then, as we shall see, the question of the construction of new structures of global government.

Europe is an ugly beast. If the imperial order is similar to what Polybius describes – I mean, if it is a cross between an American monarchy, multinational capitalist aristocracies and a new global class that we call multitude – we need to remember that the failure of the monarchic plan over Empire results initially from a victory of the imperial aristocracies. The European constitution of Giscard d'Estaing is an aristocratic constitution: we cannot avoid it, but we cannot accept it either. The schema that the imperial aristocracies are proposing is for the constitution of a new Magna Carta. The multitudes are excluded from this project. Social policies – above all, the innovative ones related to citizens' income – are today, in this condition, subordinated to the imperial–aristocratic project. The closures of 'Fortress Europe', in addition to creating blockages to the international movements of labour, are mechanisms for an imperial hierarchization of world markets, closely related to the multinational relationships which today (at the same time) are strengthening globality and blocking American unilateralism. How are we to get through this necessary transition (necessary because it is a peace transition) to reopen the struggle against the constitutional Magna Carta of Empire?

This is the question that we have to raise. However, only the movements will be able to raise it: certainly not the parties, whose institutional representation is necessarily included in the process of imperial constitution. The advantage of the movements is that they present themselves at the global level with all the expressive power of the multitude. Political parties today have, for what it is worth, a function of mediation of the trade-union type, which proposes itself within individual continental instances of the new pact between monarchy and imperial aristocracy. This function of mediation can be important. However, it is and remains purely instrumental as regards the theoretical–practical function in the struggles of the multitude. So on the one hand the question of Europe becomes a key location for transition in the alternative game which comprises the conquest of peace and the affirmation of the political power of the multitude; on the other, it becomes a key location for experimentation in new forms of representation.

The problem of the European constitution needs to be formulated in a new way, from the point of view of representation. What interests us is not the repetition at the European level of the old centralist formulae of the modern nation–state, and therefore of classic political representation; what interests us is rather the disarticulation of the central figure of the nation–state (and of 'government' in general) in order to open new processes of 'governance' which are open to the continuous pressure of the movements. It is only in these terms that a 'two-stage' theory and practice (first peace and then the constitution, but also first the social question and then the constitution, and/or vice versa) could be short-circuited. In this process, therefore, what is central is the movements and not the parties. The parties can exist, at most, as a toolbox in a process of progressive self-extinction. At this point it is worth stressing that in all the major continental areas (or at least in the driving ones: China, Latin America, India) a new relationship of sovereignty between government and movements is coming to the fore, which imposes new norms of productivity and freedom. These changes should not be viewed as secondary. The transition to Europe is being played out on the stage of the global transition to new continental powers and new forms of government. Keeping these aspects together is one of the most basic questions in the discussion of the problem of Europe.

So does the present European constitution strengthen or weaken the ability of the national bourgeoisies and/or European capitalism to create institutional – that is, economico-political – levels of command? Our answer is twofold, and articulated in various ways. In the first place, locating itself on the terrain of peace, the European constitution does actually (albeit ambiguously) weaken the central economic-political power of the traditional European élites. The multi-level structure, weak federal articulation and indecisive constitutional position mean that there are many spaces for the possible insertion of multitudinarian forces into the governing processes. Clearly this condition has its ambiguities: the flexibility of the constitutional structures and the fluidity of governance mean that it is easier to push through lobbying promotions, identity-based political positions, repressive policies and the like. Nevertheless, our view is that this ambiguity needs to be forced at two levels: on the one hand internally, trying to break the classist and sovereignist determination of the practices of command; on the other externally, pushing it towards a definitive break with Atlanticism, so that a true imperial polycentrism can be explored. Secondly, the European constitution, inasmuch as it strengthens the structures of political parties and trade unions at the European level, reconfirms the old powers: this is the terrain on which Europe and the European constitution need to be combatted, this is the terrain on which a true federalism and an opening of new procedures and machines of governance need to be affirmed. These are the reasons why all forms of Euroscepticism need to be decisively rejected, and why we should be determinedly critical of this continuing existence of institutional set-ups which the European constitution has in store for us and which the traditional Right and Left are so happy to accept.

All this would be hard to imagine, were it not for the fact that we are now in a context of new subjects of production and of life. It is vital for political debate to be utterly renewed, because the multitude (the common ensemble of singularities who operate on the terrain of immaterial, intellectual, affective, relational and linguistic labour) has emerged as the new subjectivity which is potentially hegemonic within these processes.

19
Notes on Laying the Basis for Foreign Policy in the European Union*

In my opinion, in the present phase of the debate about the European Union's constitution the question of Europe's foreign policy can in no sense be set aside or relativized: it imposes its centrality on the basis of a very simple observation: it has been on foreign policy issues – around the question of the Iraq War – that the European Union has split, but has also seen a comeback, and has perhaps also emerged as a driving force. In any event Europe has shown the weight of its presence at the global level. Now, if we want to lay the basis of foreign policy for Europe today, we have to address two problems: that of the form in which the governance of our globalized world is being set up, and that of the way Europe poses itself as a subject within this constituent process.

There are many general problems around the issue of the European constitution, and a number of structural indications have already been provided in order to get the process started. Perhaps the most fundamental element of this constituent methodology is the assumption of the 'multi-level' mechanism. What does 'a basis for foreign policy' mean, when it is framed in terms of 'multi-level' structures? This is the first question we have to ask. Secondly, we have to ask ourselves: what formal and/or structural analogies with the constitution of the global order can the construction process of a 'multi-level' European constitution offer? Will it be compatible with a 'unilateral' constitution of the global ordering, or it will be compatible only with a 'multilateral' constitution? I shall offer some hypotheses around these questions, albeit without any claim to have the answers.

---

* Speech given at the Seminar on 'Europe and Social Movements', Istituto Universitario Europeo, Fiesole (Florence), 27 May 2003.

The European Union: multi-level structures and imperial multilaterality
The juridical theory underpinning the constitution of the United
Nations from its foundation to the present day was clearly multilateral, in the sense that it envisages a universal participation of the
nation–state – even though this multilateral universalism has been
much weakened by a centralization of decision-making on the
Security Council. Nevertheless, the broad outlines of the San
Francisco constitution are enlightened and multilateral. However, as
world markets have gradually become globally integrated, thereby
requiring the existence of a sovereign power of regulation, the UN
model of multilaterality has come in for a lot of criticism and has run
into obstacles which are often hostile and sometimes insuperable. It
is worth remembering that multilateralism has a basically European
perspective. As we have said, the UN emerges as the final perfecting tool (and inner guarantee) of classic international law, both
Westphalian and modern.

However, today, in laying the basis for the European constitution,
the ongoing presence of the modern ideology of the nation–state as a
source of legitimacy and efficacy of international contractual law is
still clearly visible. The real advances in the construction of Europe
have come when the absoluteness of the principles of modernity has
been weakened and translated into 'multi-level' forms of constitutional organization. In summary: the sovereign independence of the
nation–state is here mediated towards supranational union, in a
'multi-level' process with 'subsidiarity' as its driving motor. This operation is relatively effective, but only as a preliminary, prior to the
definitive juridical setting up of the Union: it is obvious, for instance,
that the organization of a common European foreign policy will not
be possible unless the 'multi-level' aspect of the constitution is in some
sense taken further and therefore altered.

Furthermore, in global multilateralism as it is expressed in the
United Nations it is obvious that we are now well beyond the crisis
point. Developments around the Iraq War show that the unilateralism
of the United States has no intention of bending to UN multilateralism. (Since the installation of the Bush administration there have been
many policy decisions opposed to UN multilaterality and to decisions
taken in that context – from America's refusal to sign the Kyoto Treaty
to its refusal to participate in the International Criminal Court. Some
commentators have suggested that the US has actually followed an
'exceptionalist' line ever since the first formulation of its foreign
policy, and that therefore its membership of the United Nations must
itself be seen as exceptional in the development of American policy.)

But let us return to the question of Europe. If global multilateralism is in crisis, it is entirely obvious that Europe's 'multi-level' models will be incapable of operating for as long as they continue to be inhabited by the ghost of national sovereignty. This is what is happening. It is no accident that, with both the global constitution and the European constitution, the European élites are seeking to construct institutions and policies which have a close analogy with the models of national sovereignty. We seem to have, simultaneously, both a nostalgia for the nation–state and a projection towards a global or continental super-state. People seem to be incapable of imagining anything different.

In this situation, laying the basis for the European Union's foreign policy will always be difficult, if not impossible. Should a foreign policy develop, it will have difficulty in developing innovation. More probably it will be subordinated to the policies of whatever national power happens to be hegemonic at the given moment, will be tugged precariously in different directions and will be rendered impotent at birth.

Hegemonic unilateralism   It is obvious, in terms of the present global order, that the orientation of the Bush administration produces policies designed unilaterally as expressions of the hegemonic will of the United States. In particular, as I have argued elsewhere, the war in Iraq has effectively been a global *coup d'état* carried out by the Bush administration – an attempt to bend the processes of imperial constitution to the imperialist will of the American nation–state. The Bush administration imposes, against the multilateralism of the United Nations, a Byzantine relationship of sovereignty, in other words a relationship of domination and a continuously activated mechanism designed to create divisions and hierarchies in the world. In the policies of George W. Bush, the structural conditions of modern sovereignty are represented in their entirety, whatever their theoretical foundation (it is clear that the basic theoretical foundation is indifferent: it may be democratic–federalist or organic–Schmittian, or the legitimation may be Christian–authoritarian or Islamic–fundamentalist, to mention just the particularly active traditions – all these various theoretical foundations have very different intensities and extensions, but their mechanism is always absolutist and unilateral).

The problem of unilateralism, however, is that the very paradigm of power has been completely transformed in the transition from modernity to postmodernity, from Fordist production to post-Fordist production, in the fulfilment and transcendence of the national conditions of development. Bio-power now has to operate in a context which is biopolitical; the exercise of force is legitimated not simply in relation to its own constitutional conditions, but in relation to the biopolitical determinants of the global cohabitation of peoples and nations. If we do not understand that the context of legitimation has radically changed, no new order (which must of necessity be global) will be able to be established. When the situation is seen in terms of the critique of political economy, for instance, the cost of wars (as the new exclusive foundation of sovereign legitimation) has not yet been related to forms of taxation which can allow their financing: we recall that in earlier times the attempt to solve this problem is what produced constitutional democracy. Moreover, the risk of nuclear flare-ups or epidemics limits the operability of sovereign coercion and restrains it, since it requires high quotas of global consent. In short, global power discovers the weight of global public opinion. Consequently, in the biopolitical condition there are few possibilities for a bio-power to realize itself, except at the price of producing huge catastrophes.

We stress these determinants not for the pleasure of describing America's demonic power over the world, but rather in order to show the difficulties, if not the impossibility, of unilateralism; and hence to make it clear that the creation of ways of running the European Union's foreign policy will have to rule out from the start all unilateral determinations, every temptation to resort (in the constitution of foreign policy) to analogies with the foreign policies of the nation–states comprised in the Union. Certainly the 'multi-level' (multilateralist) conception has major limitations: in particular, how does one resolve the problem of the effectiveness of a foreign policy which can only take shape through a 'multi-level' system and which, furthermore, cannot operate as a unilateral force?

Thinking open-mindedly about multilaterality How might it be possible to imagine a multiplicity of subjects – not simply through the relatively weak mechanism of subsidiarity, or formal 'multi-level' structures – which can successfully explore a perspective of cosmopolitical foreign policy that is both multiversal and effective? How might it be possible to establish a mechanism for running the foreign policy of the European Union, assuming as a premise the conditions we have outlined thus far?

In formulating this problem, a shift of viewpoint might enable us to see the moment of political decision not as an emanation from an original substance of power (however organized, whether single or multilateral), but as the product of a dynamics between democratic base and government, between multitude and political expression. Sovereignty is not given by nature, it is not an essence, and it is not Byzantine; it is a relationship between government and multitudes.

A possible mechanism for running the foreign policy of the European Union can only begin to be identified when it expresses itself as an outcome of social movements, as a continuous dialogue with continental public opinion, and as an encounter between multitudes.

If we want to identify a theoretical schema that might enable us to construct this process, we first need to recognize that, when one multitude meets with another multitude, it is not a meeting of completed subjects – it is an intersection of the singularities that make up given multitudes. To clarify this hypothesis, we say that any eventual decision that might eventually be legitimated at the constitutional level in the European Union (and, in particular, all decisions regarding foreign policy) is in no sense to be seen as a princely act, as an act of absolute force, in a crushing and perverse unitary form: all decisions (including foreign policy decisions) will have to be formulated through procedures which allow for a confrontation and proliferation of the opinions, needs and desires which go to make up the political subjectivity of the multitudes. To the objection that this kind of democratic decision-making process is not up to dealing with the urgencies and unexpected twists and turns of foreign policy, we say that the ultimate act of force (and, at the same time, the first foundational act of the new imperial community) must consist in creating a universal uniformity in the procedures of decision-making in matters of foreign policy. Furthermore, as the process of imperial constitution and constitutionalization of the global market progresses, what will 'foreign policy' still mean?

What I have said so far is purely methodological, too abstract to be true, and frankly irritating when it comes to the constitution of juridical categories. Nevertheless this abstract representation at least allows us to fix two basic points for the system of foreign policy in the European Union:

1   The operating structures of foreign policy must be open to an encounter with the multitudes at the global level. The European Union is not an island, but one building block of the globalized world we inhabit. Its foreign policy has to be able to grasp the movements of the multitudes; in other words it has to be animated by a universal and cosmopolitical spirit. The behaviours of the

central states of the European Union in the present crisis over the war in Iraq are exemplary in this regard.

2   The construction of a foreign policy for the European Union is an operation that will have to prove its effectiveness around the fundamental problem of the dissolution of national sovereignty (in our particular case, in the European constitutional process) and the extinction of the very concept of national sovereignty in any superstate that seeks to impose itself at the global and/or continental level.

The crisis and disarticulation of national sovereignty, to the point of its extinction, form the necessary basis of any democratic project within globalization. The EU's foreign policy, if situated at this level, will give the will of the multitudes a real opportunity to express itself. These initial reflections were written some months ago. Now, in the post-Iraq period, I have added new points, since new perspectives have been established for the creation of a foreign policy for the European Union.

A conflict is under way in the global agenda – which will be neither short-term nor superficial – between the military, financial and commercial policies of the US and corresponding positions in Europe. If we examine this, and if we assume a resistance to the American *coup d'état* by the central governments of the European Union (probably in agreement with the élites of multinational capitalism, that is, those actors in the global order whom elsewhere we have referred to as the 'imperial aristocracy'), we have to define the original perspectives which the foreign policy of Union must assume. In particular, we have to view these new perspectives in relation to the functions (relations between member states and policies which are external in a real sense) which the EU's foreign policy has to cover.

For the sake of argument, let us assume two levels of analysis and policy proposals: the first will address the relationships between states; the second will address foreign policy in the fuller sense. So first I shall address the question of the European constitution.

The question of European enlargement   Right from the start, people were aware that enlargement of the European Union possibly represented a trap, a trick designed to introduce unresolvable elements of imbalance into the European constitutional process, at the moment when Europe was undergoing a qualitative leap. To this objection by some of Europe's leaders, it was replied that there was no alternative, that it was impossible to rule out admission of the ex-socialist states, and that anyway this difficulty could be transformed into a resource. Arriving without warning as it did, the Iraq War clarified the real terms of the problem: when it came to enlargement, the European Union had to deal with a political situation that was diversified but completely homogeneous in its fidelity to the US. The old Stalinist bureaucracy was happily converting itself into a satellite of American influence: let no one talk of membership of the International Criminal Court or of European aeronautical projects unless the Americans allowed it! The US administration's attempts to generate friction between the 'old' and the 'new' Europe were relentless. In such a situation, clearly the creation of a European foreign policy would need to gear enlargement and the admission of new states to the basic principles of Europe's independence and/or autonomous participation in the globalized world and in the structures of its governance.

The question of NATO   Here too we have a huge problem: the European Union cannot be imagined as being prefigured by the structure of NATO. This has been the tendency in discussions concerning the admission of the countries of Eastern Europe, as well as in Britain's renewed insistence on privileging the Atlantic alliance over and above all other values. In fact the relationship between the European Union and NATO is in crisis in every respect. We no longer have the Soviet Union as a compact and common enemy, in a relationship of bipolar antagonism, and the American administration has a hard time theorizing supposed 'coalitions of the willing' . . . There are, moreover, economic and technological urgencies – related to the development of scientific innovation – that cannot be conditioned unilaterally by the relationship with the US. Thus it is absolutely necessary that the development of the European Union does not take place as a reflection of the needs of NATO.

A second problem, which we have already raised, relates to the economic system which is hegemonic in the Union.

The social agenda   As we know, in the countries of central Europe there is a more or less general consensus around a value system of solidarities which have a material constitutional importance. Europe, as many writers have argued and as the present constitutional debate illustrates, is a society which foregrounds the values of solidarity, as opposed to the radical neo-liberalism of the American empire.

Moreover, the quality of working and biopolitical cooperation in Europe expresses values which are opposed to all monocratic claims over the management of society (and even more so to militaristic claims for unilateral management of the global order). This context needs to be highlighted in the process which leads to the European constitution, whatever its eventual political figure.

The European currency With the euro, the European Union has given itself the possibility of constructing, transferring and communicating systems of values. Currencies always have the ability to prefigure orders of values, and in post-Fordist society (where the hegemony of immaterial labour is now a definitive fact) the monetary factor reveals not only systems of power but also relations of cooperative potential. The break with the Washington Consensus – that is, with monetary policies that are the vehicle for capitalist decisions and for the centralized system of imposition of neo-liberal values – here appears as an absolute precondition for an independent value of the euro. Such a condition applies not only to Europe: it also applies, or will shortly apply, to other regional systems at the global level (starting with the one which is being created in Latin America, around Brazil).

I could continue examining the material perspectives of European foreign policy around other areas and issues. For the moment, however, I prefer to address the articulations that these policies might and must have with the social movements. Framing the problem in these terms does not only mean arguing for the constituent efficacy of the movements and posing the problem of constructing a real cosmopolitical democracy; it also means understanding how the movement can develop a 'strategic–tactical' relationship in its daily action, both at the local and at the global level.

A first consideration. At this time, in the face of America's unilateral initiative, two central difficulties have been defined. First, looking at things horizontally, there has been a clear break in the power balances between the countries which are central to capitalist development. There is no doubt that this break represents a crisis of the aristocratic multinational élites, which reckon the military dimension of the American government to be fundamental, but not sufficient, in the constitution of the global order world-wide, and inadequately proportionate to the biopolitical conditions of economic production and reproduction of the system. It is seen as being dangerous because it is liable to have uncontrolled and uncontrollable repercussions. The first problem the global movement must address is therefore the following: is it useful and productive to seek out tactical occasions of alliance between aristocratic forces and multitudinarian forces against American unilateralism?

A second consideration has to do with the increasingly obvious tendency towards 'regional' or 'continental' configurations of state systems and global policies. The consolidation of the European Union and its attempts to arrive at a constitution have equivalents in Latin America, in south-east Asia and, above all, in regionally significant positions such as China. These regional realities are already engaged in a 'struggle for recognition'. The issue which the movement has to address is: how might it be possible to find in these regional groupings – in the light of a strategic project which has to be defined as global and cosmopolitical – conditions of tactical alliance in resisting and struggling against neo-liberalism?

Returning to the question of Europe, we could therefore fix the following two points regarding the 'strategic–tactical' alternatives implied in the relationship between global political situations and social movements of contestation. In terms of Europe:

1   The debate under way between 'sovereignists' and 'communitarians' appears to be incapable of opening up debate between the aristocratic and the multitudinarian components of resistance to American and neo-liberal unilateralism. Thus, in defining a tactics that makes it possible to operate in this direction, we need to re-launch a democratic European federalism: this is the only option which might provide open spaces for discussion, cooperation and struggle, rejecting both the essentialist conception of power that the sovereignists are constructing (Europe as a nation–superstate) and the functional and bureaucratic conception of the EU prevailing among the communitarians. There is only one tactics appropriate for the movements: a tactics of stops and starts, retreats and inventiveness in the strategy of the construction of the common. A democratic framework can be maintained and developed only in terms which are federalist.

2   Can Europe work as a basis of ideological and practical resistance against the neo-liberal promoters of *coup d'état*? Can it be the basis for the emergence and strengthening of a proliferating insurrection of democratic proposals and global solidarity? Is it possible to imagine a postmodern Europeanist strategic line which might mount a critique of the exportation of modernity, as it has been pursued over centuries by capitalism and the European nation–

state, and propose instead solidarity and the exportation of freedom? This is the strategic indication around which the movements need to make a federalist choice that can pull together a tactics and a strategy in favour of the European Union.

PART THREE
POST-SOCIALIST POLITICS

20
Social Alternatives to Neo-Liberalism*

I am proud to be here to discuss with you the alternatives to neo-liberalism, since you are putting them into practice. I don't mean discussing them in general because that would not be useful to you, nor do I mean talking specifically about what you are doing today because I wouldn't be up to it. The responsibility here lies entirely with you: you are the ones who have the threads in hand (by virtue of the counter-power that you are exercising) to be able to weave a web of alternatives. All I can do is introduce a few issues regarding the politics of the multitude, questions which you are already addressing (or so it seems to me), and which therefore do not need to be formulated in analytical terms for us to verify, rather, what we need to do is develop them in political terms, above all in order to deepen their efficacy.

Multitude is, first and foremost, a class concept. Better, it is a class experience. We could say that it is an extended class concept, in other words a class concept which is wider, more extensive and more all-embracing than the old concept of working class. Multitude includes within it women who do housework, workers in the service sector, workers in agriculture, students, researchers, and others. These categories of workers were at one time seen as being marginal to the concept of working class; of course, they were not actually excluded (how would it have been possible, from a communist point of view, to exclude them?), but they were not taken into account, they were kept on the margins, not considered essential in the organization of labour and in the intensity of exploitation, and hence from a political point of view they were considered as 'allies'.

---

* Talk given in an occupied factory in Buenos Aires, 27 October 2003.

But there is a further point of view we might develop: this stresses the new quality of labour, the immaterial and social elements of productive activity, the transition from the massified indifference of people's jobs to their subjective difference, to the real difference in the jobs people do and to their reconfiguration in the production of subjectivity.

Comrades, how could you have reacted in such an active and powerful way to the economic crisis in Argentina and to the disarray in the industrial system of your country – how could you have done this if the labour power that you represent had not only been aware of itself and of the mechanisms of production within which it reproduces itself, but also, and above all, if you had not been intelligently capable of reappropriating the functions of organization, both productive and social, which were born with you and developed by you, by your intelligence and in your body?

Furthermore, when we speak of multitude as a class we mean that a new quality of exploitation is being imposed onto the multitude in order to exercise control. If what is now being exploited is the social dimensions of production, it follows that your resistance presents itself immediately as resistance within a context of social production. The antagonism which runs through the new systems of capitalist development and has found the basis for its development in the social and the immaterial – this antagonism needs to be redefined within a set of experiences which are within, and characteristic of, postmodernity: in other words, experiences which place themselves beyond the continuous pressure of the refusal of wage labour which has characterized modernity and brought about its demise. Now, the field in which we find ourselves is that of the multitude as the ensemble of the living labour of singularities (which, at the very moment in which they operate, are continuously under attack by bio-power); here we cannot permit ourselves errors. Because if we are within the mystified reality of capital, if we are within the real subsumption that capital has enacted over society, then we have to create a space of action and subversion independent from capitalist development, not somewhere outside of it but a protected and antagonistic 'from within', a base from which it becomes possible to reappropriate wealth.

When we discuss multitude in the terms we have used thus far, a further consequence follows: namely that this multitude, this ensemble of singularities, this heap of differences is not prepared to have itself represented in the old manner.

The experience of Argentina, in its complexity, has attained the pinnacle of movement and its theoretical dignity through the refusal of representation. Representation is always an expropriation of the multitude. This is obvious and comprehensible to anyone who stops to think about it. Between Hobbes and Kant, in all of modern politics there is an ontological limit arising out of the concept of representation (or rather there is the assertion that an abstract unity of representation has the upper hand over the multitude of subjects). So here we need to address again matters of representation. How many times has the continuity of struggles against, and in relation to, power been blocked and destroyed precisely by perverse traditions and/or functions of the political representation of the workers . . . I do not know which God we have to thank for the fact that today, at last, so-called popular representation finds itself ludicrously blocked and closed into a rigid impossibility of acting. Anyway, the new problematic is the organization of the multitude; and, while it has never been posed so forcefully in the last decades as a mediation between state and movement, it will be posed with increasing intensity in the years to come, because every constitutional theory needs to measure itself against reality, and a tradition of struggles (such as you represent here), if it addresses itself to the state, will not find anyone capable of resolving it abstractly; nor, more particularly, will it find any social referent (proclaiming itself as such) capable of usurping it.

So – is it possible to undertake a reconstruction passing through the social and without passing through neo-liberalism? We have seen that this is the requirement which traverses the negative moment, the critical phase of the liberal call for liberty. But here, in Argentina (as previously in nineteenth- and twentieth-century Europe), we have now arrived at the start of a positive reconstruction. To take the social as the basis from which to raise immediately the problem of the political reform of the state seems to be the winning proposal today. So, while it is right to go towards the factories, above all we need to go from the factories to the city, to the social. Let us grasp the new meanings contained in exploitation: not simply as a system of torture of individual human beings but also as the instrument for neutralizing their social force. Let us move in the social in order to liberate living labour

Here in Argentina the movements have again called to arms living labour and placed it in the front line. In Argentina the social has always been conjugated with the political, and now this synthesis has at the same time to be both criticized and reconstituted. This is precisely the critique and the synthesis that we have in mind when we speak of the biopolitical. The Argentinian movement seems to have understood that the problem of a reconstruction of welfare applies not only to the factories but to the whole of society. There is a radical democracy that lives and and will continue to live in the experience of the workers, but which prepares to express itself in all the citizens, once this experience becomes extended to the entire society.

The Argentine revolution offers a formidable example of what it means to fight in order to rebuild a new and powerful public space. It has raised the problem of how the governments of Latin America will bend to this obligation. It has worked in depth, our Argentina movement, to rebuild a space which is social and common.

In addressing you, workers of the factory struggle committees, I feel I should conclude by saying that we can and must continue to advance the revolutionary programme. But, as well as defending ourselves, this continuing also means attacking the aggressor, going beyond the enemy's defences. And it means above all, as your experience has shown, putting the common at the forefront of the struggle. Putting the common at the forefront means rejecting the idea that the reconstruction of welfare can simply be managed by the state; it means placing the working-class multitudes in a position to express a power also in relation to the deferred wage and to all the problems of social reproduction and organization. It means, finally, practising a tactics which is equal to what we have discussed thus far. As soon as one of the pillars of neo-liberalism (in other words, the capitalists' ability to manage) goes into crisis, we have the possibility of taking the economic management of the country into our own hands and of elevating this *potenza* to the government of the state. Let us play this opportunity – as Machiavelli termed it – with an appropriate *virtus*.

21
A Post-Socialist Politics within Empire*

Today we want to address four questions related to the contemporary world order and to possible political strategies for the construction of alternatives.

These are questions that need much deepening, and for this reason we shall deal with them only partially. We hope, however, to offer an analysis which is sufficiently substantial to enable us to open a discussion, today and in the next few days. We shall begin with a brief explanation of the concept of Empire, a concept we use to describe the new global order that confronts us today. Secondly, we shall analyse the new emerging forms of production, and in particular we shall analyse the hegemony of what today we call immaterial production. This analysis of production will then enable us to move on to the third question, the question of socialism, its inheritance, and today's need for a post-socialist programme. Finally, we shall suggest some possible geopolitical strategies and regional alliances that could provide ways for the transformation of today's imperial order of domination.

(1) *Empire: Neo-liberal order and global war* Our central hypothesis is that a new form of sovereignty is emerging today, at the global level, a decentred form, in a web of sovereignty that we call Empire. In our analysis, this new imperial sovereignty is fundamentally different from the imperialisms which in modernity initially developed in Europe, the United States and Japan. Modern imperialism was founded on the sovereignty of the dominant nation–state and it implied the extension of that national sovereignty over foreign subject territories. Many

---

* Talk given, together with Michael Hardt, at the East China Normal University of Shanghai and at the Tsinghua University of Beijing, May 2004.

imperial nations had global aspirations, but each of them was able to dominate only a part of the world. These imperialist powers of modernity ended up in conflict with each other, and the outcome was horrific world wars and numerous other atrocities

We are in a position to identify three central characteristics of the modern age of imperialism which have now changed. First, the structure of imperial sovereignty, which was substantially based on the nation–state. Secondly, when a sovereign national power was extended to foreign territories, a clear division was created between the dominant subject and the dominated subject – be it a territory or a nation – and between inside and outside. Finally, in modernity there was not one single imperialist nation, but several, and, moreover, imperialism always implied competition between imperialist nations and an ever-present potential for conflict.

The Empire which is emerging today, in contrast with the imperialism of modernity, is not based on national sovereignty: it is truly global in the sense that it obscures all distinction between the inner and the outside. However, to say that Empire is not founded on national sovereignty does not mean arguing that nation–states are no longer important. The nation–state certainly remains important – some, obviously, more important than others. The power of Empire implies nation–states, but it extends far beyond their prerogatives. Imperial sovereignty is founded on a mixed constitution. As a first approximation we could say that imperial sovereignty is defined by a constant collaboration in the world between monarchic forces and aristocratic forces. One could think, for example, of the Pentagon as a monarchic power within the global military dimension: the Pentagon often acts on the basis of unilateral decisions. Or think of the United States government, which assumes a monarchic role globally when it governs de facto international political and economic transactions. Secondly, among the global aristocratic forces we would include, beyond the US, the other dominant nation–states, and also the forces which are not states, such as the principal capitalist multinationals, international institutions such as the United Nations, supranational economic institutions such as the World Bank, the International Monetary Fund and a series of other powers. The monarchic forces cannot govern this Empire on their own, but must constantly work with the various global aristocracies. That means, in other words, than no nation–state can govern this Empire unilaterally, not even the most powerful nation–state, not even the United States.

The notion of a mixed constitution, which involves collaboration between monarchic and aristocratic global forces, is a good introduction to the concept of imperial sovereignty. A more articulated and innovative conceptual approach, which in some ways defines the concept better, is to consider Empire as a network of power and imperial sovereignty as a form of distributed network. A distributed network does not have a centre; rather, it presents a number of nodes which can connect each other in various ways. In this conception, the dominant nation–states, the bigger capitalist multinationals, the supranational institutions and the other global powers would be simply many nodes in the network of imperial sovereignty, and these nodes would work together in different combinations and at different moments

The network model clarifies our previous statement, namely that the distinction between inside and outside tends to become obfuscated in Empire; there are, obviously, external elements in every distributed network, but every node of the network can potentially be included, so that the border between inside and outside becomes undefined.

We shall dwell on this point in order to avoid certain misunderstandings which can easily occur. First, we should note that, when we say that national sovereignty is not at the base of the Empire, as it was for the imperialism of modernity, this – again – does not mean that the nation–state is no longer important. In the debate about globalization, too, often this fact is seen as an alternative, an equation: on the one hand people say that, since globalization is a reality, the nation–states no longer count; on the other they say that, since the nation–state is still effective, there is no globalization. We say that this is a false alternative. The dominant nation–states are still powerful, but they are not the ultimate power. The network structure of the global Empire includes the dominant nation–states, as we have said, together with numerous other powers. In the second place, when we say that Empire is not characterized by conflicts and intra-imperialist wars, this does not mean that there are no longer conflicts between the principal nations. It means, rather, that the conflicts and contradictions between the various nodes of the imperial network are internal to the imperial structure itself. At the same time, when we say that there is no longer an outside of Empire or, more precisely, that the distinction between the inside and the outside is constantly obfuscated, we do not mean that there is no longer hierarchy and subordination in the world, that there is no longer a division between those who have power and those who do not. On the contrary, Empire functions by means of a proliferation of hierarchies and through the divisions internal to its structure. However, these lines of division cannot be understood in terms of national borders or global lines which divide the North from the South, the East from the West, the First World from the Third World, and so on. The lines of hierarchy and exploitation are much more complex and interlacing, and they run through every national and local space. If we want to describe imperial sovereignty as a network, then we must remember that the net is in no sense homogeneous but what is developing is a dramatic conflict and a hierarchy between the various nodes

We hope it is clear that this network structure of Empire is perfectly in accord with the needs of the global market and with the productive circuits of global capital. Capital always needs this kind of inclusion between its spheres of production and consumption; this inclusion must always work through the existing hierarchies and in fact it generates new divisions of power and well-being. In this sense Empire could appear as the political form best suited to the neo-liberal global regime.

Now we would like to move on to the more serious objection to our notion of Empire: that the unilateral actions of the United States, in its 'war on terror' and in particular its invasion of Iraq, refute our hypothesis. According to this argument, the United States shows that imperialism is very much alive and kicking! The war in Iraq, however, in our view, demonstrates exactly the opposite. It is true that the rulers in the White House nurture imperialist ambitions and have constructed a plan for the US to govern the global system unilaterally. The American doctrine of security and preventive attack, the exemption of the United States from international law and international agreements and, finally, the arrogance of American leaders in dealing with all other nations are all part of this imperialist project. Indeed, American unilateralism wants to break the ongoing collaboration between monarchic and aristocratic forces which, as we have said, characterizes Empire, and seeks to assert the autonomy of the global monarch.

Today, however, more than a year since the invasion of Iraq and the 'taking of Baghdad', the projects of these would-be imperialists are not working. It is increasingly clear that, despite the huge asymmetry in military armaments, the United States is not in a position to maintain global order unilaterally. (Clearly military force on its own is not sufficient to maintain order.)

In Iraq, on the contrary, the imperialist projects of the US have generated only chaos and have increased the areas of so-called 'disorder'. In other words, with this negative experience, the aspiring imperialists of the White House are substantiating our hypotheses on Empire:

their failures demonstrate that, today, an imperialist regime cannot exist. Only Empire – which is a decentred form of power network, characterized by an ongoing collaboration between the monarchic and aristocratic elements of global power – is capable of maintaining the hierarchies of global order.

Finally, before we leaving the question of Empire, we want to clarify another specificity of our thinking. Today we see Empire not as an accomplished fact but as a tendency. This method, of the tendency, is also a characteristic of the writings of Marx. Halfway through the nineteenth century, when capitalist production extended only to a part of the British economy, to a still smaller slice of the European economy, and to a tiny fraction of the global economy, Marx recognized capital as a tendency projected towards the future, and thus he analysed a society which was entirely capitalist. Our reasoning on Empire is similar. Empire is the only form through which global capital and its neo-liberal regime can maintain and guarantee their global order, and this fact makes the imperial tendency a necessity. It is interesting to ask what was the date that inaugurated this transition from imperialism to Empire – perhaps it was the social movements in China in 1989, perhaps the collapse of the Soviet system, perhaps the defeat of the United States in Vietnam, perhaps the global chain of revolts in 1968. In any case, Empire is not fully realized today, but we say that it is the emergent form of the power we shall have to confront tomorrow. It would be a good idea to analyse it today, so as to be in a position to fight it tomorrow.

(2) *The new forms of production: The hegemony of immaterial labour*   In the transition towards these changes in imperial sovereignty, which we propose with the concept of Empire, today too we are seeing significant transformations in the productive processes. In our view there is an emergent hegemony of immaterial production compared with other forms of production. This fact replaces the previous hegemony of industrial production.

In every economic system there coexist, side by side, numerous different forms of labour, but there is always one figure that exercises hegemony over the others. This hegemonic figure functions as a vortex which gradually transforms the other figures, so that they assume its same central qualities. The hegemonic figure is dominant not in quantitative terms, but in the extent to which it has the power to transform the others.

In the nineteenth and twentieth centuries industrial labour was hegemonic in the global economy, although it was still minoritarian in quantitative terms compared with other forms of production, for example agriculture. Industry was hegemonic inasmuch as it drove other forms of production into its own vortex: agriculture, mining . . . even society itself was forced to industrialize. Not only its mechanical practices, but also the rhythms of life of industrial labour and its working day gradually transformed other social institutions, for instance the family, education, military service and so on. Working practices which were transformed, in areas such as industrialized agriculture, although they always remained distinct from industry, also shared with it an increasing number of factors.

In the last decade of the twentieth century, industrial labour has lost its hegemony and in its place 'immaterial labour' has emerged, in other words labour that creates immaterial products: knowledge, information, communications, linguistic and emotional relations. Conventional terms such as service work, intellectual work and cognitive labour all refer to aspects of immaterial labour, but none of them fully grasps the generality. In an initial approach, immaterial labour can be thought of in two main forms, which generally merge in the actual practice of work. The first form involves work which is primarily intellectual or linguistic: for example problem-solving, symbolic and analytic operations, elaborating linguistic expressions and the like. This type of immaterial labour produces ideas, symbols, codes, texts, linguistic figures, images and products of other kinds. We call the other main form of immaterial labour 'affective labour'. Unlike emotions, which are mental phenomena, the affects are equally to do with mind and body alike. In fact affections such as joy and sadness reveal the state of the life of the entire organism, they express a given state of the body inherent to a way of thinking. Affective labour, therefore, is a labour that produces or manipulates affects such as feeling relaxed, feeling well, satisfaction, excitement, passion and so on. Affective labour can be recognized, for example, in the work of legal assistants, flight assistants and fast food workers. A sign of the growing importance of affective labour, at least in the dominant states, is the tendency of employers to play up good manners, education, attitude, 'social' attitudes, character and behaviours as prime necessities in their employees. A worker who has a good attitude and social abilities is a worker who is dealing in the area of affective labour, so to speak.

We should stress that the labour implicit in immaterial production remains material – it involves our bodies and our brains to the same extent as other forms of work. What is immaterial is its product. We recognize that the phrase 'immaterial labour' is ambiguous in this sense. It would be better to call this new hegemonic form 'biopoliti-cal labour', that is, labour which produces not only material goods but also relations and, finally, social life. The term 'biopolitical', more-over, indicates that the traditional distinctions between the economic, the political, the social and the cultural are gradually becoming less distinct. However, 'biopolitical' introduces other conceptual com-plexities, and in our view the notion of immateriality, although it has ambiguities, seems easier to grasp initially and works better in indi-cating the general tendency of economic transformation.

When we say that immaterial labour is tendentially assuming a hegemonic position, we do not mean that the majority of the workers in the world today produce immaterial goods. On the contrary, agri-cultural labour remains, as it has been for centuries, dominant in quantitative terms, and industrial labour is not globally and numeri-cally in decline. Immaterial labour constitutes a minority of global labour and is concentrated in some of the dominant regions of the planet. Rather, we mean that immaterial labour has become hege-monic in qualitative terms and has imposed its tendency onto other forms of labour and onto society itself. In other words, immaterial labour is today in the same position in which industrial labour was 150 years ago, when it engaged a small fraction of global production, con-centrated in a small part of the world, but actually exercising hege-mony over all other forms of production. Precisely in that phase, all forms of labour, and society itself, had to industrialize – while today labour and society must informaticize themselves and become intelli-gent, communicative and affective.

In certain respects the subordinated classes, in the period of indus-trial hegemony, provide a key to understanding the main character-istics of the hegemony of immaterial labour. Agricultural workers, for instance, have always deployed the knowledge, intelligence and innovation of immaterial labour. Certainly, agricultural labour is labour-intensive in physical terms, but agriculture is pure science. Every farmer is a chemist who puts the right seeds into the soil, who transforms fruit and milk into wine and cheese; every farmer is a geneticist who selects the best seeds in order to improve plant vari-eties; and is also a meteorologist who observes the skies. The farmer has to know the earth and work with it, in tune with its rhythms. Deciding the best day for sowing, or for harvest, is a complex calcu-lation; it is not a spontaneous act of intuition, nor is it a cyclical repetition of the past, but a decision taken on the basis of traditional knowledges in the light of observed present conditions, constantly renewed thanks to intelligence and experimentation. (At the same

time, and similarly, many farmers must also be financial brokers, able
to read the constant fluctuations of the markets so as to know when
best to sell their products.) This kind of open science typical of agriculture, which moves with the unforeseeable changes of nature, indicates the typologies of knowledge central to immaterial labour rather
than those of the mechanical sciences of farming. Our notion of
immaterial labour should therefore not be confused with the 1990s
utopian dreams of a 'new economy' which, many thought, would
make all work interesting and satisfactory, democratize well-being and
ban the recessions of the past – mostly through technological innovation, globalization and widening of the financial markets. The hegemony of immaterial labour does not make work pleasurable, nor does
it generate greater rewards, let alone lessen hierarchies and command
in the workplace. Nor, finally, does it lessen the polarization of the
national and global labour markets. Although it shares many of the
qualities of immaterial labour, as we have just shown, agricultural
labour continues to be subordinated in the global system, and the
order of hierarchy between city and countryside has not changed.

The hegemony of immaterial labour, however, tends to change the
conditions of work. Take for example the transformations of the
working day in the immaterial paradigm, in other words the increasingly indefinable division between labour time and free time. In the
industrial paradigm, the workers produced almost exclusively during
the hours they spent in the factory. But when production involves the
solving of a problem or the creation of an idea or a talk, the labour
time involved tends to extend to life in its entirety. An idea or an image
is not just created in the office, but also in the shower or in our dreams.
Once again, the traditional characteristics of agriculture and domestic labour can help us to understand this change. Agricultural labour,
as we know, does not follow traditional timetables: in the fields the
working day extends from dawn to sunset, when necessary. The traditional articulation of the domestic labour of women destroys in even
more obvious ways the divisions of the working day, and ends up
invading every part of life.

Some economists use the terms Fordism and post-Fordism also to
indicate the transition from an economy characterized by the stable,
long-lasting employment typical of industrial workers, to an economy
marked by flexibility, mobility, precarious working relations and so
on. Flexibility because workers have to adapt to various tasks; mobility because workers often have to change jobs; and precarity because
no contract guarantees a stable long-term job. An emergent, post-
Fordist form of agricultural production, for example, is characterized

by such technological changes. Agrarian modernization is very much based on mechanical technologies, from the Soviet tractor to Californian irrigation systems, but agricultural postmodernization develops biological and biochemical innovations, together with specialized systems of production such as greenhouses, artificial lighting systems and hydroponics. These new techniques and technologies tend to separate agricultural production from large-scale production and they permit more specialized operations on a smaller scale. Moreover, postmodern manufacturing production is itself becoming digitalized, for example through the integration of communication technologies into the existing industrial process; in the same way, agriculture is also becoming information-based, and this can be seen clearly in seed production. One of the more interesting struggles in agriculture – for instance – centres on ownership of the genome of the plant, that is, the genetic information contained in the seed. The seed multinationals patent new varieties of plants which they themselves produce – often by means of genetic engineering; but peasants through history have discovered, conserved and improved the genetic resources of plants without any claim to ownership. Our aim here is not to support or to condemn these practices – some scientific involvements in agriculture have brought benefits, others have brought harm. Our main interest is to show how the process of change in agriculture and the battles over rights depend increasingly on the production and control of information, in this case the genetic information contained in plants. And this is one way in which agriculture is becoming informaticized.

In general, the hegemony of immaterial labour tends to transform the organization of production passing through the linear relations set up in the modality assembled by the indeterminate and innumerable relations of the distributed networks. Information, communication and cooperation become the rules of production and the network becomes its dominant form of organization. The technical system of production thus corresponds specifically to its social composition: on the one hand the technological networks and on the other the cooperation that the social subjects set to work. This correspondence defines the new typology of labour, and characterizes the new practices and the new structures of exploitation. From our point of view, exploitation in the hegemony of immaterial labour is no longer mainly the expropriation of the value which is produced by, and in the time of, individual or collective labour. Exploitation becomes rather the expropriation of value which is produced by cooperative labour and which becomes increasingly common through its circulation via social networks. The central forms of productive cooperation are no longer generated by the capitalist as part of the project of organization of labour; they emerge instead from the productive energies put into place by labour itself. This fact is the main characteristic of immaterial labour: it produces communication, social relations and cooperation.

Someone might object at this point that such a notion of immaterial labour would be more apt for describing the transformations of the economy in the dominant areas of the world, and that it has very little to do with the subordinate regions, where the workers are still tied to fields and factories. We, however, still maintain that this tendency towards the hegemony of immaterial labour applies to all sectors and regions of the global economy, in at least three respects. In the first place, and obviously, the hegemony of immaterial labour brings about new global divisions of labour: for example, some forms of immaterial production remain in the dominant regions while many types of industrial and manufacturing production are being moved to the subordinate regions. In the second place, as we have explained, the qualities of immaterial labour tend to transform all the other forms of production. Every hegemonic form of labour undoubtedly generates common elements: so, just as economic modernization and the hegemony of industrial labour have technologically updated agriculture (along with all other fields) and have also homogenized industrial and economic practices and relations, in the same way economic postmodernization and the hegemony of immaterial labour have produced transformations. In part these are a product of bases newly created by the common and in part they are an induced effect: today we can clearly identify long-standing bases of the common, for instance in the role of information and scientific knowledge in agriculture. This does not mean, we should stress, that conditions of labour and production are becoming the same all over the world or in the various fields of the economy. Rather, it means – from our point of view – that the many single determinations of the labour processes, of conditions of production, of local situations and of lived experiences coexist with the becoming-common of the forms of labour and the general relations of production and trade – and that there is no contradiction between the singularity and the common

In the third place: we must recognize that the hegemony of immaterial labour also involves a dramatic expansion of the socialization of labour and provides new bases for the independent organization of labour. From a certain point of view immaterial labour has a different, more intimate relation with cooperation by comparison with previous forms of labour. The creation of cooperation, communication and collaboration is part and parcel of the production process itself, and is completely in the hands of the subjects who work. From another point of view, immaterial labour is different from the other forms of labour for the reason that its very products are, in many respects, immediately social and common. To produce communication, affective relations and knowledges, as opposed to the production of motor cars and typewriters, can directly increase the wealth of what we put in common and share. From both points of view, production is becoming more clearly and directly the production of subjectivity and the production of society itself. In other words, the greater abstraction created by the hegemony of immaterial production also implies a greater socialization of labour. This constant creation of the common and this becoming-common of the different forms of production reduce the qualitative divisions which have separated the different classes of workers, thereby creating the conditions for a common political project of labour which we can call 'the multitude'.

(3) *A post-socialist programme, or what is still alive of socialism, and what is dead?*   This analysis of contemporary transformations in production gives a vantage point from which to re-evaluate some central aspects of the political and economic strategies of the socialist tradition. Let us note, as the first element, that the socialist strategies of economic modernization were based on a concept of stages of development which is now unusable. In fact these socialist notions of modernization were entirely modelled on the capitalist model of development. One could also question whether this strategy ever actually had any value in the past; but it should be obvious that today it does not. All this should be clear from our previous analysis of the hegemony of immaterial labour. It is beyond doubt that today there are hierarchies and divisions of labour in the global economy, some of which are even more rigid than they were in the past; but these different sectors function contemporaneously, in the same temporal dimension, and interact in the global system without there being any relation between stages of development. Development, here, has a different inflection: it proceeds together with the ever-greater socialization of production, with the formation of common relations, circuits of communication and cooperation. Today, in fact, there can be no development without a simultaneous advance in the socialization of production. What of socialism is dead, therefore, is the notion of transition which modelled itself on the capitalist system of development.

In the second place, these economic transformations have also led to the emergence, from the foundations of the state, from the bottom, of centralized and authoritarian mechanisms of state control. (We should emphasize that this notion of the progressive role of state in economic development also modelled itself on the imperatives of the capitalist organization of labour and was seen as a means to overcome the lag accumulated in relation to capitalist development.)

Today the economic horizon can be sustained only directly, by a series of common goods. We must therefore find a way to move away from the socialist paradigm – according to which the distribution of social goods and the rules of investment are determined from the outside – towards a conception based rather on the common precondition of the socialization of production. In other words we need to shift from the authoritarian and centralist practices of socialism to practices of economic self-organization. We feel the necessity of this shift, as we have said, and the necessity of making it starting from our analysis of the transformations in the economy: the hegemony of immaterial labour in the global economy renders the old paradigm of state control non-viable. But we would also emphasize the political attractiveness of such a change, which requires a far-reaching re-examination of the state form itself, as well as that of the concept and institutions of political and democratic representation. This means that, while we attack the capitalist forms of state control (together with their horrible neo-liberal permutations), we also need to criticize the forms developed by the socialist state. This goes far beyond simply a critique of the totalitarian model of the Union Soviet and obliges us to reconsider the democratic character of the socialist state as a possibility for exploring new forms of democratic representation.

What is still alive of the socialist tradition is mainly the desire for equality and democracy that has characterized socialist politics since its origins. Wang Hui explains brilliantly, in his article published in English in the volume *China's New Order*, how the heritage of struggles for socialism teaches us that the demand for democracy cannot be separated from the demand for social equality. It is certainly true, as he says, that the Maoist project to eliminate the 'three differences' – between industrial workers and peasants, between city and countryside and between intellectual and manual labour – is still extremely important, together with the struggle to eliminate numerous other hierarchies: between men and women, between racial groups, between regions of the world, and so on. If today a post-socialist political programme can exist, its first order of interest has to be the development of a new notion and new institutions of democracy both at the national and at the global scale, and this notion must incorporate struggles for equality.

In this sense, we view as rich and promising the many movements emerging in various parts of the world against the dominant global and capitalist order of Empire. These are movements which are being constructed on the inheritance of socialism, and they are moving it in new directions. There are many situations in which the political battles are directed to ends that are specific and local, but at the same time they manage immediately to touch the global structure of power, the nature of Empire in its entirety. Take for example the movement against the construction of the monstrous dam on the river Narmada in India. This is clearly a local and national event which has to do with the right to land, with national debt, with the redistribution of national wealth and so forth. But the people who are opposed to the dam immediately find themselves also up against the World Bank, which encourages these kinds of big works and lends money to the Indian state. Or consider the Zapatista revolt in Chiapas, Mexico. There too the issues are both local and national: racism against the native populations, reform of the system of land redistribution, legal rights and representation in Mexican society. But from the start the Zapatistas have also mobilized against the NAFTA agreement, recognizing that the neo-liberal construction of free trade areas was a factor in deciding the policies of the Mexican state. We would also have to include among such struggles those of the Sem Tierra workers in Brazil, those of the indigenous movements in Bolivia, and also the various movements in Europe and North America which define themselves as 'anti-globalization'. (Wang Hui maintains, in fact, that the 1989 social movements in China, that is, the Tiananmen revolt, have an 'inner connection' to this whole cycle of struggles.)

It would be much simpler to consider these, and the other innumerable struggles which are taking place all over the planet, as split off from each other, inasmuch as they focus on specific and local problems. But we need to recognize how they share (not as a lowest common denominator but as a maximum common aspiration) the construction of a global democracy or, at least, a democratization of the global system which should be based on social equality. Every such movement comes into conflict, from different points of view, not only with the undemocratic character of its own national government but also with the undemocratic character of the global Empire itself. Each of them recognizes its damaging nature, and demands democracy and equality.

These movements are a resource which makes itself available for the construction of a post-socialist programme. Obviously, however, a lot more is needed. The project to develop not only the institutions but also a real concept of global democracy is an enormous task, which will require incredible resources.

(4) *Regional geopolitics and New Deals*   Having outlined such a high purpose – global democracy and equality as a post-socialist programme – we want to end with an argument that has a more modest scope, namely the question of regional political projects. It seems to us that the regionalist projects in Empire have two distinct faces. It is useful here to return to the simplified notion of monarchic forces and aristocrats in Empire (the notion that we presented at the start), because the issue of regionalisms relates to the question of aristocracies. Thus on the one hand we have the properly imperial model of regionalism, in which each regional aristocracy collaborates faithfully with the monarchic elements. As a reductive example (but nevertheless useful) of what we are talking about, let us consider how the US government is involved in every area of trade and in every military alliance. In all these lines, each regional alliance includes the presence of the United States – a European regional alliance is made up of European nation–states plus the United States; similarly, a Latin American alliance consists of the states of Latin America and the United States; ditto with alliances among countries of the Far East, and so on. This is the face of the regionalism that maintains the stability of Empire.

On the other hand, it is possible that the regional aristocracies (the nation–states together with the regional economic powers), instead of aligning themselves with the monarchic elements, might ally with the multitude. Such an alliance might constitute a kind of regional New Deal, that is, a compromise by which the aristocracies would give political and economic guarantees to the multitude, thereby developing the forces of production and favouring their own interests. This face of regionalism potentially creates a distance from Empire and is oriented in a different direction. In other words, instead of strengthening the imperial order, these regional alliances could constitute a counter-imperial strategy. We should not forget, however, that the interests of the regional aristocracies and those of the multitude are not in any way the same. Such regional alliances would constitute a strategic effort to which the multitude would have to apply itself in view of its own objectives.

A contemporary example of such an alliance can be seen in the southern cone of Latin America, in particular between Argentina and Brazil. The Latin American example shows clearly that a regional

New Deal needs to involve two developments at the same time: the proposition of democratic policies at the international and global level (including challenges to the World Trade Organization, the International Monetary Fund and the USA) and the development of internal democratic policies (including the redistribution of welfare, agrarian reform, labour policies, and so on). The democratic proposals directed to the outside cannot be separated from the internal democratization. The Latin American example is suggestive, but up until today only small steps have been taken. It is not at all clear how a democratic process can be articulated in the present conditions.

What we would like to explore with you – and on this point we end – is how a regional New Deal project might be possible in China, and in what way such a process is already developing today. Is it possible to identify in China inner processes of struggles for democratization, struggles for equality which could merge with a project for a democratic east Asia and therefore raise an alternative to the global system of Empire? To what extent can the socialist heritage and the tradition of communist internationalism form a reservoir of well-being which China can use in that process? In what way can domestic movements in China productively articulate themselves with the various movements we have previously cited, which are demanding global democracy – for example the movements against neo-liberal capitalist globalization? These are questions that you can answer better than us. We hope, however, that China's past places it in an extremely powerful position in any project of regional alliance against the rules of Empire and for a global democracy.

22
The New Phase of Empire*

Whenever I come to Padova, which happens rarely (and then only when I am visiting family and relations), I have a strong sense of embarrassment . . . This is the city where I was born, where I grew up, a city to which I am tied for all kinds of reasons, and also where I developed during my university years. I want to tell you now, perhaps for the first time since my arrest twenty-five years ago for those so-called 'heinous crimes', that I actually experience a kind of shame in returning to Padova. Shame because here we have a university that still has not made a public act of self-criticism over the fact that it opened this academic year with an outpouring from Professor Ventura (published in the *Rivista Storica Italiana*, where you can find it). In that speech, the 'Calogero thesis' – in which I and my comrades, some of whom are present here today, were presented as murderers (and cowards because we did not admit to being such) – was accorded the value of a scientific truth. At other times, if people had said that kind of thing in the University of Padova, they would have been dragged from the platform. When will it be possible, in Padova, to drag from the platform these scientifically non-existent gentlemen who continue to make these kinds of accusations? When will it be possible to change the editors of our newspapers, who have never undertaken self-criticism? When will it be possible to get public prosecutor Calogero to recognize the falsity, the calumnies, the shameful accusations that were heaped onto us, ruining whole families in the process?

For my own part, I am lucky. I came out of all this still standing. But, out of the group of comrades who were arrested with me, fifteen

---

* Talk given at the Radio Sherwood Festival, Padova, 6 July 2004.

have died young. Of cancer. If a God exists, I might wish that he would talk with these judges, and tell them how much misery and unhappiness they have succeeded in producing – something which of course the law, the responsibility of the law, does not cover. Padova owes us too many things for me to be able to forget it; Padova should thank us for the fact of still being alive. For our part, we thank Padova for our good character, for our good temperament, for the fact that we were able to get through all this terrible stuff and still emerge as strong people, continuing to study, to work, to propose ideas – and continuing to propose political movement. These are the forces which today everyone considers to be fundamental in dealing with the world.

Has the idea of democracy as being constrained within a given constitution been superseded? It seems so. Democracy, in fact, is not one of the forms of management of government, as also are not monarchy, aristocracy or democracy, according to the teaching of the Greeks: these are forms through which the chaos of society is reduced to one. Democracy, in that case, is nothing other than the government of the people; but the people (in that perspective) is one, exactly as democracy is one. Bodin, an old and formidable theorist of the sixteenth century, said that all forms of government reduce to monarchy, because they all seek to be a government of the one, of oneness. Today this is no longer true; when people speak of democracy (assuming that they are not talking *à la* George Bush), they are referring to something else: democracy is the expression of desires, of living labour, of production, of the ability to put together differences; democracy is the formidable ability to unite through labour the continuous dialectics of differences, a capacity for reaching agreement and building in common.
Recently I was re-reading a series of papers produced – all over the world, and also in the University of Padova – by historians of philosophy and of political ideas. This meaning of democracy – which is no longer that of Plato and Aristotle, of the city–tribe able to unite everyone, but is rather the production of different identities, of various desires – cannot still be presented in the form of sovereignty. It comes to represent itself in the interplay of expressions of the desires and resistances of minorities: these kinds of conceptions are widespread these days. This, in fact, has been the great contribution of the 'no-global' movement: a new idea of democracy. An idea of democracy that has little in common with Lenin and communist democracy, and likewise with federalists such as Madison and with the great American tradition, which none of us disparages. Rather, democracy reveals

itself as a *clinamen* of freedom which runs through the desire of the multitudes. A democracy which, inasmuch as it is the expression of a multiplicity, is not chaos, because we live in community, we live immersed in a language which communicates, we live immersed in a production which takes the form of networks, we live immersed in affects which are a single substance that unites us, even when it is in the form of hatred or negative feelings. Let us ask – what do government and sovereignty count for in our lives? Ten per cent, more or less, and the rest is the things that we construct and do spontaneously, because that is the way man is brought up: as a great political animal of multiplicity. What we construct is not chaos (the accusation always directed against us), if we construct it freely: it is a quest for a higher complexity and togetherness [*comunanza*].

Now I have a little joke, about the the typology that Michael Hardt and I identified seven or eight years ago at the time when we were writing *Empire* – it feels like a century ago! – in which we said: there is this Empire being constructed, and it has a new kind of mixed government, which is a combination of monarchy, aristocracy and a form of democracy which lies below us and which we call multitude. Ten years ago the United States was king: Washington commanded the armies and imposed order on the world after the 1989 ending of the Soviet splitting of the global market; New York ran the world market in monarchic fashion and Hollywood ran the communications market. This was the schema of monarchy. There was also a world aristocracy, made up of the nation–states and their intermediaries, but above all made of the great movements of the multinationals, which were not co-terminous with those of the American global Empire and which occasionally tried to re-balance the system in their own interests. And then there was the great pressure of the movements – the liberation movements and the workers' movements – which by now had acquired a new figure. This figure – the worker who was mobile, flexible and migrant, the intellectual worker, the services worker, the worker in communications – was a person who embodied a new heritage of production and freedom. It was no longer possible to produce without producing freedom, nor was it any longer possible to produce without putting oneself into a circulation. The multitude was no longer a mass, but a new ensemble of singularities, of people, men and women, who put their spirit and their freedom into play in production. There was no value produced without this capacity for commitment.

No longer massified and undifferentiated, but with a maximum of differences: we therefore found ourselves in this extremely dynamic and shifting situation. Now, in the face of the first general insurgence of the multitude (this new reality of labour), what has happened? An attempted *coup d'état*, pure and simple, over Empire, by the American government, by the neo-conservatives and by Bush. Jokingly we refer to this as 'The 18 Brumaire of George W. Bush'. But was this really comparable with the situation described by Marx in his critique of the *coup d'état* carried out by Napoléon le Petit, nephew of Napoleon Bonaparte, against the development of the French republic?

A *coup d'état* which said '*L'empire, c'est moi*' and which amounted (in Bush's case) to unilateralism. A precise attempt at a *reductio ad unum* of new tendencies which were appearing within globalization – and here we should remember that they represented, first and foremost, a powerful aristocratic resistance. Chirac and Schröder were certainly not the kind of people to be interested in the movements of the new productive freedoms of the multitude. They were more concerned with the interests of their multinationals and their financial markets, and they saw Bush's position as an attack and a forced subjection into unity within the American empire. This is why they opposed it, not because they loved peace. The love of peace didn't even enter their minds! Yes, maybe Chirac was momentarily nervous that the extremists in the French *banlieues* might rise up, but this was secondary to the real reason for their position. Then the Americans accused the French of being shirkers because they were not prepared to go to war; of course they were shirkers – it suited their interests that way. However, the most important fact was that – albeit in accord with their interests, and under pressure from world-wide public opinion and from the newly organized global multitude – these men rejected war, despite the fact that, in the mixed alliance of the Empire that was coming into being, these aristocracies were in some sense obliged to collude with the American monarch. This was a great victory of the multitudes: the fact that the Iraq War has become a war which has in some ways led to the isolation of the United States.

I imagine that I am probably the least anti-American of all of you. I have always liked the USA. As a kid I even wanted to emigrate there . . . However, the problem is not whether we love it or hate it, but to consider objectively what is going on in the world: what we have seen is a *coup d'état* which has been defeated not only by struggles, but also by a fracture in the alliances of power. It is this fracturing of alliances that we need to analyse, since we are going through a phase in which the American defeat complicates things enormously. In our view, the fact that the Americans did not succeed in getting their hands on all the energy in the world through the Iraqi operation, and were not able to consolidate their unilateral power, is a victory, but it also opens enormous problems. I believe that the movement's thinking needs to take account of this picture, and I also think that many critical attitudes within the movement need to be read within this overall framework.

For my part, I think that in the next few years we shall see a 'constitutional' recomposition of Empire. It is likely that in the next few years Chirac and Schröder, or whoever replaces them, will arrive at an agreement with Bush, or whoever replaces him, and that the imperial alliance between the monarchy and the aristocracies will be recomposed. At that point, however, the subversive and democratic possibilities of the multitudes, the workers and the oppressed classes will be posed in new terms. I would say that, within the transition we are living there are some irreversible elements. The first of these is war, and the concept of preventive war.

'Preventive war' does not mean 'imperialist war' but 'imperial policing'; it means the transformation of armies into policing structures which are able to move from this recomposed global centre and intervene to order all the spaces of the world in terms of capitalist development. What we have is no longer war between nations or the 'imperialism' of a strong nation over a weak people; instead we have a network of police powers which intervene everywhere. This new structure of repressive apparatuses has already penetrated so deeply into the organization of the armed forces as to constitute an irreversible reality. By now the armed forces of the world are no longer armies that march to fight on the frontiers of nations, wielding the banner of the destructive potential they have in their arsenals. The world's armed forces have become mobile, dynamic, more or less mercenary (as the police also are mercenary), available to intervene promptly when required in order to impose order, organized in networks and around mobile units, and providing simultaneously both a capacity for intervention and a capacity for assistance, organization, nation-building and 'democratic constitutions'. Soldiers and missionaries at the same time.

The shameful Italian experience in Nassiriya, and the still more shameful propaganda that has been made of it, are a small paradigm of what the organization of power is becoming: think what a wonderful world is in store for us, with *carabinieri* distributed all across the planet! This networked 'counter-insurgency' (a word that is nearly untranslatable into Italian, because it is not 'counter-guerrilla' but 'counter-uprising' or 'counter-freedom') has to contain within itself everything that goes to make up this fine capitalist world we inhabit:

non-governmental organizations, banks with pretensions to being benefactors, men of religion and secular missionaries – a fine cocktail! This is a threshold from which they will never turn back in the organization of legitimate imperial violence. What a contrast with the democracy that I was discussing before, which is an expression of needs, desires and capacities for the common, for community; the expression of will from below, of federalism . . . all those wonderful things that we feel in ourselves and perceive as natural, as part of our lives, in the same way that language, its enrichment, research, and so on are also part of our lives. Standing against these ways of common thinking which have become so widespread, there is now an irreversible horizon of war. The Iraq War was a defeat for the unipolar, monarchic and exclusivist tendency of the American governing group, but it also initiated and generalized this new situation of war.

The second element to note is the ambiguity of the new alliance between the monarchy and the aristocracies. An alliance which is somewhat ambiguous, because the Americans knew that they would arrive at this kind of situation sooner or later. We have a splendid example of something similar in Anglo-Saxon history, namely the drawing up of the Magna Carta. At a certain point in the thirteenth century, England's King John had to pay for the wars he had embarked on (crusades, war with France and so on), but he found himself up against the nobles and the aristocracy. They told him: 'Friend, we have no more money to give you unless you give us some power.' From that moment the relationship between the aristocracies and the king becomes a relationship which is contractual and constitutional. The Magna Carta, which they now tell us is the foundation of democracy and liberty, was in fact an agreement between the king and the warrior aristocracies, who said: 'Before going out to get ourselves killed, we want a part of the power you have.' Today we can suppose that this is more or less how things are going to turn out: Chirac, Schröder or the Chinese will go to Bush and will say: 'Pay up!' – pay up in terms of political agreement and a redistribution of power.

So to speak of the end of monocentrism is a good thing. But the ending of American monocentrism is matched by the emergence of a polycentrism which, insofar as it concerns us – as the multitude of exploited proletarians, the multitudes of workers – is interesting, but only interesting to a certain extent. Knowing that they were going to have to deal with the situation I have described, the Americans have tried the strategy of *divide et impera*, 'divide and rule'. In relation to Europe, this has happened in quite vulgar ways. The attempts to break

Europe have witnessed some fairly horrible scenes – the buying of Poland, the giving of money to Aznar . . . Not to mention poor Berlusconi, who's hardly worth it! The same goes for Latin America, and for relations with the former Soviet Union, and for the issue of China and its membership of the World Trade Organization. However, when we try to define this transition we need to see it in all its different aspects: differences which can be taken as revealing the enormous power of the revolt which has taken place.

So what about Europe? Ever since 1953 and the demise of the idea of the European Defence Community, Europe has been trying to unify itself. The breach caused by the Americans' attempt to prevent a United States of Europe and by the possibility of European unification as a market and a political power has never been healed. The fact of Europe unifying itself is hugely important for us, but at the same time it is of secondary importance. Hugely important because a politics at the global level can only be conducted from within European dimensions; of secondary importance because a Europe created exclusively by the aristocracies, by the likes of Chirac and Schröder, can be of only relative benefit for the workers. But this is also true of Latin America, where the new, globally oriented politics, basically those of Brazil and Argentina, are creating tendencies towards unity and the construction of continental poles which are proving fundamental in the balance of world power and as a counter-power against the United States and its monarchic intentions. The same is also true for China, which is far from being a unitary country governed by a mighty Communist Party: as we all know, China is a country very much in movement, where two or three hundred million persons are now inserted in the beginnings of the capitalist process, but where a billion wretched peasants are pressing for their freedom. How can the new imperial constitution, in which monarchies and aristocracies are combining, open spaces for the new movements?

As things stand today, the world-wide movement, in the form in which it emerged against the Iraq War, is finished. Why? First: in large part it was a sovereignist movement, that is, it thought that the restoration of nation–states and of what nation–states do was sufficient in itself for defeating imperialism – in this case, American. Secondly: in the countries of the South especially, people were once again entertaining notions – based on sovereignty – of projects of independent development. This, too, is a lot of nonsense! Thirdly: the general mechanism of the alliances was not engaging with the movements.

But the movement has been stronger than all this. Although today we find ourselves in a relative *impasse* in the face of the new process which is being configured – or the new alliance between an American monarchy and the European, Latin American and Chinese aristocracies, and so on – we also find ourselves up against a number of other fundamental things.

In the first place, we have the elimination of the sovereignist terrain, of the nation–state. This is no longer a terrain on which to conduct an effective struggle for the liberation of the multitudes. The nation–state is a place in which the imperial structure – particularly in the new forms in which it now appears – and with the coupling of American imperial power and the various associations of capitalists and local political élites – must be superseded. Politics can no longer be made at the national level. The national level is a level at which nothing is decided any longer: neither the value of currencies, nor the possibility of the exercise of force, nor issues about language and communication. The national level is by now completely consumed in the experience of the liberation of the multitudes.

Secondly, we have the elimination of a particular idea of government, related to the kinds of concepts of democracy we discussed earlier. In this regard there have been important developments, both in China and in the countries of Latin America: governments no longer shut themselves off from the movements; it is no longer possible for governments, at a certain point of development, to plan their countries' normative and regulative systems, the general mechanisms of social organization, unless they also bear in mind the dynamics of the forces of counter-power, of movements within it. There is no possibility of developing production and wealth without keeping ever-present the mediations and resistances of multitudinarian counter-powers. This is not only because a new conception of democracy has penetrated into the ranks of the movements. The point is that these days, in the world of work, where people participate by applying their intelligence and mental abilities, putting their freedom into play in their work, in that situation it is not possible to produce wealth except by creating spaces for the acceptance and acknowledgement of this subjective freedom of living labour, of this new force of production. This not only applies to the classic trade-union forces with which we are familiar. In general terms, it also applies to the actual social structure of work. Take the example of the peasants, that huge mass of the world population that still produces foodstuffs and agricultural commodities: here we find extremely interesting changes. Looking at the peasantry, we see great multitudes who are no longer simply drawn into the great mechanisms of mass production, but live a continuous and singular differentiation of productive capacities. Like all workers, the peasant has always been a remarkable figure, whose working life involves a relationship with the weather, with the atmosphere, with nature, and with changes in cultivation patterns, and who is able to carry this singularity into production. Today these processes are becoming increasingly intellectual and are expanding on all sides: if you want value added in agricultural production, you have to act singularly and intellectually – in other words, as a multitude of singularities. These developments can be seen not only among the peasants of the Po Valley or those of Bourgogne, but also in the great agricultural economies of South America, the United States and China. The proletarianization of the peasant is finished: agricultural labour too is immaterial!

Another huge (and completely revolutionary) change is what has been happening in service work, affective work and relational work: these forms of labour now also require increasing degrees of freedom and capacity of expression.

That being said, governments find themselves at something of a loss – they are able to express normative substance only if they succeed in putting themselves into relation with this new form of life and labour. The attempts made by the Lula government in Brazil and by the Kirchner government in Argentina, and their relations with the big social movements which have emerged in those countries, are paradigmatic from this point of view. Certainly today, on this terrain too, we find ourselves facing major obstacles and difficulties, obstacles which sometimes turn into moments of crisis; but the experiences are there, and we have to place them at the core of our analysis of the situations of transformation we are living through.

It happened that I was in Madrid in the days following the election defeat of Aznar. I was able to grasp, from the accounts of many comrades, but also from people outside the movements, the emotion of those days. An emotion arising out of the fact that a huge number of citizens, having been served an obvious government lie (the accusation that the Basque ETA had been behind the bombing of the Atocha station), organized themselves in singular and multitudinarian ways. It wasn't the Socialist Party of Zapatero that organized all this, but groups of people who were saying 'NO, these lies must be fought, and I'm going to communicate this need to my friends by sending them text messages, or phoning them, or going round to see them . . .'. In the space of a day and a night this multitude of singularities succeeded in overthrowing a government. But, more than that, this popular upheaval took Spain out of the Iraq alliance and shifted it towards Europe. The Spanish comrades call this movement 'the Commune of Madrid' – it was in effect a new insurrectionary form, which passes through the masses to the extent that it passes through the awareness and desire for truth of each single individual. So don't be surprised if and when you find the same kinds of demands being made against the new ordering of the world of work! It could happen!

But all this also happened in ways that were absolutely unexpected: the instruments of power, from public opinion polls to the unanimous pressure of the mass media, were all giving victory to Aznar. But that's not how it turned out! The opposite happened, with irresistible force. I believe that the movement is aware of the great transition which is under way. It's no longer a matter of fighting only for peace and against American war, with a large collective coming to awareness; we are also fighting for peace through the resistance of the multitudes, and for the transformation of the social order through the action of all those who work every day, generating day-to-day resistance.

The third point I would like to make is that the forms of organization and representation which are developing today are different from the forms we have seen in the past centuries, which now reveal themselves as obsolete and empty. The resumption of the social struggles, linked to the new form of the proletariat and working multitudes, becomes once again a fundamental transition. This is why we say that what is needed is to formulate a post-socialist programme. Socialism, that great experience which we all lived and in which we also include Soviet communism, was a programme based on the proletariat's take-over of power in order to develop the productive capacity of capital. Today, in the new conditions of production, we are beginning to advance a programme which is not wishful thinking or anarchistic, but which aims at conquering power within the common, in order for us to be able to express productive *potenza*; in order to construct wealth through the production of freedom. Today there are new social strata, which are central to social production and which are right there, concentrated at the key points of productive development: these strata are intellectual, digitally cooperational, relational and networked. These are the strata which (with their desire) will have to construct a political programme.

On the one hand, the movement we have lived has obliged power to recompose itself in its functions of command, between monarchy and aristocracies; on the other, it has given expression to new subjects and to a new subjectivity. This subjectivity is born out of the new forms of labour, out of the new forms of communication and the new forms of production which, with immaterial labour, also affect peasants, women, care workers, domestic labour . . . in short, the entirety of social labour, and which generalize the networked content of the production of the multitude. We need a programme capable of matching this development. This is the new communist manifesto which awaits us, the new kind of perspective we must construct. We can already identify some key questions for the construction of a post-socialist programme. The first is the global issue of cosmopolitanism, of the knocking down of national borders and of the construction (for example) of Europe or of the unity of Latin America: in short, the expression of all those potentials which exist at the continental level and which have a capacity for conditioning imperial power. The second theme, which is fundamental, is the possibility of creating specifically new forms of income, that is, the possibility of a redistribution of wealth. The issue of citizen income should not be seen simply in relation to unemployment, but in relation to general social production as a whole: if the whole of society is being set to work, then everyone should have the possibility of profiting from that work! The third question relates to the production and development of subjectivity. In other words, on the one hand a systematic break with all the forms in which communication is commanded, and on the other the constructive singular reappropriation of the forms of communication, both those which are immediately subjective and those of the big mass media. The fourth question is the project for new forms of government. What does it mean to take power? Nothing, if power means the management of capital. What might it mean if we say instead that to take power is to express a rich freedom, a freedom of production and thought, a freedom in every possible respect? This is a project in which the excedence of our lives, of our activity and our happiness, comes into play. We still run the risk of falling into extremism, but we are most cautious in this: it is not extremism to ask for something which is already ripe and mature. Who could call the Abbé Sieyès an extremist, when he says that the Third Estate wanted everything because it produced everything?

The problem is how to construct forms of government which are capable of investing the common, founding themselves on a grassroots political activity which has the ability to break down institutional obstacles and to deploy from below a real capacity for revolutionizing the real. These are things we have always said, but now they take on a new relevance, because now the federal structures, the structures of participation, in which the creation of wealth is activated, are extremely well developed.

There is also another critical element: this power accepts nothing of what the multitude expresses. Power has taken on war as the validation of itself, and this for a very simple reason: capital is becoming increasingly parasitic, the employing class no longer has the ability to understand the future. This is the reality that the present phase of movement and struggles has shown us. The bosses no longer have the measure of production. When production becomes social and common, when it shows how we are all more intelligent, the bosses can no longer command. In the old days the bosses plucked our grandparents from the fields, brought them into the factory, hung alarm clocks round their necks and told them: 'When it rings, pull that lever'. Then, gradually, they started to put them in front of machines they didn't even need to answer to: in order to produce it was enough just to obey . . . Today, for our children, things are different. Production is intelligence and intelligence cannot be commanded. And this freedom is no longer containable: capital then becomes the world gendarme, in the form of global policing, just at the moment when production is no longer containable within capitalist logic and the employer no longer serves any useful purpose!

These are the changed circumstances which must be taken as the basis of the post-socialist programme. It will require a radical change in the practices of representation. The new intellectual proletariat will no longer accept political parties which tell them: 'This is the line. If you are with us, you are with us. If not, then not. We are the representatives of the movements.' No, you are the representatives of nobody. The movements of the multitude can only be represented in/by a constituent process. The political parties, insofar as they serve any useful purpose at all, can only be servicing structures for the movements.

The same applies to administration. We need to be present in all the changes at the administrative level, knowing that all of them will have to be thrown out, and that their normativity will have to be shattered in order to enable the emergence of new energies; we must be present in all the trade-union struggles, but here we need to know that the problem is not the cost of labour, because the cost of labour is no longer the issue: the real issue is the need of productive society to reproduce itself. Thus we have to generalize the demand for income; we must be present in all the struggles in education, in the knowledge that this is a central productive resource; we must be present in all the struggles of women, in the knowledge that women's difference constitutes the very essence of the revolutionary transformation of society from a patriarchal society into a society of open production. We have to be within all of this, because this represents the only possible and adequate programme. And we need to remember that we find ourselves in a situation which is new and, as always happens with the new, also difficult.

23
Urban Democracy*

We have been invited here to offer some thoughts on culture in urban situations. According to the organizers of the 2004 Year of European Culture, Genoa and Lille are reference points for the debate. We shall say more about Genoa and Lille later. For now, since we have the Lille–Roubaix city councillors here among us, I want to discuss a few things which seem to me crucial if we want to deepen our approach.

The question of urban territory is vital if we want to understand what capitalist accumulation is today. Urban territory is the factory of postmodern accumulation, the laboratory of immaterial valorization, the biopolitical environment within which the activity and the exclusion of labour power confront each other. We live in a period of transition, and the city still offers itself as a place of contacts and relations between people, cultures and productions. On the other hand, it also manifests itself in ways that are completely new – either as if inserted into global networks of communication and exploitation organized around globalized productive energies which are concentrated in soaring towerblocks, or as ghettos of social subjects and proletarians forced into situations of international flexibility and mobility of exploitation. It is this dual reality that I would like to address today.

Genoa and Lille   At first sight it would be hard to find two cities which are more different. Why on earth should they be bracketed together? Why do these European cultural projects try to impose a fraternity onto populations and ways of life which are so very different, between horizons and climates which are so radically opposite? Why should intellectuals spend their time inventing reasons for meetings and a

---

* Talk given at VivaCités Nord-Pas de Calais, Lille–Roubaix, 6 September 2004.

shared terrain of discussion spanning such a vast difference? Of course there are some similarities. For instance, Genoa and Lille were both major industrial cities during the period of Fordism. They invite comparison because of the big working-class neighbourhoods that each of them once had, and for the powerful political identities that each expressed in the past. But today? Today they seem to resemble each other only in their urban decay, in the crisis of that way of life and that way of producing, in the destruction of their entire manufacturing landscape and in the weariness which derives from all that.

Apart from that, Genoa is in the South, Lille is in the North, and one is warm and the other is cold. One has the Mediterranean as its heart and soul, the other has the freezing winds of the English Channel. So why insist on this twinning, which is not even a *métissage* but seems to configure a monstrous figure of opposition?

Perhaps, however, North and South are relative notions. For instance, I remember a Genoa that was full of North. The sea was close by and the sky was probably blue, but who ever saw it? The chimneys of the Cornigliano steel works put out so much smoke that Sampierdarena was black inside and out – both the façades of the buildings and the hearts of people. The sing-song dialect of the Genovese seemed only able to create songs full of sadness. In comparison, the Lille that I remember seemed like a Mediterranean South. A city bustling with Italians and Spaniards, with those resonant voices of the South – and also North Africans, many of them – from all the countries of the Mediterranean and all the professions which the Mediterranean imagination knows how to invent

Perhaps the reason is that Genoa and Lille are both port cities: from Genoa you embark on the Mediterranean, from Lille you emerge onto the North Sea . . . Harbour cities, cities of nomadism, nodes of a Europe which is struggling to find an identity for itself and for its people, or to free its multitudes. Lille lies at the base of the crescent that reaches from Paris to Berlin; Genoa lies at the centre of the south European crescent which today runs from Barcelona to Naples, and tomorrow will run to Athens. And within these spaces we see the nomadic movement of a new multitude, a multi-coloured Orpheus: Genoa and Lille are full of them . . . Nomad cities, cosmopolitan metropolises, riddled with postcolonial tensions and with racist and imperialist contradictions . . . nevertheless cities where, unstoppably, a new fabric of European dialogue is being constructed, not simply among white people and well-educated citizens but above all between the latter and these nomads who in these days bring colour to our common, shared existence.

They are also cities of major social turnover. With the crisis of Fordism having destroyed their old social fabric, both have become privileged locations for precarious labour. The populations of these two cities, Genoa and Lille, consist of what we would call 'socialized workers' [*operai sociali*], a new workforce which is mobile, flexible and precarious . . . This is the new proletariat: intelligent and poor, aleatory in its job prospects and radical in its desires . . . They are cities, this Genoa and this Lille, with a multitude which increasingly expresses the productive force of the social and industrial service sectors; they are places with a growing phenomenon of self-employment among a precarious proletariat which carries with it, in people's brains, the tools of their labour and seems not to need a boss to supply the work. From this point of view Genoa and Lille are simultaneously very rich and very poor – rich in intelligence and poor in wages. A new phase of capitalist development? Certainly, but a phase which brings with it a series of political consequences, because if you carry the tools of your labour in your head, you see no reason why you should need a boss. And above all you don't see why capitalism, the capitalist market, and nowadays the capitalist globalization of trade must be considered 'natural', in other words necessary and essential, which results in a situation where poor black people are driven into work amounting to slavery and white proletarians are left without work. Also, these young people don't understand why poverty is becoming such a common condition and ostentatious wealth has become the only morality.

Social turnover in these cities is very strong. New generational strata are coming onto the labour market. The metropolitan and multitudinarian proletariat which the crisis of the 'old economy' had destroyed is being recomposed downwards, towards young people. The young people who work in the metal-working and transport sectors are no longer distinct from those who work in dot.com start-ups or those who are at university preparing for a future of precarious employment: the unification of these singular fragments takes place in the movement of intelligence and knowledge.

So finally we have arrived at a real point of similarity between Genoa and Lille. Don't go looking for it in history or similarities – look for it in change and difference . . . in the difference of a new labour power which seeks to invent another world for itself.

Having found one common element between Genoa and Lille, let's continue and try to find others. Indeed, if we can't find them in the past we shall have a hard job, because who is able to read the future? And here we find ourselves facing subjects and forces which constitute a genealogy of the future, and only in this future are they recognizable as common . . .

On the other hand these youngsters, these people, these populations do not act in a void, but within cities which themselves have been transformed, as a result of changes in the organization of labour and in the reproduction of life. Take Genoa and Lille: at one time they were different, dominated by different capitalist and working-class corporations, and both of them were in some sense telluric, ancient . . . Nowadays these two cities could be defined, if we wanted to be provocative, as one single non-place, because they are both unified in that consumption of life and colonization of desire which capitalist culture imposes at this stage of development. But stopping there would be insufficient, indeed wrong, because these cities were strong enough not to accept the destruction which, under the Fordist system of production, sought to carry away, snatch away a shared way of life. The destruction of welfare has not succeeded in destroying the bio-political communities of these cities. If Genoa and Lille had been obliged to add to the destruction of the Fordist mode of production also the destruction of the productive social fabric, of the skills of their workers, and if, in addition to the weakening of their welfare systems, they had had to cope with the ending of the interaction between society and the structures of administration – in what kind of desert would we be living today?

That is not the way things have happened. The elements of the new – in nomadism, in *métissage*, in precarity, in the intelligence of the new labour power – have inserted themselves into the old fabric of the socialist and communist traditions in the local administrations. These are traditions which are often tired, with administrative actors who are sometimes past it, but nevertheless the contact with the new, the radical critique, the necessity of answering to new requirements sometimes brings even some of these traditions back into the game . . . We are witnessing the paradox that the 'only renewal is that which returns to first principles'. Machiavelli discovered this in the great transformation of the 1500s – and why should it not also apply today, in the great social transformation of postmodernity?

And then there is the presence of women, which is increasingly marked in this metropolitan situation. They carry the burden not only of a large part of social production but also of the control over the flows of difference. The becoming-woman of labour and of politics is central here, not only because the quantitative presence of women's work is enormous, but also because on them weighs (and they are now capable of controlling) the entire context of the relationship between production and reproduction, between services and care in the metropolitan context.

They are not really a non-place, these cities of the new social composition of the proletariat: they are cities of a multitude of differences, which nevertheless succeed in working together and, probably, in producing subversion. Faced with the productive force of the new multitudes and with the hopes for renewal which live in them, faced with restlessness and moments of rebellion, these cities also become privileged locations for experiments in repression. We saw in Genoa, not so long ago, the police turning out on a new war footing; they seemed no longer even humans, but automata, cyborgs brutally unleashed against young people's demonstrations. Carlo Giuliani was killed. Many other young people were beaten in barracks and hospitals, in the streets and the improvised prisons: the city became a place where you could no longer distinguish between police actions and low-intensity warfare. Similarly in the *banlieues* of Lille, in the *cités* of emigration and marginalization, the CRS (Compagnies Républicaines de Sécurité) have taken the place of the local police, and there too the territory is patrolled like the towns of the West Bank.

But if you don't go into these neighbourhoods armed, if there is still a bit of joy in your heart, then you can feel the actions of social resistance, rather than as violence, as new music, as incessant rap. Movement and sound which become one, songs which organize life . . . and then, once again, resistance. In this tendency Genoa anticipated Lille. As I said before, people used to say that in Sampierdarena even the dialect seemed to murmur sad songs during the hard times of the rule of Fordism. But then, already in the 1970s, a new songbook was being born there, which sang of open landscapes and the sea, of deep emotions and of revolt ever-renewed . . . It was in Genoa that the Italian *canzone d'autore* was born, creating a revival of popular song: it was born there, the only place where it could have been born, among the discontent and the suffering which had emerged from the factories to assail the city, its way of life, and the spirit of its young people.

Where there is repression there is resistance, and where there is resistance a new culture is born.

But now back to ourselves. What can intellectuals say in this situation? What is it that these European projects want from us in the light of these social and political upheavals? Perhaps that intellectuals might bring spiritual calm and a diversion from the more immediate needs of the populations of these cities who are struggling to survive? Often this is what those young rebels suspect. So then, if they want to avoid these suspicions, what might the intellectuals say to these movements of resistance? Can they offer political alternatives, or even simply inspire moments of organization – here, within this poverty and this strength?

I do not really think that intellectuals have a lot to say here. Indeed, if they are honest and not corrupted by power, they won't say anything at all. All they need to do is look at what they themselves have become, precisely in those cities where the transformation of labour and social conditions has been deepest, where the confrontation is not between workers, immigrants and intellectuals, but within a block of unitary labour power where the distinctions between workers, between all workers, are becoming harder and harder to distinguish. There are no longer intellectuals, apart from those who are paid to do special pleading and are offered pulpits and masses to recite in exchange for cheques with lots of zeros. Because intellectual labour is by now labour *tout court*. Now we no longer have the figure of the intellectual who stands between the workers, the unemployed, the single mothers – and power. Intellectual labour now exists as matter which traverses the entirety of labour. This is why labour has become precarious, it is for this that the whole of society has been set to labour. What can intellectuals say in this situation? They can only say: we are the same as the rest of you.

I would attempt to interpret the cultural relationship between Lille and Genoa in terms of the generalization of struggles against power. In this sense the European cultural initiative has some meaning, but probably the opposite of what the official documents intend: a subversive meaning, which implies that the cultural initiative is within the multitude and that it has the capacity to shake off all the elements of repression it has no wish to endure.

But at this point our discussion needs to go back a bit, re-addressing these differences subjectively, reinterpreting them from below, and not simply deconstructing the crossings and complications of the journey. What is important to bring out here is a young person talking directly about what interests her – or him. We are not observing this person, we are not interpreting this person's words, we are simply listening to them. This is a creature of Lille and Genoa and a person who knows many other places . . . It is there, on the inside, that this person lives, within these metropolitan and multitudinarian dimensions; and it is there, on the inside, that this person seeks to build moments of antagonism and resistance.

The quest for antagonism by this new subject first has to deploy itself against the fragmentation and dissipation of the world of life.

The singular experience of precarity is what puts this young person simultaneously within creative labour and in a situation of resistance to the deployment of the processes of social transformation. Such people ask themselves why their creative faculties, their language, the wealth of their social relations, their capacity for learning and their emotions should be ground down by the private and privative dimensions of the capital relation they see happening before them. They are deprived – or so they feel – of the very possibility of emancipation. They must therefore place what they are (singular labour power, creative) into tension with the organized and commanded situation which surrounds them. There is a gap, a very big gap, between the tendency of intellectual power and intellectual freedom to express themselves and the actual nature of the relations of production. And within this gap the decision is located: the wretchedness of relationships imposes exodus, removal, autonomy, production and incessant reappropriation of the life nexuses of common being. The fact is that global movement can only be constructed if it passes continually through the local, through those small and continuous revolutions which constitute the gap that each of us experiences between domination and the experience of creation. 'Power is local because it is never global, but it is not local or localizable, because it is diffuse': thus Gilles Deleuze.

So we have now reached the point where transforming the city becomes our prime necessity, the very condition of our existence. It is a militant decision, this. Even when it doesn't know how to organize itself, but it knows where to try, it knows that it has to build creative tactics of deconstruction and exodus, gathering the spontaneous, diffuse behaviours of self-valorization . . . It is there, in the city, where living the wealth and the networks of social cooperation becomes the sole decision of political militancy.

In the natural sciences a distinction is made between ontogenesis and phylogenesis, that is, between the becoming of the individual and the becoming of the species: here, in our case, we have the impression that these two processes develop together and that the reconstruction of the individual can only take place through the reconstruction of the species. But do not Lille and Genoa show us precisely a modification of the species?

24

For a New Welfare*

I want to start by detailing the critique of the welfare state which has developed in the radical Left from the 1970s to the present day. I shall then go on to what the radical Left can say about the crisis of welfare as it stands today.

As we know, the welfare state was introduced from the 1930s onwards, and particularly in the second half of the twentieth century, as an attempt to regulate the movements of the working class within the requirements of capitalist development, which is capital's valorization of labour power. Welfare policies were a high-level (and effective) response of capital to the breakdown of capitalist order brought about by the October Revolution, which became endemic after 1917. When we frame things in this historical context it is easy to see how the development of the welfare state was conditioned by the marked and continuous working-class offensive characterizing the various cycles of struggle that spanned the twentieth century. I am saying that welfare policies were not only a function of the capitalist tendency (in the Fordist period) to create high demand in order to match the mass production of industrial goods: welfare policies were, above all, an attempt to close the successive waves of struggles that the industrial working class had unleashed during the twentieth century.

If, from a certain point, the capitalist classes of the welfare state (here I am referring to the '30 glorious years' which followed the end of the Second World War) permitted themselves to use those working-class struggles as the motor of capitalist development, this is not a

---

* Talk given at the Guido Pedroli Foundation, Università della Svizzera Italiana, Lugano, 2 October 2004.

functional response of power – it is, first and foremost, the revelation of the constituent power of working-class struggles.

Thus capital's requirement to find alliances with the trade unions (and, to a lesser extent, with the peasants and the urban middle classes), with the aim of democratically legitimating its own power, led to the birth and diffusion of a system of universal welfare. In the short term, this process represented a powerful increase in aggregate demand, designed to guarantee the processes of realization of surplus value. However, in the subsequent years, and particularly from the early 1970s onwards, this same process, under continuous attack from successive major waves of workers' struggles, put national accounting systems completely out of control. Hence the financial crisis of western societies in the 1970s. What needs to be understood here is that this crisis gradually became irreversible; that in this situation the wage relation itself was brought into question; and that this crisis thus concludes with the working class (through the struggles of the mass worker) breaking out of the regulatory limits dictated by the Fordist pact.

We need to stress this transition. The break which happened during the 1970s involved a transformation of the subjects in the field. On the one hand capital reacted by modifying the organization of labour, increasing the intellectual and immaterial quota in the production of value and thereby raising the level of exploitation. By this operation capital set the whole of society to work. With its modification of the organization of labour, it put itself into a position of subsuming all social labour under its own command. It is here that the concept of multitude is articulated, as a simultaneous understanding of the modifications taking place in living labour, of the singular and/or subjective imputation of living labour itself and, above all, of the recognition that the immateriality of labour and the cooperation of singularities always go hand in hand. It is, furthermore, imposed by the necessity of recognizing the 'active elements' of the political composition of the multitude.

We should always remember that the action of the working class (yesterday as well as today) is constitutive/constituent. As we have already said, in the Fordist period the welfarist state is not simply a figure of control, but actually a product of resistance – of the articulated, dynamic, unexpected and always powerful resistance of the working class. And, when labour becomes transformed and caught within new networks of control and globalization, at that moment it has an immediate alternative to offer: it is living labour which recognizes value in the capacity to produce excedence, it is living labour which creates a prevalence of cooperation over every other determination of production, individual or massified.

Therefore, when capital tries to respond to the breaking of the Fordist pact and the financial crisis of the state and tries to go beyond the limits imposed on it by working-class action, it sets in motion the deregulation of the welfare state and a series of processes of privatization. Spurred by the crisis, capital and its state substantially renounce the various mechanisms put into operation by the Fordist pact. This is what happens inside the central countries of the capitalist area; and this is followed, externally, by the push to the process of economic globalization which, on the planetary scale, is given a free hand with the collapse of the Soviet Union. What role remains for the welfare state in this new context? Does the welfare state still have some space of development? It is useless to attempt theoretical answers to these questions. The welfare state is dead: long live the welfare state! It needs to be said that the welfare state is so rooted in the very capitalist mode of production that its radical destructuration becomes problematic and in fact appears impossible. The welfare state is perhaps an irreversible characteristic of the capitalist mode of production – in the maturity of capitalism. Even the likes of Thatcher and Reagan often had to check themselves in their attempts to dismantle the welfare state. In the present phase of ebb of neo-liberalism, during which some fundamental aspects of the welfare state (demography, schooling, pensions and the like) are still holding up, we see the falling heads of many politicians who tried to give the final blow. If we consider the welfare state for what it has always been – namely, not as a concession by the state but as a product of workers' struggles; not as a projection of capital's needs but as something constructed by the *potenza* of the multitudes – then it becomes obvious that the battle over the welfare state is still completely open; indeed it is expanding, in line with the expansion of the ability of labour to affect and influence all the nexuses of the social process. In the real subsumption of society into capital, in biopolitical postmodernity, the struggle of labour power is metropolitan, urban-based and social – and therefore everywhere.

The battle over welfare is reopening. The question of citizen income has barely been initiated by the struggles, but it has already imposed itself as a pivotal element in the reconstruction of a welfare project. However, since we do not believe that one central element can resolve the problems, or that a monistic conception of social labour can enable us to confront the multiplicity of the aspects of exploitation, we think that thousands and thousands of alternatives will need to be produced, constructed and theorized by us in order to make possible the definition of a new programme of welfare.

A new common programme, then. And here the 'common' is to be understood as meaning that we no longer cede to the state, or capital, or any other external power (the churches, the mosques, the synagogues – in short, to the force and madness of command, which works by way of charity) the role of managing what is ours. The difference between the 'public' and the 'common' is that, in the public, social production can be managed by the state, but in the common it is managed by the subjects, who reappropriate it in common and reproduce in common politically.

As well as being a historical experience, the welfare state was also an anthropological experience: it was a desire of humanity that came true. There is no going back on that experience. From the point of view of workers' struggles, welfare is an established reality, and is irreversible. Furthermore, we have the present decline (incipient but none the less real) of the neo-liberal cycle and its likely defeat – as the proof of what I am saying.

PART FOUR

POLITICAL PHILOSOPHY IN IMPERIAL POSTMODERNITY

25
Postmodernity and Liberty*

In discussions in late modernity the concept of liberation has often been taken to be central. In fact this is true not only in late modernity but throughout the whole of the twentieth century. It seemed that liberty – 'freedom' – was not a valid and autonomous value. In fact the watchword of liberty was handed over to the conservatives, to the advocates of natural law and to the defenders of neo-liberalism and capitalist development. Handed over to hypocrisy. What did it mean to defend liberation against liberty? It meant seeing liberty as being completely subsumed within the circle of power, completely closed into the dialectical relationship which made it part and parcel of the capitalist and democratic order of things as we know them today. The concept of liberty thus came to be a lifeless concept, incapable of being developed as part of an expansive process; liberty became homologous with the constitutional form of capitalist power.

In contemporary debates in the social sciences, this reduction of liberty to power, this homologation (which fancies itself to be critical but is only passive) repeats itself. But, while it is true that in modernity liberty functioned within capitalist development, and while it is true that freedom has become a slogan of the dominant bourgeois classes (and thus liberation seemed to be the only viable concept, another way to say freedom, another desire), today we can say that the situation has changed, and everyone recognizes it. The real subsumption that capital has perpetrated in its absorption of society – and the globalization of social, economic and political relationships – has created a horizon, a reality, which is totally new. In calling this reality

---

* Talk given at the Pordenonelegge event, Pordenone, 21 September 2003.

postmodernity, we correctly define the difference it entails in relation to modernity. There are people who disagree with calling our present reality 'postmodernity'; they prefer to call it 'hypermodernity'. What does this terminological difference have to do with questions of liberation and/or freedom? Suffice to say that here again we are emphasizing liberation rather than . . . [sic]

We define postmodernity as a situation where the antagonistic relationship of capital dominates all social relationships, all nexuses of life, whether in production, culture or ways of living. In other words, the world that surrounds us is now characterized in biopolitical terms. The transition from the modern biopolitical (as described by Foucault in the various genealogical schemata he constructed) to the postmodern biopolitical is simply a deepening of power's invasion of the existential conditions of the whole of society. The technologies of power invest the social composition of labour power. In our research we have widely documented the transition from the phase of work organization dominated by the mass worker to that represented by the socialized worker, and we have illustrated the changes in the nature of labour, from materiality to immateriality, intellectuality and so on. Now, to construct a description of the social transitions of and within biopolitical technology, within the reality which power builds in its relationships with the social, means no longer placing our trust in processes of liberation which may (or may not) be closed within – or produced by – the dynamics of subsumption (the possibility of their not being thus enclosed depends on the balance of power between subjects rather than on the effective conditions of development); rather, we must place our trust in the emergence and the powerful declaration of freedom. We have entered an epoch in which freedom presents itself immediately as *potenza*, as alternative constitution. Freedom is a material *potenza*.

If we want to describe the political transitions taking place in the age of communication technologies and socialized knowledge, in the age of the postmodern biopolitical, we have to remember that the fundamental element traversing this reality is living labour as it places its hegemony in intellectual and affective, cooperative and excedent action. This is what biopolitical production is: can there exist something different from this new fabric of socially useful labour? Assuredly not. In such a situation, however, if liberation is the project, then freedom is the subject, the precondition, the condition without which there is neither production nor living.

Freedom is today, in a fundamental sense, part and parcel of the labour process, that is, of the erogation of knowledge and all those intellectual and/or affective possibilities that constitute excedence, difference and, therefore, in a radically alternative way, capitalist surplus value or common reappropriation of life. I hold very dearly to this concept of freedom as coming before the concept of liberation, and I insist on it. Liberation means liberating freedom: freedom is what stands at the root of things.

If we return to Spinoza's definition of freedom, we see that it is not just the construction of a consciousness of necessity, but above all an irrepressible tendency/tension towards the construction of being. Freedom means the ontological construction of the free person, and the social and conscious construction of the common. If we take the process of freedom in this sense, we can see how it superimposes itself on (and removes meaning from) that of liberation: the meaning of the process is constructed by the relations which extend between passions in the construction of social institutions. In Spinoza, freedom can become absolute freedom in real democracy.

Now we come to the question of general intellect, not only as intelligence but also as eros. The becoming contemporary of freedom has nothing to do with liberation (from a series of obstacles), but has everything to do with the traversing of those obstacles, with a process of singularization, as strong as it is anthropologically articulated. Freedom is asserted within an ontological compact of matter and spirit, between material labour and immaterial labour. Freedom bows to the ambiguous relationship between production of goods and services; but, in submitting to this, living labour discovers itself as social activity, as an excedence which is no longer containable, as a given freedom.

Furthermore, from a metaphysical and ontological point of view, the concept of liberation has little meaning. Liberation is a concept tainted with the theological–political. There, liberating oneself means liberating oneself from sin, from matter, from the heaviness of reality. Today these are not the kinds of question that concern us. We do not have the freedom to sin, but only the freedom to create being; in other words we do not have the freedom (and who can still call it that) to lack a constitutive act of being. Resistance must be considered in exactly the same way. It is not a withdrawing of oneself or a limiting of oneself within horizons which are established by power. Resistance is either production of subjectivity and constitution of new reality or it is nothing. Resistance is a radical alternative to the capitalist colonization of life, but it succeeds in being that only to the extent that it is an appropriation of the common (or of the conditions in which we live) – in other words an ability to break – radically but in ways that are original, ingenuous, spontaneous, autonomous and self-founding – with command.

If we now turn to examining the problem of liberation and freedom from the point of view of moral philosophy, we find many similarities, but also many differences, what we have said thus far. First we have to consider our existential condition. We live in solitude, misery and fear. This is very often the case. That negative which, viewing the thing in terms of political phenomenology, seemed almost not to be there, or rather seemed to represent itself only in a ghostly fashion . . . that negative that faced us in metaphysical forms . . . well, this is now physically present. What in political philosophy presents itself as limit, in our life presents itself as priority: in effect, the miracle of political philosophy is that of eliminating dissent, of using increasingly effective instruments of neutralization. On the contrary, it is here that the first action of freedom presents itself as necessary. And it seems negative, negative in itself. It is rebellion and refusal; it is the strength of saying 'No'. It is strange that the concept of freedom, necessarily given outside of liberation, that is, as a tendency towards the affirmation of singularity, reveals itself immediately as refusal, as negativity. And yet this is the phenomenological figure that we find most widely generalized; it is the figure of a freedom which manages to assert itself in the sphere of language, of a desire for autonomy which succeeds in affirming itself in the sphere of communication . . . Rebellion and refusal are, immediately and against all expectations, positive elements in the construction of an ethical awareness.

If we extend our view from the singularity to the common, if we assume this affirmation of freedom in its singular consistency – but if, at the same time, we subject this experience to the capitalist subsumption of society – we have to pose another series of problems. Here I mean that the statement of freedom as the primordial and essential element in no sense cancels the difficulties, ruptures and obstacles created by the structure of power.

(Here I would like to make a second observation, namely that in postmodernity this theory of freedom is quite different from a concept of freedom formulated in purely idealistic terms: the freedom of which we speak is that of bodies, of wages, of the material construction of a possible life . . .)

A materialistic philosophy of freedom in postmodernity offers us two roads, whose validity and/or effectiveness we shall have to gauge. The first is the road which follows the theory (and practice) of the excedence of labour power; the second is the road of residue, of the rupture of the historical flow by labour power. I believe that neither of these theories has, in itself, the ability to develop a possible alternative, unless they open themselves to major modifications, corrections or wholesale transformations.

The theory of excedence often draws on the sociological tradition of the gift. The theories of residue draw on the deconstructionist philosophies, and therefore on those slight variations that can occur at the edge of capitalist domination. Now, this is not what the philosophy of freedom in postmodernity can ask for and obtain. A philosophy of freedom, in postmodernity, takes its distance from philosophies of excedence and the gift, and also from deconstructionist philosophies of the interpretative residue [*scarto*], because it recognizes in them a structuring that is dialectical. This dialectical figure, which dominates the exit routes from modernity (in order to flatten them anew on modernity), no longer resorts to historical exemplifications and to physiologies of the spirit (as happened in Hegel), and no longer entrusts temporal–ontological determinations. The transitions these theories imply are passional and ethical – and yet they remain dialectical. They are rooted in transcendentalism. They require a star that can be referred to for redemption. They move, in reality, on the terrain of liberation.

But the problem today is no longer that of liberation as much as that of freedom. Freedom is a material foundation. Freedom does not need to be put into a machine which could find it a genealogy or could subject it to metamorphosis in order to adapt it to the present. No, it is there, just as it was created by the struggles of the proletariat, the class struggle which by now has been going on for centuries: freedom is living labour, the production of subjectivity. Freedom is antagonism pure and simple, which presents itself in the face of the real subsumption which capital has operated over this society. A subsumption which, at the very moment of becoming total, has determined the rebellion of the totality, freedom in the face of totality and domination.

Today the multitudes of freedom present themselves simultaneously as figures of the catastrophe of the capitalist world and as figures of the recomposition of passions, of the multitudinarian inter-crossings of singularities – the multitude is the figure of the recomposition of the contemporary sensible, not only that of language but also – and above all – that of desire. There is an absolute critical point which here touches on the difference between destruction and *potenza*, the destruction which capital cannot avoid imposing and the *potenza* which the multitude cannot avoid proposing. Here we are in contact with Spinoza and we try to read him as our contemporary. Spinoza followed the path which lies between the quest for freedom and the love of freedom, identifying it in the phases, in the dimensions, in the sensible transitions of a process which led towards the opening of the individual to social cooperation. Within this opening, the individual was eliminated and became singular. The ontological characteristics of the singularities are much stronger, in cooperative terms, than the egoistic and destructive Hobbesian and Hegelian characteristics which define individuality. This path we have covered, both in political philosophy and in moral philosophy, leads us towards the common, that is, towards a true democracy . . . conceived of not in terms of gift, not in terms of residue [*scarto*], but in terms of ontological construction.

26

The Communism of Immanence*

Modernity has been traversed by two lines of thought, corresponding to two opposing positions regarding the state, obedience and the definition of sovereignty. The first is the line which runs from Hobbes, through Rousseau, to Hegel. This line considers sovereignty, power and the possibility of human cohabitation in society as the effect of an order rooted in transcendence. The second line, which runs from Machiavelli through to Spinoza and Marx, sees power and sovereignty as products of experience and association between human beings. The first line, in its radical statement of transcendence, establishes power as a unity: sovereignty is a 'God on earth'; the second line sees sovereignty as a process of constitution which is increasingly open and increasingly efficacious for the freedom of the individual. In this per-spective 'absolute democracy', in other words a democracy of all and for all, proposes itself as a continuous construction on the part of social subjects.

Today the transcendent view of power and sovereignty, as opposed to practices of absolute democracy, is once again on the agenda of neo-liberal conservatism. Just as, after the French Revolution, the French and German counter-revolutionaries invented political theol-ogy in Romanticism, so today American neo-conservatism is rein-venting the transcendental nature of sovereignty. From Leo Strauss to today's apologists of Bush's warmongering policies, we find the same conviction: that power needs no legitimation except in its reference to an abstract and immutable idea of justice. Plato has been put at the service of ideological positions which are hard to distinguish from

---

* Talk given at the Catholic University of São Paulo, Brazil, 16 October 2003.

religious fundamentalism or political fascism. But what is most characteristic of these positions is a particular kind of sociology which underpins the performative declarations of war: the negation of social conflict and the invocation of *raison d'état* lie at the basis of claims for the autonomy of sovereign politics at the global level.

But, facing this reality, we have to recognize the existence of poverty, slavery, exploitation . . . in short, of everything that the theory of power (qua transcendence) determines and excludes as negative. The negative is being that does not exist . . . But this negative is charged with *potenza*: it is there, and it has to fight at every moment against the negation and/or neutralization of its own existence: and yet it is inescapably there . . . Poverty, slavery and exploitation are continuously in a state of rebellion: we use the term 'multitude' to refer to this set of potentialities, to this ensemble of *potenze*. Furthermore, if we examine the concepts which inform these political alternatives, we perceive immediately how the 'being which is not' produces instead an indignation of *potenza*, its irreducibility to the given state into which it is constrained. We are not performing a dialectical operation here: the dialectics assumes negativity as substratum and motor: no, here the dialectics disappears because there is no longer a final purpose to be brought into being but only a freedom to be expressed. The two prevail over the one. Here it is the multitude that appears, or rather the multitude as subject. Here immanence presents itself as the sole possibility for political discourse.

But if things are this way, how is it possible to fix, beyond dialectics, the development of an immanent, endogenous *potenza*, the force of an ontological *potenza*?

Today this is probably the area in which the main efforts for a renewal of Marxism are being carried out. In other words, here communism is no longer considered as an inevitability which has to come but as a tendency, subjectively active, moving forward in the present time. There is, in this problematic dimension, a maturity of the times which synthesizes both the crisis of capitalism and the force of the new proletarian subjects. The renewal of Marxism, if it comes about, will be effected within these theoretical dimensions.

When we say that the multitude is an ontological *potenza*, a number of real definitions are proposed which renew the framework of the critique of political economy and political critique *tout court*. In the first place, the multitude presents itself as a *potenza* of living labour, that is, as the expression of the new technical and political composition of productive labour. We say that this *potenza* of living labour is a *potenza* of immaterial labour: in saying this we are laying out a series of tendencies, which are headed by the *potenza* of cooperation (and the birth of an increasingly intense ontological common) and, on the other hand, by the *potenze* of affective labour and the continuity of bodily and intellectual aspects in the construction of proletarian subjects. The multitude is this extremely strong determination of articulations and networks of singularity and difference. When we speak of the common, the term covers things which are very different but are unified objectively through the techniques of organization of labour (for instance, never has agricultural work been as close as it is today to the work of those who operate in the knowledge department; never has women's housework been as close as it is today to the becoming-woman of work in the services; and so on). But this objective transformation has to be interpreted as a transformation into a subjective power.

Spinoza helped us to find our way into postmodernity. When he speaks of the *potenza* of love, constructing it on the ontological continuity of metaphysical *potentia*, of physical *conatus*, of ethical *cupiditas* and, finally, of rational *amor*, this is where the multitude subjectivizes itself and becomes the basis of every thinkability of absolute democracy.

Here it would also be worth indicating a further transition: within the continuity of *potenza* between *conatus* and love, the constitution of being presents itself as a production of subjectivity. It is difficult to think this successfully in terms which can match the political dimensions of the present, the asphyxiation of theoretical thought and the repression of the disobedience of movements. Nevertheless, it is only in immanence that resistance can occur, it is only in the immanence of communism that a strong tendency can cut across – and pose itself against – the postmodern softness of weak thought, let alone of conservative thought, against command as a metaphysical principle and against tradition as a sinking swamp for theoretical innovation.

27
Bio-Power and Subjectivity*

When we discuss contemporary society and the form in which command and obedience are exercised in it, and in which resistance and life-alternatives express themselves, we do so from a basic initial understanding, namely that this society has been subsumed in real terms into capital. Power has invested life. Foucault explained in his major works how sovereign power was transformed during the centuries of modernity into bio-power. Bio-power is a concept which invests the dimensions of the economic, those of the political, those of consciousness – bio-power is a concept which represents the synthesis of modernity insofar as it is a functional rationality of power that invests life, an instrumental rationality of economic action that brings about an increasing spread of capitalist domination, and also an effective communicative action that affects consciousnesses. However, in talking about bio-power we are also talking about the biopolitical. In other words, bio-power is that force which, investing the totality of life, embraces the totality of the events which constitute life. Probably, in order to understand this process of total subjection of life to the economic–political rules designed to discipline and control it, we need to return to that homologous conception of power which modernity has produced: from Carl Schmitt to Max Weber to Lenin, the concept of power as a transcendence acting on the life of singularities – the old slogan of a command which holds things together (as Heine put it) – Richelieu, Robespierre and Rothschild. This is the power which invests life.

---

* Talk given at the General Assembly of Psychoanalysis, Rio de Janeiro, 31 October 2003.

As we move forward in postmodernity, we take this perception as our starting point. The world of life is closed and compacted within power. The world is reduced to system. This is the perception, this is the experience of the world that we feel and suffer. How should we react? There are resistances, and they appear always and continuously. Giorgio Agamben, for example, has defined its ways with extreme intensity: it is a resisting which is both absolute and marginal, which finds the force of absoluteness in marginality. Naked life, the resistance of human beings in the concentration camps: this formidable insistence on one's own self is what determines the limit of control. Is this individual, subjective quest for independence and/or autonomy sufficient to save oneself from the invasion that bio-power determines, from its control over the world? Silent and passive resistance assuredly have a significance. Already in the history of modernity we have an example: in the seventeenth century the 'libertines' went under the motto *'Bene vixit qui bene latuit'* – he who has lived hidden has lived well.

The reaction to bio-power and its invasiveness in postmodernity, as we have outlined them thus far, has been seen to be insufficient by most of the writers we have cited. In effect, the debate begins when the pervasiveness of bio-power is gone beyond, in other words when we begin to understand that, prior to bio-power, not only is there a biopolitical fabric, but this fabric is also open, and the clash over it and the dynamics which traverse it are central and irrepressible. Deleuze/Guattari and Foucault lived this transition. From the start, they interpreted the reality of bio-power as an open environment of struggles over the lived and political fabric of life. Deleuze defined the biopolitical as an ambit of conflictual and irreducible singularities. Structuralism (revisited and critically analysed by Deleuze in *Difference and Repetition*) is at this point broken: the laws and the structural isomorphisms are interrupted through the identification of events and a constantly renewed analytics of desire. There is a world unified by bio-power: well, yes. But it is a surface criss-crossed by events and differences, singularities and diagrams, and, finally, rhizomatic alternatives . . . A possibility of conceiving the postmodern fabric as a biopolitical reality of resistances . . .

After *Anti-Oedipus*, which theorized and explained this destructuring action, Foucault takes a further step. On this split terrain, between events, differences and singularities, he begins to unfold a singular motor of the production of subjectivity. With Foucault's last writings we are beyond the Deleuzian analysis of bio-power and the critical prospecting of the biopolitical fabric: with Foucault, a constituent element is inserted into the framework of the control which bio-power exercises over life. Resistance is no longer simply an abstract defence or alternative; rather, 'passing through bodies it is the construction of a different human reality . . .'. What more formidable example could there be of this alternative living material than that which Foucault produces in his reconstruction of ancient and mediaeval sexuality and in the new proposals he offers us for the present?

This takes us to a fundamental transition, that of an alternative within modernity, but an alternative which goes beyond modernity. When Foucault refuses the destiny of modernity, the destiny which ends in bio-power and which – in transcendental manner – constructs a destructive and terribly nihilist conception of being; and when Foucault, through Nietzsche, rejects Heidegger, he reconquers a constitutive instance. When, against transcendentalism, he speaks to us of production and subjectivity, in reality he is repeating the Spinozan adage: 'You do not know what a body is capable of!'

It is strange to find ourselves, around Foucault, repeating an interpretation of modernity which sees 'modernity' exactly as a split world: on the one hand an ontological, democratic and immanentist line, which goes from Machiavelli to Spinoza to Marx; on the other, an idealistic and deeply anti-democratic line, which traverses modern thought between Hobbes, Rousseau and Hegel. But this repetition is not really repetitive – the issue that we are addressing proposes a completely different horizon: a biopolitical horizon, in other words a horizon in which life and politics, living and the collective conditions of living are completely intermeshed. Here again the adage applies: 'You do not know what a body is capable of!'

Shades of Marx, or rather from philosophy to the critique of political economy. Resistance – that strong resistance theorized and characterized by Deleuze/Guattari at the exit-point from modernity, and the resistance newly constructed in constitutive terms by Foucault – well, this resistance is carried into the system of the world. That is what I mean by 'shades of Marx': a spectre, a monster, an image, a light which continuously transforms the real. The system of the world is not – as the spectre of Marx tells us – only the trajectory of dead labour, and not even the deposit of a living labour which has exhausted its constituent force. The world is rather a system continuously interrupted and fractured by the constitutive trajectory of living labour. The world subsumed in capital is the world of a split relation; it is the world which diffuses the cleavage of split in the capitalist relationship. The concept of capital becomes, in real subsumption, a dual relationship: plural, dissipative and active.

It is important to follow this transition through: it reveals the radicality of the break which capital effects in the transition from modernity to postmodernity. The relationship of exploitation becomes something which is continuously dislocated over the totality of social relationships and in the continuity of the global relations which capitalism determines, both from the temporal point of view and from the spatial point of view. Living labour is, in this situation, completely metamorphosed. By this I mean that living labour changes not only because it is subject to the changes in the organization of labour that capital decides, but also because the struggles and collective movements determine, in deep and structural ways, the metamorphoses of labour.

We can take the various changes in the capital relation as a way of defining the various stages and periods of the political composition and technical composition of labour power. Today, in the present structure of capitalist organization and at the present level of proletarian action, we can define an organization of labour which is intermittent and changeable, related to a technological and political regulation which is articulated on a complexity of relations. Between the biopolitical and bio-power the screen of social and productive relations is broader than ever. When we trace the transition from the Fordist factory to post-Fordist social production, and through to the hegemony of information technologies in industrial production; when we pass from the material labour of the mass worker to the immaterial labour of the socialized worker, through to the socially significant productive activity of the new social subjects via information technologies – in all this the central question becomes that of how we are to identify resistance at this very high level of real subsumption of society in capital. What is the difference between the labour of the subjected human and the labour of the liberated human . . . or rather the human in struggle?

Immaterial labour is living labour. Labour, that thing which we knew as manual and physical activity, although still remaining such in large part, is becoming transformed. There is a becoming-intellectual of labour: in other words, a labour which is mobile in space, flexible in terms of time, often independent in terms of how and where it is carried out. Here one can speak of a reappropriation of the tools of labour by the worker. Posing the problem in these terms is, of course, an exaggeration. However, it remains a formidable option, this option represented by the development of immaterial labour viewed in terms of the end of every reabsorptive dialectics of capital. Capitalism, according to Hegel, was based essentially on the dialectics of the tool, in other words on the fact that the capitalist offered the worker the instrument of labour and life in common was constructed around this instrumentation. Well, today this Hegelian instrumentation is removed.

A second element defining the transformation of immaterial labour as living labour is the becoming-woman of labour. Within immaterial labour are contained affective labour, caring work, relational work and many other forms of labour which throughout history have been characterized as feminine forms of labour. Just as within the becoming-immaterial of labour its autonomy is asserted, in the becoming-affective of labour its difference is asserted: in other words, the impossibility of reducing this psychological excedence and ethics to the rules and measure of capitalist control.

But there are also other forms in which labour is defined as living labour that is unattainable and ungraspable under capitalist command. A first level of this new nature of labour is the becoming-nature of labour: this is not linguistic game-playing. The fact is that work in nature – peasant labour, the labour involved in transforming nature – has by now become intellectualized and complexified to the point of embracing within itself the entire scientific heritage and the entire informatics and instrumentation of labour. Peasant labour in production transforms traditional knowledge (which is also enormous) into reappropriation of technological knowledge. To the autonomy of intellectual labour, to the difference that the becoming-woman of labour asserts, a new quality is now being added, namely that of a recomposition of labour and of nature, of its inner transformation, of a necessary metamorphosis.

Finally, we have linguistic expression, in other words the expression of signs, the communicative constitution of labour as becoming-linguistic. When we think from the point of view of production today, we constitute new languages; this is the form in which language is expressed and labour is effected.

Naturally, this whole series of elements is recomposed by a becoming-common of labour – labour is no longer abstract but is rendered concrete and singular in continuous and substantial ways by this series of active elements which comprise its becoming. The becoming-common of labour is not the rediscovery of some natural essence and activity it has, but it traverses the transformations in the nature of of labour: the common is realized homogeneously, in relation to the common transformation of labour. Once again, our analysis leads us back to the alternatives of modernity. It now fixes elements which are completely irreducible in the definition of labour and in the constitution of the social (through labour), and every conception of the transcendence of the value of labour and of the common order. Here we can complete in open and constituent ways – understood in terms of the new figures of postmodernity and of the power of general intellect – the intuitions we already find in Spinoza and Marx: an ontological line of passional constitution of the new human being who, moving from *appetitus* through *cupiditas* to *amor*, can construct a new world.

When we define the multitude, we define it as a web of relations, as cooperative activity, as a multiplicity of singularities. The multitude is posed because it is a multiplicity of singularities, against every possibility of defining the political as transcendence. People and action, as paradigms of modern sovereignty, are here bankrupt.

Again, the multitude is balanced against all those categories, more or less tied to the concept of socialism, which identify the multiplicity as mass, as an undifferentiated ensemble of subjects. The multitude is an ensemble of singularities, and this must never be forgotten. In the final analysis the multitude presents itself, from the ontological point of view, as a productive capacity, as a constituent power, as a determination of productive and social excedence.

This latter concept (which is also an experience) brings us back to the relationship which develops in the multitude between subjectivity and cooperation. But subjectivity and cooperation constitute the common – in other words, that dynamic and continuously open relationship which in no case closes into flat and organic communities. The relationship between subjectivity and cooperation constitutes – and at the same time reveals – the common which is at the root of the concept and reality of the multitude.

Today we are living a major moment of transition in the construction of the structures and global figures of Empire. There are forces trying to refeudalize the common which has been constructed by multitudinarian activities. The global movements, and above all the continuous daily production of subjectivity, oppose and resist these attempts at normalizing the transition to Empire in unilateral ways. At this point, by way of conclusion, it would be worth stressing that this imperial transition, within globalization, is extremely contradictory. In fact we are living through an interregnum: that is to say, a period in which the various alternatives all present themselves as, so to speak, incomplete. Global struggles and global movements, phenomena of *métissage* and anthropological metamorphosis coexist side by side. The barbarians are no longer simply at the window, at the borders of

Empire, but they traverse its consistency and follow in the wake of its expansion. It will be hard to imagine the nature of the years ahead if we do not adopt this framework and do not take on board its dynamics, however painful and ambiguous it may prove to be.

28
Multitude and Bio-Power*

Here I shall try to create an articulation between two sets of concepts, the first regarding the dimension of immanence in philosophy and politics, the second considering the concept of multitude in philosophical terms, as a biopolitical dimension in the making of history.

Politics is born as ontology. Philosophy, when it is born in the West, offers itself in turn as political argumentation. It is not accidental, therefore, that in classical philosophy ontological principle and political command are both expressed by the same word: *arche*. Platonism and its tradition consist of – and insist on – treating them as one and the same. It is only in modernity that this line is interrupted – namely, precisely at the beginning of modern philosophy (in humanism), when the political principle once again emerges with its own autonomy. Immanence is balanced against transcendence: in other words, what is given is only the human being's (absolutely pertinent) claims of domination over nature and the affirmation of the *potenza* of living labour, of cooperation between individuals, of social togetherness and, finally, of the ability to construct history. It is within this insurgent reality that modern philosophy is able to requalify itself. It assumes increasingly secularized forms of political expression, it touches on horizons of absolute immanence, and it invents those dialectical processes which (transforming philosophy) paradoxically make transcendence the motor of history and so forth. Having said that, philosophy will conquer, politically, the claim to absolute democracy, to being truth on earth, to progressive humanism; it will reconquer the progressive sense of the pragmatic revelation of 'God on earth'.

---

* Talk given at the Schauspieltheater, Hamburg, 12 December 2003.

The terrain of transcendence is being re-proposed today with increasing violence by conservative philosophies which are religious or traditionalist in origin. Political theology has once again come to the fore in the analysis of the history of our times. The theological–political horizon unites defenders and detractors of democracy, American neo-conservatives and Islamic fundamentalists. We seem to have returned to that gloomy (but, from a theoretical point of view, extremely productive) period of post-revolutionary and counter-revolutionary reaction and Thermidor in the first half of the nineteenth century. In that situation, too, political teleology was renewed very forcibly, except that it was then cancelled out by that insurgence of national identity and nation-thinking which, at one and the same time, exhausted the reactionary drive of the counter-revolution and lit the fires of the new theological–political heresies of contemporaneity.

If we examine this moment in history from the perspective of what was happening in philosophy, we can identify in modernity a repetition of political positions which had characterized the most acute period in the crisis of humanism and of the Renaissance. There the opposing positions distanced themselves from each other: on the one hand we encounter the concept of modern sovereignty (Hobbes and all the idealist philosophers from Descartes onwards), on the other, a radical democratic thinking which often manifested itself as republicanism. We can read this tendency through from Machiavelli to Spinoza.

We need to signal a weak variant of the political theology of modernity. This emerges with a claim to mediate immanence and transcendence and to relocate republican thinking within the revolutionary desire for freedom. It is in Kantian philosophy and in the theories of liberal Hegelianism that we most particularly find these trascendentalist tendencies, which refuse to line up on the frontier of immanence or on that of political theology. Here the horizons which are established are spurious – formal and transcendental, precisely: the fixity of mediation (as a natural need of human beings) could show the possibility of gauging and sustaining a well-organized democracy. But all this is no more than a vain attempt to escape the radicality of immanence, the heaviness of a horizon which is completely human – of existing, of living in community and of exercising power.

As modernity moved forward, transcendence in politics became more and more strongly established. What is paradoxical in those who reckon politics to be entirely subsumed to capitalist bio-power, what is paradoxical in the position of those who, in this picture, would still aspire to republicanism, is that a metaphysical rule is here superimposed on the articulations of subjectivity. From the Frankfurt School to French structuralism we have a double paradox: on the one hand, the real subsumption of the whole world within capitalist bio-power; on the other, the global opening-up of individual resistances, which certainly traverse the terrain of the biopolitical but which, since they are marginal, are unable to develop and spread the moments of rebellion (as would be suggested by the very fact of the extension of capital into every relationship of life).

We need to find a way out of this condition and to break these blocs of thought. We need to move beyond this reality which, while it provided the fabric of political analysis, at the same time left us drowning in the shifting sands of postmodern weakness. The problem is how to recompose political thought around immanence, taking as the starting point the reappropriation of the rules of living together on the part of the multitude and asserting at the same time a radical defence of freedom. Only bodies are capable of critique.

This brings us into the field of political considerations about post-modernity – a postmodernity which is not weak – and it is here that the concept of 'multitude' seems to us to be central. It is a class concept based on the concept of labour, on its exploitation and on the antagonism which is created within exploitation. When we speak about a becoming-intellectual, a becoming-woman, a becoming-nature, a becoming-linguistic/relational/cooperative, and finally about a becoming-common of labour, we are not proposing a notion which is generic; rather, we are identifying an absolutely determining historical transition –the moment at which immanence is determined in a global way. From now on, any theological conception of the political will be per se mystificatory.

It follows, however, on this multitudinarian basis, that exploitation is exploitation of the common. What does exploitation of the common mean? It means that capitalist command and capitalist appropriation/accumulation no longer focus simply on a single operator in the organization of labour and life but they attach themselves to, and enmesh with, the common relations that labour determines in order to be productive. Exploitation will therefore be extremely intense, particularly inasmuch as it extends to the global dimension. But the antagonistic character of this condition of exploitation will also become extreme, since here it is not only the single worker who is touched by the violence of capitalist appropriation; rather, what is being exploited is the working activity of the whole of society.

We shall return shortly to the characteristics of exploitation. Here I would like to stress the fact that, in order to become meaningful, the concept of multitude needs to construct itself in the biopolitical. Now, biopolitics is the limit to which global labour power and the social conditions of its reproduction tend; it is the place in which the reduction of life to productive activity (as capital wished it to be) rediscovers life as a *potenza* for production. On the other hand, the biopolitical is also the conceptual and ontological dimension within which the extent to which life is the motor and subject of historical transformations is revealed. The changes in the nature of labour and in the social organization of the exploitation of labour are the product of class struggles; and it is in this transition that the production of subjectivity continues – incessant, increasingly powerful – and proposes itself as a biopolitical horizon. Where capital has conquered politics, there life reappears, taking apart the dimensions and figures of capitalist activity, and it is there that life (appropriating the product of accumulation) attacks exploitation.

The biopolitical fabric is thus characterized by capital's wholesale invasion of life but, at the same time, by the resistance and reaction of labour power, of life itself, against capital. This transition is not dialectical but metamorphic. In other words, the configurations assumed, in biopolitics, by the subjects who confronted each other therein are neither reversible nor recuperable within new unitary dimensions. Capital, and above all sovereignty – within this new biopolitical condition – are no longer configured as forces of synthesis, but appear as elements exercising an activity which is partial and unilateral: the worker and the political subject stand before capital and sovereignty as elements which are irreducible, as independent variables, as points of reference, resistance, revolt and insurrection.

Moving ahead in our account of the transition from modernity to postmodernity, we note the intensity of the change of paradigm. I began this talk by highlighting the multiple forms in which the theological–political has been counter-balanced to the modern conception of immanence – in other words, of absolute democracy. We have seen how this opposition between the theological and the political was imposed, and we have seen the impossibility of effecting dialectical paths which can embrace and subsume the adversary. Today, when we say that there has been a change of paradigm, we are referring basically to the radical discontinuity that the becoming-multitudinarian of labour brings about. Within this radical discontinuity is rooted the centrality of exodus, and also the constituent activity of the multitude; here is the opening of the transition we are living.

When we speak of multitude and the biopolitical, we are thus referring to the triumph of the *potenze* of immanence. The 'love of God' (of the Spinozan tradition) is not a crepuscular and decadent episode; rather, it is the statement of the *potenza* of a life which has become entirely political, around a human activity in labour which has revealed itself to be creative.

29

Empire and War*

1   While I was preparing this talk I happened to come across a col-
lection of the writings of Karl Löwith on Marx, Schmitt and Weber.
I knew these writings from fifty years ago. However, I had not read
the Preface which accompanied them in this particular edition. It
was written by Ernst Nolte. In it Löwith was transfigured into 'a
political figure who refused to take a position' in the struggles of his
time, because he was a philosopher of the eternal human nature and
of the transcendence of thought. The betrayal which Nolte perpe-
trates in his interpretation of the thinking of Löwith (because it
really is a betrayal) is interesting here as an option for transcendence
in politics – something which would be perfectly in tune today with
the American neo-conservatives and with the neo-liberals in the
present phase of imperial war. As I say, it is a betrayal: for Löwith,
transcendence was entirely within the ambit of historical truth; he
was shaking it and eventually directing it. This way of conceiving
transcendence, unlike what the revisionist Nolte might think, was
revolving around immanence and assuming a dramatic aspect in
contact with it: this is what Löwith had recognized in the tendency
which modernity had attributed to Marx, Schmitt and Weber. If we
had examined closely Heiner Müller, we would have found ourselves
in a similar situation: what interested him was this fact of passing
through an absolute immanence – which saw the tendential defeat
of transcendence. And yet it was a tension which remained – an
arrow fired into the void. What I want to do in this talk is to discuss
philosophical – and therefore political – immanence in relation

* Talk given at the Heiner Müller Conference, Akademie der Künste, Berlin, 10
January 2004.

to the dramatic, philosophical and political thought of Heiner Müller.

What is the thought of immanence? Simply put, it is the thought that this world has no outside, that its construction and its necessity are within this world, and that – in its structure – anthropology and ontology are not separate. One does not need to be a revolutionary to recognize that this world has no outside. Postmodernism (the great heresy of Marxism) has generalized this affirmation. It has recognized, in power, not simply a machine for the subsumption of society but a motor of production of society as a whole. Power has become bio-power. But postmodernism has forgotten resistance; it has put it at the margins of the imperial totality. In other words it has not imagined the uprising of the multitude, the possibility of carrying to the heart of Empire something which is no longer a counter-power, but resistant varieties of singularity: the statement that 'another world is possible' is rooted in the analysis and development of subjective genealogies, of an alternative production of singularity and resistance.

It is on this terrain of immanence, of true immanence, that Heiner Müller urges us to move, because he anticipates in this our own moving, because he forcefully pre-empts the falsifications of an eventual transcendence imposed on the crisis of being, above all of the kind offered by Ernst Nolte (and by the strong revisionism of weak postmodernity).

2 Power has become bio-power. What does bio-power mean? It means the investment by power of the totality of social relationships; hence the construction of social relations, the control of social cooperation in global time and space, and domination over life. Power invests the biopolitical context of the reproduction of life in its every aspect, in all of its various articulations of production and reproduction. We owe to Foucault the insistence on this transition, which today is confirmed by the analysis of the modes of production, of the organization of labour and of the general anthropological condition (in the warmongering crisis imposed by neo-conservatism).

Nota bene: it is not that the invasion of the space of freedom and life is anything new. The historical phenomenologies of slavery and patriarchy have extensively documented these biopolitical experiences of domination and social and political hierarchy. Today there still exist countries which are dominated by this determination of power. But taking into consideration these traces of the past, even where they are still effective, does not mean forgetting the novel quality of the situation we are now living. On this terrain, Heiner Müller has, so to speak, reasoned in unison with Foucault. Like Foucault, 'he has walked masked' in the political context of modernity and socialism, in order to bring to light the gravity of the biopolitical experience of slavery, newly re-proposed in the crisis of real socialism.

Empire, the definitively constructed paradigm of a new figure of sovereignty, interprets bio-power not simply in terms of discipline but increasingly in terms of control; not simply in terms of production but also of hierarchy of organization and of productive spaces; no longer simply in terms of the construction of social nexuses but through continuous attempts at the production of subjectivity.

What we have in Empire is a structure a bit like a Russian doll: life contained within discipline, discipline contained within control; and – since power is violence which legitimates itself through its own exercise – in response to the expression of difficulties or resistances, Empire imposes the state of exception. Today the state of exception is called preventive war, never-ending war.

3   The old materialistic dialectics is also always immanence. But how is it possible to move in this picture, within this postmodern totality? The old dialectics – for example as Bertolt Brecht interpreted it – gave us the inevitable crisis of the process of domination as a crisis internal to capitalist development, and the material necessity of breaking (at some fateful moment) the articulations of domination. Economicism and the dialectics between structure and superstructure were fundamental elements of this perspective. Dialectical materialism established a framework in which the violence of factual necessity was accompanied by the dramatic and/or eschatological opening of liberation.

We do not play this game. And neither did Heiner Müller. We have seen how far capitalist violence and destructive command can go, including also the world of so-called 'real socialism'. We want to understand the world as it emerged after Hiroshima and Auschwitz, after the Soviet gulags, but also within the new imperial wars; we feel that, going beyond dialectical separation, another version of immanence exists. It is based on the discovery of a subjective possibility, of an irreducible event, of a sense of a reality which is revealed. To the dialectic we oppose antagonism, the insoluble crisis which is descending on humanity, and therefore the genealogy – and, even before that on this anthropological terrain, the archaeology of these changes and the *potenza* of the metamorphoses.

This is where we find Heiner Müller. Somewhere in the introduction to his Italian translation of the works of Müller, Peter Kammerer notes this with great intelligence. He says that, in the face of the dialectical development of the history of which Brecht remains convinced ('even the flood does not last for ever'), Heiner Müller takes a different path. He indicates, emphasizes and develops the emerging of an anthropological crack [*incrinatura*]. 'All that is human becomes alien.' The Brechtian thesis and antithesis are not followed by didactics but by the abyss: rather than being didactic, the theatre of Heiner Müller is terroristic, in the sense that terrorism is lived as the breaking of the dialectics.

Heiner Müller lived within – and anticipated dramatically – the great ontological transition we are living: we need to interpret the actuality of this immanence. Heiner Müller reads the presence of a great non-dialectical tragedy in the coincidence of what was lived in the western world and what was lived in the socialist world. For humans, everything becomes alien: there were people in the western world who thought they were humans but were probably monkeys, and monkeys who lived in the socialist world but who often acted as humans. Perhaps only Spinoza could have interpreted this relationship between being a brute and being a human (both in the West and in the East) as a paradox which extends in time and which can transform physical *conatus* into desirous *cupiditas* and into the more ontologically constructive intellectual *amor*: once again, a paradox where ethics (the free behaviour of the free individual) presents itself as ontology, as ethical institution (no longer of an abstract subject but) of a free human being in the development of his or her real history.

4   How can this new version of immanence be represented dramatically? How is drama possible in this situation? How is it possible for there to be a politics without an outside – in other words, when thought and utopia, and the critique of the project, no longer have distance? Does this happen when the representative exchange of the symbolic (*mimesis*) for subjective reality (*catharsis*) is immediate? In order to answer these questions we have to:

• define a place of theoretical and dramatic action (at the centre);
• identify a force which determines the movement and the figure of the (multitudinarian) movement;
• define a common constructed by us which can be part of our experience, both in a passive and in an active sense, both in an archaeological and in a genealogical sense.

Reading the plays of Müller, one seems to be fully within this onto-logical reality. Each of his plays constructs a place which is no longer dialectically recuperable, identifies a critical force which, although dis-persing itself in the complexity of the plot, recomposes itself in a moment of decision; and at the end all this constructs a common to which we may or may not hold, but there is a fabric of action and hope that runs through it continuously. Let us not limit ourselves to waiting for the expansion of these tensions. We could easily find ourselves facing an implosion (suggests Müller); rather, we should always believe that, outside of all necessity, outside of every dialectics, this process can occur. Tragedy is not only a literary form, it is also a figure of being.

5   On the points signalled at the end of section 4 we have already made some progress:

a We said that Heiner Müller seeks to define a place of dramatic and theoretical action which is not marginal but placed at the centre of the ensemble of relations founded on the control of bio-power; hence a shift of the dramatic discourse to the centre. Here we clash with the postmodern conceptions of immanence and resistance, which see them only as marginal elements subject to naturalistic temptations and therefore do not grasp the centrality of resistance as a genealogy of the singularity. What we have called the anthro-pological crack in Heiner Müller we find here, in this place which has become philosophically and politically central. Compared with Derrida and Agamben, for example, this shift of the locus of resis-tance is fundamental and brings us into the real situation, where antagonism is unceasing and conflict is perennial. Permanent war and the state of exception oblige us to an answer conceived within (and against) the centre of the production of command in a non-dialectical way: thus what is proposed is not a subject of counter-power but a dissipation of tension, an anthropological innovation centred on resistance. The genesis of the singularity is also a geneal-ogy of the multitude.

b We asked whether it is possible to identify a force which determines movement, and the figure of the movement, starting from the centre of the crisis. We asked whether there is a force with the capacity to oppose. We say that it is the multitude, in other words a multiplicity of singularities. When we speak of multitude, we mean that labour presents itself as cooperation and that the ensemble of singularities presents itself as language. If critique had asked the material subject of the class struggle to become the active motor of the process of liberation, here the hypothesis approaches verification. However, it is no longer possible to confuse *raison d'état*, the state of exception and bio-power with revolutionary reason, resistance and the rebellion of singularities – the uprising. Philoctetes wins this time: that is how Heiner Müller would have characterized this fundamental transition. Immanence has not only won here, it has also absorbed the transcendent refrain of innovation. The revisionist infamy of Ernst Nolte here stands completely exposed, since thought and action – and this is clear – do not need any reference point outside of, and beyond, human beings' desire to be free, not to suffer, and to claim their existence outside of identity. Philoctetes wins. But this does not mean that all the questions we have touched upon so far have a solution. On the contrary, the difficulties become concentrated – so that now one can ask: is a theatre for the multitude possible, a theatre which takes as its subject the swarm, the multiplicity of singularities attracted by a common objective?

c Let us begin with a quotation. Friedrich Nietzsche: 'The question of whether humanity has a tendency to the good is prepared by the question of whether there exists an event which cannot be explained in any way other than by that moral disposition' (*On the Genealogy of Morals*). Such is the Revolution. Kant: 'Such a phenomenon of human history is no longer forgotten, because it has revealed the existence in the human nature of a disposition and of a faculty towards the good, which no politician has hitherto thought out on the basis of the course of things' (*The Conflict between the Philosophical and the Legal Capacity*, 1798).

We asked ourselves how we might define a common, constructed by us, which would be part of our experience, in both a passive and an active sense, both archaeological and genealogical. We asked whether it was possible to identify a sense of the common that could guide the experience of the multitude. We have discovered that this sense exists both passively and actively (as Kant shows in the revolutionary event, also taken up by Nietzsche; we see it again in the tension of the spirit in the struggle for *Aufklärung*, as Foucault has shown in his formidable text), and that it lies at the basis of the critical method of dramatic construction. It is genealogy, as Heiner Müller interprets it, for instance in his *Mommsens Block*.

There is one single, enormous opposition to this plan: it is that represented by the state of exception, by war as imperial figure, by the new sovereignty, all of which confirm and redouble the experience of death. Death is the content of bio-power, the ultimate content, which does not exclude discipline and control but understands them as the guarantee of the effectiveness of power. The giving of death is and continues to be the operational mode of power.

So, to sum up: in Heiner Müller the meaning of drama is fully regained, but we also have the immanent critique: giving life, creating, having revolution in one's heart and guts. In Empire, a theatre for the multitude has to develop, through the action of a swarm of resistances and rebellion, the anthropological crack that Heiner Müller understood so well. Theatre today has an ontological function.

30
Let us Reform the Political Lexicon!*

I am here to answer a series of questions which have been put to me: how might we think politics in capitalism? Or rather, in more concrete terms, how do we think an anti-capitalist politics in the present conjuncture, namely when historical capitalism seems to have entered a phase of global turbulence and systemic chaos? How do we think politics once we have new historical modalities of the existence of the antagonist political subject, and in particular the hypothesis of a general intellect as the dominant figure of collective labour power in the capitalist world economy? Finally: what relations can we establish between the new forms of production, the new forms of political struggle, of constitutional construction and/or revolutionary political practice?

In all probability, in order to answer this series of questions we shall need a new political lexicon. The real, historical transformation of this world that we are experiencing brings with it the transformation of the languages of politics. In the case of myself and my own theoretical history, I cannot but recall how profound the modifications, indeed metamorphoses, have been of the categories used to analyse the political and technical composition of the working class in the twenty years which elapsed between the key events of 1968 and 1989. Reforming the political lexicon is not, however, an operation which simply has to take account of the transformations of history. Transforming the political lexicon, in our situation, also means establishing a genealogy internal to the process which has led from modernity to postmodernity (a genealogy which is also able to grasp continuities and

* Talk delivered at the Círculo de Bellas Artes, Madrid, 13 April 2004.

discontinuities, facts and innovations). Moreover, since by now we are within a situation which is entirely globalized, our lexical effort will have to be matched against other experiences that have also taken place at the global level. For my part, I think I can claim to have conducted a thorough-going lexical activity in my writings, which run from *Constituent Power* to *The Labour of Dionysus* and, finally, *Empire* and *Multitude*. It is on the basis of this work that I permit myself here to embark on the discussion of a new political lexicon.

However, setting in motion a new political lexicon requires not only much courage, but also a number of precautions: in part that was already stated above, when I said that the lexicon needs to follow and describe a new reality. None the less, the precautions become even more important when what is at stake is not only to describe but also to deepen the new technical, social and political composition of the multitude (or proletariat, if you prefer). A new political lexicon describes new political subjects, but it must also enable them to speak. In order to construct a new political lexicon one has to count on a kind of ripeness of the times, languages and practices – on the ontological weft of history.

So let us approach this opening. What are the fundamental terms of a new political lexicon? They are multitude, immaterial labour, general intellect, difference, singularity and the common; but they are also Empire, nation, sovereignty, discipline, control, war . . . and then: democracy and communism. I do not intend – nor indeed would I have the ability – to carry out the work of definition which each of these terms demands in order for them to be taken into political debate today. Here I shall simply indicate some important elements in the general process of constructing the lexicon. What I would stress, however, is this: the construction of a political language cannot be separated from the *potenza* of the person speaking that language. For instance: if one speaks about immaterial labour, it is obvious that the people best placed to speak about it are the immaterial workers in computer science or scientific research. Yet in constructing a political lexicon we are not simply referring to this obvious linguistic relationship, but to the forms in which 'immaterial labour' can be taken, for example, as a term referring to the productive activities of peasants in the new mode of agricultural production, or to the work of women in the affective services and in social reproduction. A new dictionary term therefore only works to the extent that it has political currency, in other words to the extent that it is assimilated/assimilable by many singularities in the development of their activity. This is something which has to do with the aesthetic constitution of new objects in the construction of political language: we can appreciate its effectiveness exactly to the extent to which the singularity, the singularities, the language of the singularities take control of the new term and of the eventual practical and political indications which are potentially contained in them. It is, as in poetry, an event.

The fact remains that many of the terms we want to redefine here (not simply in this conference, but in the work we are setting ourselves) operate in the first place as descriptions: when we say 'Empire', what we are indicating is in fact a tendential emergence of sovereignty over the world market. To that extent it is a descriptive term. But it is also clear that every descriptive term is articulated both by a specific spatiality and temporality (in the case of the Empire, by the tendential spatiality of the single world order and by the temporalities which traverse this unitary becoming and articulate it) and by more or less effective political tensions (for instance, the American determination to achieve and fix a unilateral hegemony over Empire). We could say the same for other terms which are important to us: for instance 'nation' (its critique, the analysis of the dynamics of its overcoming and so on); 'war' (the new forms in which war presents itself); 'discipline and control' (in the new articulations which the imperial dynamics imposes on them; and in the transformation of modes of production), and the like.

But it is absolutely fundamental to introduce into this thematic and defining project the democratic passions of the multitude, the political presence of the common. People talk of a new world being possible. The struggles against neo-liberal globalization have now been followed by struggles for peace, and now new struggles are opening which indicate new transitions of conflict and new programmes of social reform. The most important episode in the struggle against the neo-conservatives and neo-liberals, at the level of the contestation of neo-liberal globalization, was certainly the big Genoa demonstrations against the G8. Here a multitude, an ensemble of subjective forces unified by the refusal of capitalist domination and by hopes for a new world – so here, in Genoa, a 'Commune' of resistance was introduced, which formed a new plan of struggle and the strategic consolidation of a new antagonism. The struggles against neo-liberal globalization found in Genoa a very high and exemplary coefficient of expansivity and at the same time accumulated an irreversible potential. Equally important, on another terrain (that of the struggle for peace and for the construction of a new, democratic international order), was the Madrid revolt against the lies and opportunism of Prime Minister Aznar. There is no doubt that in those days in Madrid we lived the experience of a 'Commune' of the multitude. Previously, in Genoa, the movement successfully attacked the imposition of the 'red zones' through the generalized and continuous documenting of the repressive behaviours of the police, through their denunciation and through continuous rearticulation on the part of the multitudinarian masses; so also in Madrid, through the effective, commonplace but universal use of diffuse networks and text messaging, the multitude organized an upsetting of the relationships of force which the power apparatus did not expect to have to face. The speed of the movement, its dynamic and plural articulation, the uncovering and public statement of the truth: these are some of the elements which define the concept of multitude, no longer from a sociological point of view but from a political and creative point of view. 'A new world is possible' is not simply a statement of a programme, but is a reality, a presupposition, a powerful latent quality of the movement: the multitude is an actual new world. When the political lexicon is renewed, it is within this kind of linguistic articulation that it has to renew itself.

I do not believe that it is a hazardous hypothesis to open a debate on a new political lexicon which might at the same time lead into a constituent discourse. Certainly the levels are different: on the one hand we have the elaboration of a body of analysis and political dynamics (which have to do with subjectivity) and on the other we have – as regards the constituent discourse – an antagonistic, hard and violent relationship which creates a relationship between the subjectivity of behaviours and the objectivity of institutions. But it is precisely to this contradictory intersection that our attention is continuously redirected. Even if only in order to construct language – because the construction of language is not a neutral operation. The fact that the new lexicon is not simply descriptive is confirmed to us also by the requirement – which all the multitudinarian subjectivities (the emergences) express – to build a new programme: a programme which extends and articulates fully the instances of rupture that the movements succeed in building against the imperial capitalist order. Now, it may be that – in this new situation we register – governments put themselves at the service of the movements (here is, for instance, a new singular definition of government and governability). It may also happen that political representation weakens and/or loses its character of maximum abstraction (here is, for instance, a new definition of the concept of representation and, in general, of the institutions of representation, which could then be defined in an original way as 'service structures'). I could carry on listing new possible figures, both linguistic and functional, in which there might be a new articulation of sovereignty (of its monistic character). But the more important problem is not to weigh the many hypotheses which the historical situation offers us, but to connect the definitions of the new lexicon to a political action which can anticipate (and at the same time accumulate resistance against) the capitalist restructuring of relations of production and relations of domination. It is not accidental that the terms most open to an effort of redefinition are those which are connected to a dualism (by now rooted and radical) of the concept of sovereignty: sovereignty is no longer able to recompose the opposites dialectically, it must instead assume them to be contradictory within itself.

In *Multitude* Michael Hardt and I tried to define this situation as a temporal and substantial transition which is unique in the centuries-long history of modernity (of which we are just now seeing the exhaustion). From the temporal point of view, this twofold articulation of sovereignty corresponds to a definitive crisis of the capitalist order and therefore defines a transition (an interregnum) to which the political relations between capitalists and multitude are constrained, in twofold form and in irreversible terms. From the substantial point of view, the exercise of sovereignty shows itself to be in crisis because it is conditioned by the continuous pressure which the movements exercise on governments, thus rendering impossible, in such a situation, monistic practices of power. The construction of a new language in order to represent a new reality: this is our task.

31
The Biopolitics of General Intellect*

The first characterization of the biopolitical order today is the general condition of war: imperial capitalism subjects life to war.

It is clear, therefore, that any renewal of political language – a renewal that is adequate to the biopolitical condition in which we find ourselves – is particularly difficult; or rather, it is as fascinating as it is worrisome. If it is the case that renewing the political lexicon means carrying out a metaphysical act and an ontological rediscovery, that renewing our political language means operating through the multitude, this brings us immediately to a paradoxical status of this new language, which is all the more undecidable as the relationship of war bears increasingly heavily on us (is imposed on the language of freedom). We shall need to proceed through pauses and breaks, through deepenings and discontinuities, which is precisely what the general biopolitical condition, traversed by war, imposes on us – imposes on everyone, with equal violence. However, let us examine some new conditions of this research.

When we defined the imperial structures of domination and placed them under the name of the biopolitical, on the one hand we were expressing the continuity of state control and command as it tends to expand and organize itself on the imperial terrain (and with effectiveness); on the other hand, within this picture, we were able to identify a fabric built from the action (that is, from the resistance, struggles and imagination) of the movements. When we speak now of a 'biopolitics of general intellect', as well as recognizing the difficulties mentioned above, this will also mean developing (extract-

---

* Talk delivered at the Museu d'Art Contemporani de Barcelona (MACBA), Barcelona, 16 April 2004.

ing and generalizing) the potentialities of the movements within the
perspective of globalization. Thus, while we know that the current
political lexicon, at the same time as it is being reconstructed, is interrupted and blocked in its performativity by the gravity of the condition of war in which we live – we nevertheless know that in general
intellect (from both the productive and the affective point, from the
point of view both of the emergence of the singularities and of the
common establishment of relations between single entities) innovative
(and excedent) syntheses of languages and bodies are determined,
tendencies that cannot be permanently blocked, whatever the war or
police pressure exercised against them. The biopolitics of general
intellect has living aspects which cannot be eliminated; it has common
dimensions which cannot be repressed. It also has to be said that
general intellect has an aspect which is, so to speak, erotic and
Dionysiac: immaterial labour is not abstract labour but always a (concrete) trajectory between singularity and the common. Our terminological labours will need to address this ontological circumstance.
    Certainly we should not exaggerate the physics of freedom in the
development of the biopolitics of general intellect. We know, in fact,
that it is precisely the free constitution of the common which today
has become the object of appropriation by liberalism (by capitalism
and the state). It is beyond doubt that the extraordinary maturity of
the multitudinarian usage of the means of production (and therefore
the extraordinary maturity of the productive and constituent subjects)
– has to be continuously attacked. Neo-liberalism can only be defined
on the basis of this continuous hysterical reaction; it would come to
nothing if it did not react in these areas.
    Here we immediately have a problem: how concretely to define, and
form new practices of, militancy in the biopolitics of general intellect.
It is obvious that when we speak of militancy in this situation we have
to recognize the importance of differences. This means that the first
thing that needs to be eliminated is the vanguardist model – a model
which is traditional, but always external to the immanence of the
biopolitical process, of the organization of the multitude. The
differences which are important here are those given as immanent:
singularities, actions which justify themselves in the immediate exercise of resistance, and subjects which are born from the networked
nature of the relations between actions. The militancy of differences
presents itself, first and foremost, as a labyrinthine polyphonic front
of linguistic connections.
    All this does not mean that a terrain (and a point) of decision
cannot be asserted. Indeed, although it may appear paradoxical, this

necessity imposes itself as a priority and traverses the militancy of differences and resistances in primordial terms – it is a strong and transversal decision that is proposed here, strong in its transversality. Now, the problem which arises (and which is part of the biopolitics of general intellect, translated into the political language of subjects) is how best to analyse diversities in order to arrive, through the transversality of struggles, at a moment of common decision. This means being able to recognize the new constituent dynamics of the organizational process, bearing in mind that the organizational order is not born from command but from the common definition of a new political lexicon, of a new recognition of the enemy and of the new subjects of biopolitical production: to organize means to traverse the entire biopolitical process of general intellect.

Let us now introduce the concept of exodus. I suggest that talking of the biopolitics of general intellect means at the same time talking about exodus. Now, to use this term is already to define a programme: a programme to which I have already referred when I spoke of a transversality of struggles that can represent (prefigure) political organization. Putting this in more abstract terms, exodus seeks to signify a new form of mediation between *potenza* and power. Note that there is no intention here to establish any form of homology between *potenza* and power, between movements and governments . . . there exist transversal and effective homologies only between languages and bodies, between a new lexicon of the political and the new productive movements of general intellect. So, when we speak of mediations between *potenza* and power, we are speaking of an antagonistic dynamic which sees the movements as standing up against the institutions and – only from a relation of power – as using (or rather overturning) the administrative nexuses which traverse that entire society, which has been set to labour. Bringing things back to a traditional theoretical level, we can add that, if there is no longer exchange value, there will probably be new use-values, inasmuch as these use-values are interpreted as the ability to put every condition of social life at the service of the rupture of the system of domination. The networks which constitute the space of biopolitical production, the technologies which function in this space, the subjective energies which are here put into play can constitute exodus every time the inner, transversal, multitudinarian decision opens itself to the action of reappropriation of the productive processes of society.

People are going to say that, with this notion of the biopolitics of general intellect, we are simply repeating the Marxist (or neo-Marxist) theory of the prerequisites of communism. Some will say that, operating in this way, we are re-establishing in reformist terms some of the illusions of socialist progressivism or of modern productivism *tout court*. Perhaps some will add, with malevolence, that within this repetition there are illusions of homologation between proletarian power and capitalist power, and thus a possibility of repression: starting from these symptoms, the status of our proposal of revolutionary biopolitical language could be denounced as a repetition of paranoic conditions. The opposite is in fact the case – namely the fact that here (far from repeating apologies for socialism or the productive force of the proletariat, or dreaming up new Leninist programmes under the slogan 'Internet plus Soviets') we are in practice restoring a single theoretical decision: the one which allows us to see the class struggle as producer of every transformation of the social horizon; and thus to remove, through this affirmation, all teleology of historical processes; to study the processes of mutation through which we are moving today as real and actual metamorphoses. Here the transformation and the innovation that biopolitics imposes through the Marxian conception of general intellect turns out to be radical.

32

The Philosophy of 'Old Europe'*

I have to admit I am a little moved to be back at Collège [de France]. I remember how, in 1984, when I began to give courses here at the Collège at the start of my exile, it was a very strong thing, even heroic, so to speak. The comrades who came to the seminars were not from the Parisian philosophical *grand milieu*; they were comrades who had come to France from Italy and had a real need to exchange ideas with each other after a period of extremely hard struggle. Today, in summing up those beginnings, I would like to say this: I think that France and Collège de France have been very important in modifying and helping to develop new forms of agitation, thought and struggle in Italy, and that the change of critical thought which has taken place in Italy is related to certain experiences which have happened here. This is important also in our appraisal of the Battisti case and thus in the solidarity we feel with these less fortunate people. In this case too, however, it is a solidarity intensified and modified through participation in the new debate and in the new experiences which have been lived here. In some senses I am in a privileged position. I was able to return to Italy – albeit with heavy consequences in terms of imprisonment – but I have also regained the possibility of travelling around the world and of comparing notes with very large numbers of people. There are others who, given the wretched situation of justice in Italy, have not had this possibility. I invite you – if you are able – to reflect on this.

Now I come to the theme of this talk which, as our chairman François Noudelmann said in his opening remarks, is an introduction

---

* Talk given at the Collège International de Philosophie, Paris, 4 May 2004.

to other problems which I intend to address here, next year, in a set of seminars at Collège de France. I shall speak about the philosophy of 'Old Europe'. That is my title. I want to examine the polemic that has arisen around the idea of an 'Old Europe'. This polemic, as you know, was initiated by American neo-conservatives, who have found polemical references in 'Old Europe'. One, between Mars and Venus . . . Mars, that is, the warrior capacities and the creative capacities, through war, of America; and Venus, that is, the tiredness and corruption of the old Europe. Another provocation has been entirely internal to Europe. This involved contrasting the old central powers of Europe with the new nations which have recently joined the European Union, that is, with those countries which were seen as having been regenerated, through the anti-Soviet struggle, in the struggle against real socialism. So, taking as my starting point the presumed corruption of old Europe, I would like, on the contrary, to speak in defence of old Europe, and from a certain a point of view. I say 'from a certain point of view' – and only from that. I shall speak in defence of old Europe, defending the idea of a Europe which, in spite of everything, has been the producer of a series of democratic values that are deeper and more real than those offered by the American empire. In reality this idea of Europe was not a discovery of the American neo-conservatives. The image of an old and corrupt Europe is deeply related to that of the twilight of the West. This idea of an old Europe corrupt in the complexity and totality of the western world is widespread, from Spengler through to Heidegger: it is a fascist idea.

However, it is worth remembering that the idea of an old Europe is part of a portrayal of a crisis, or twilight, of the West which also includes the United States. The idea of the crisis of Europe is linked to the crisis of technology, to the destiny of technology, to a view that sees the process of modernization as negative. It is a reactionary idea, born between the two centuries – the nineteenth and the twentieth – and which became particularly marked after the Second World War. Therefore, to be clear, 'Old Europe' is fundamentally also an 'Old West'. But note this: 'New Europe' has for a while been tied to a reactionary and fascist ideal. And on the other hand a loyal and courageous adherence to the history of old Europe has constantly renewed the hope of democracy, for Europe and the West as a whole. In fact there has always been this possibility of referring back to European history, to an ancient Europe, to classical Greece and Rome, in order to find the source of new political configurations and images of the free spirit. I am not thinking only of Leonardo Bruni or Machiavelli and the writers who found in the Roman republic the idea of the liberation of the multitude. I am not thinking only of Giambattista Vico, with his text on the 'ancient wisdom of Italy', or only of the adoption of the ideas of the Roman republic in the thinking of the Enlightenment and of the French Revolution. These are the banal things that we learn at school; they are all, furthermore, extremely contested. And yet we inevitably have to ask: why is it that every time people return honestly to this idea of an old Europe, of a republican Europe, this means also a kind of renewal of thought? The tradition of a republican Europe, a Europe which never accepts its destiny as a *finis terrae*, this Europe which arrives always at the limit and has to press on beyond that limit, this Europe which is always teetering on some kind of edge, this is the Europe we love. I do not want here to venture into the polemic on eurocentrism; I believe, however, that eurocentrism, too, could not come about, were it not nourished by the idea of an ancient republic, a republican ideal which was possible and could always be renewed here in Europe – an ability to bring about this republic starting from a constitution in which slave wars are as important as the formation of empires. Certainly, this reference to the ancient world in the history we are trying to understand – and also to real history – has always proceeded through the jolts and leaps enacted by history. Our defence of the experimentations of this past goes through the absence of memory or the return of memory. Each time, one meets this difficulty of remembering and reconstructing. But, having said all that, the fact remains that we can define Europe, above all and first of all, as republic: as a republic of the spirit, as a republic of equality, as a republic of solidarity. And every time we think of this republic we think of it as something which removes or eliminates the alienation of power: as a power of singularities, a democracy of the multitude; and thus as the ability of singularities to present themselves as libertarian forces in solidarity and in communion, in a cooperative multiplicity.

Today we live in the transition between modernity and postmodernity, between a democratic and constitutional imperialistic system – which has come into being – and something new, of which we don't know what it is but which we want. We are in a kind of interregnum, something similar to what the English lived post-1640 and the 'glorious revolution' of 1688, between the Stuarts and the House of Orange. That moment marked the end of the Middle Ages, transformed the patrimonial state of the classic, absolutist age, and established the bourgeois and capitalist phase of the modern world – the opening of modernity. Today we are living an age which parallels that of Harrington and the great theorists of the period of the interregnum, who thought that there was a kind of original myth one could draw on in order to organize the future. Thus I think that today there is this originary myth of a European republic that perhaps we might use in order to orient ourselves during this phase of transition.

At this point my reference is Spinoza, the only one who did not accept – ever – the theory of forms of government (invented in the classical era) as theory and practice of the management of the One – the unity of power. This One, this unicity, could be managed by a monarch or a prince; it could be an aristocracy or an oligarchy; it could also be a democracy, that is to say, a power of the many. But what was to be managed was always the One. The theory of power and of sovereignty was born before Jesus Christ, before Christianity, on this sole base and urgency of power: the management of the One. But only the European re-elaboration, democratic and deep, succeeded in going beyond this idea of a power which inevitably has to be a One. Democracy itself as a form of management of the One? To this idea Spinoza says: No, democracy is not this. True, there is a democracy which has this form: but the true political form in which we live, without which society would be impossible, is that which implies the multiplicity of singularities, and it is, therefore, the multitude that constitutes society and all the forms of consistency in society. This is the republic; not the third or the second or the first republic – or the fourth, the fifth, the sixth, the seventh, the eighth. We shall continue to have numbers of institutional republics, but the other republic, the republic after Machiavelli and many others, is the republic of the conflict of singularities with the aim of arriving at agreement, living together, in order to re-unite freedom and solidarity.

So this is old Europe, the Europe of humanism, the Europe of the Protestant Reformation, the Europe of class struggles, the Europe of the communism lived by people, the Europe which has proposed everything good on the horizon of life – that Europe which, as Kant said, invented the idea that man can desire the Good. And the desire for the Good is an experience that can be confirmed by history, 'by the revolution', said Kant – because this is something politicians never envisage, because politicians have always considered people to be bad. No, the republic thinks that people are good, that they have the ability to show, in political constitution, the metaphysical, ontological condition of our existence, in every history. Thus this republic pre-dates every political form and our life is only a continuous quest for this original scheme of existing-together.

Two elements constitute this idea of republic in old Europe. First, uprising and resistance, which constitute the singularity, and therefore the affirmation of freedom; second, the relationship which exists between these singularities, and hence cooperation and solidarity in production. One thinks, for example, of the idea of native country [*patria*]. As Machiavelli has shown and Kantorowicz very well picked up, the idea of *patria* in 'Old Europe' has no truck with national individuality: patriotism is rather the free transformation of solidarity, of love between persons. This has nothing to do with national individualization or related phenomena: national pride, chauvinism, imperialism and colonialism.

On the other hand, all the ideas of solidarity mean that the social is always within the political, that one cannot separate the political from the social, and that liberty and equality are absolutely bound together. To divide them is an absurd act of violence and force. We in Europe, however, have also lived the triumph of ideas concerning the constitutional division between the political and the social. This completely false idea of democracy has been exalted by the apology for the American constitution. However, we cannot forget how this orchestration was functional to the anti-communist struggle – which at the time was called anti-totalitarianism because, precisely in that situation, the unity between the political and the social was stigmatized as totalitarian. Hannah Arendt also fell into this game of constitutional mystification and plays on words, and she bears a heavy political responsibility. It is fundamental, on the contrary, to think of the relationships between the social and the political as being entirely within each other. However, even in the worst periods of European history – for instance during the Cold War, when European ideology was flattened on a certain neo-liberal American constitutionalism – also in those periods, in reality, those old drives and tendencies, those real and old tensions of European democracy were never ever lost. I think, for instance, that the European welfare state never entirely bowed to the rules of American constitutionalism – even of the best American constitutionalism, that of the New Deal. There has always been, through the strong presence of class struggle – in other words, of the solidarity and freedom interpreted by the proletarian forces – a living republican idea which has never allowed Europe to be reduced to classic liberal schemata. Now, I would not want to go too far in defending the European constitution, which is in the process of being created. However, I am convinced that, in this case too, the relationship between market and law inclines more towards law than towards the market.

Having said all that, what is this 'New Europe' which the American neo-conservatives are proposing to us? The paradox of this story, at bottom, comes from the fact that 'New Europe', according to the American conservatives, is still a product, a sub-product of old Europe; it is, at bottom, a dissolution of political ontology operated in the theories of the twilight of the West, fundamentally in Heidegger. This fascist Heideggerian idea is opposed to Spinozism, because, whereas in Spinoza we have a constituent power, in Heidegger there is a movement of being which, from the political point of view, is privative and nullificatory. *Potenza*, in Spinoza, is an expression of liberty and solidarity, as I said, in the cooperation of subjects. The subjective realization of liberty constitutes traces and elements which become increasingly strong, institutional and loving. The transition from desire to love – the transition from impulse, from appetite, to the real constitution of liberty – is possible at every moment, if the process is not blocked. In Heidegger exactly the opposite is the case. To every objectivation corresponds alienation and the void; the consistency of every signification becomes insignificant. The whole tension which traverses Kantian transcendental schematicism is, in Heidegger – because this is his problem, isn't it? – emptied out.

But we need to be attentive to the fact that, in the last fifty years, we have been, so to speak, sucked into a negative development of western thought. I said, for instance, how dangerous some aspects of Hannah Arendt are, for instance where she separates the political horizon of constitutionalism from the social horizon, from solidarity – the American Revolution from the French Revolution. But we could say the same of Benjamin and a whole series of writers who traverse, continually, our philosophical daily reality. This happens wherever there is a surviving conception of power which remains completely monolithic, classical, ancient, in other words which does not address the reality of the class struggle, of the multitude (in Spinoza's definition), and consequently of the alternative to the traditional forms of power. This limit of thought can be experienced in different ways. In Benjamin we find it in ways which are completely messianic; in other words, it is accepted in the hope that there is something on the other side. Or, in the whole Frankfurt School, and mostly in Adorno – among others – it has been seen in terms which are completely apocalyptic, where power occupies the entirety of all possible space and leaves no margins of liberty. No, power is never a unity, and much less a totality. Power is always interrupted by *potenza*, by the republic. The transcendental idea of power is nothing but the resonance of metaphysical unity. It is Plato, Aristotle, the great philosophical tradition. *Merde* on philosophy! We have the experience of the struggles which have traversed all of this, for all of our lives. This is the role of Europe: the memory and the experience of the continual breaking of this schema.

This is the basic starting point from which we can rediscover political ontology and, precisely, arrive at considering the meaning of this transitional period of interregnum in which we find ourselves. It is obvious that the development of capitalism was a raging and total development, and that this society has been completely – as the Marxists say – subsumed, in real terms, under the domination of capital. There is no longer use-value, there is only exchange-value; everything one does is entirely alienated by this formidable machine for the production and reproduction of power. But, precisely, the big problem is to understand how it is possible to introduce the sense of alternative, of rupture, of split within this horizon, of this new narration of the real. Some have described in perfectly clear terms the situation we find ourselves in. I am thinking, for example, of the writers of postmodernity, those I know best, from Vattimo to Rorty. Here too (I have in mind the Vattimo of today, the Vattimo who is currently mounting a huge self-criticism), there are philosophers who have, in their intellectual progression, achieved terribly equivocal results. Vattimo claims as justified, in his frustrated struggle of the 1970s, the attempt to disarm Marxism, to give up Marx to Marx, 'to weaken Marx', as he has recently stated; therefore to utilize Marx insofar as he interprets the relationship between the classes, but without loading him with the violence of Marxism. But in doing this Vattimo also disarms democracy. And in his attempt to remove all determination or teleology from Marxism, from the progressive conceptions of history, he has stripped all reason from resistance. One no longer knows why one should resist. In the attempt to weaken the tensions towards emancipation which were to be found in the thinking of old Europe, Vattimo has opened up to a conception of being in which the market becomes nature. From this he has deduced that emancipation had no *raison d'être* in the face of the *natura* of the market.

In effect, all this lasted for the brief space of an autumn. On the contrary, we have rediscovered in this present interregnum the violence of social relationships and the desire for resistance and liberation. Because *potenza* is something irresistible, the only natural thing. There is a little anecdote that I would like to share with you. De Tocqueville's *Journal*, June 1848. The de Tocqueville family is sitting in its beautiful apartment in the seventh *arrondissement* and from the other side of the Seine they hear the sound of cannon fire directed against the working class which, in that month, had risen up for the first time. A maid is serving at table. Everyone sitting at the

table is worried. But the maid is smiling. For this she is immediately
sacked, thrown out. In that smile, resistance was recognized: it is this
impossibility, this smile, this *potenza* which the de Tocqueville
family cannot accept, in the echo of the guns from the other side of
the Seine.

So we see that there is a blocked situation. There is capitalist power,
which has subsumed society, but there is also this resistance, that of
the workers' barricades, that of the maidservant's smile. How can this
resistance be represented in philosophy, today, against the 'New
Europe', against this schema of domination? Various strategies exist.
One, in particular, has been very important in recent years: to take
this subsumed and dominated world by starting from the margins,
from the edges; to try to attack this world and this block – of
insignificance or of equivocal significations – starting from the
outside. I would say that Derrida was a formidable motor of this strategy. However, Giorgio Agamben interests me much more, because he
has, so to speak, exasperated, rendered absolutely strong this way of
starting from the margins, of proposing *homo sacer*, naked life, the portrayal of the 'Muslim' in the concentration camps, the total negativity
that presents itself, as an alterity – as the only alterity that resists.
Behind discourses like that of Agamben lies the recognition that the
block of power is always traversed by a biopolitical weft, that life runs
through this and every block of life. Is this merely what Marx has said
– that it is necessary for capitalism to win, so that the contradiction
can be recognized at every level of the capitalist realization of the
world? Maybe it is – but not just. Here a new threshold of experience
has been introduced: the biopolitical. And it is this biopolitical dimension, that is, this presence of contradiction and opposition at all levels
of life, not only in the factory, not only in the relations of domination,
but in every aspect of life – it is this dimension that suggests the idea
that it may be possible to start from the the margin in order to intervene, in order to go back and to contest the complete structure of
capitalist development and capitalist domination.

However, there are other, far more meaningful and effective strategies: those that try to take as their starting point not the margins but
the centre. These are the strategies which were designated, in their
grand anticipatory effort, by Foucault and Deleuze, and which today
have become entirely actual. They allow us to glimpse the possibility
of recovering, starting from the centre of this unified and compact
world, all the *potenze* which emerge there, at the centre, out of every
transition. And in every transition there can be determined different
resistances, new figures of singularity. These can be put in line, one

with the other, and can construct sequences which are sequences of transformation. Diagrams, rhizomes and genealogies.

But what is a revolution, if we follow Foucault and Deleuze? Perhaps it is a metamorphosis; perhaps it is the production of a continually open subjectivity, which must nevertheless be determined. We are no longer in the situation in which 'weak thought' tried to use the exaltation of the surface, in Deleuze or in Guattari. That period is ended. We are in the interregnum. New figures of thought can be discovered, can be invented. And these new figures can only be constructed in the light of the fact that there is a rupture and that we no longer have the possibility of defining the categories of political thought and a political ontology in the form in which they have been defined for thousands of years. For this reason I am proposing to work on a new political dictionary, one that would define, for example, sovereignty – a sovereignty which is no longer One, but which is always in-relation – with new concepts. Perhaps we need to arrive at the foundation of non-being, so to speak, perhaps we need to fall in this hole, which is that of the One, of the unicity of power, in order to show that it is an illusion. The unity of power is false also from a phenomenological point of view, because this oneness, in the ensemble of conditions which today constitute society, can no longer being experienced, and much less theorized. There no longer exists a theory of the One; there exist only claims to unilateralism. But resistance is present there, always present. Around every corner there are shadows who come out and say 'no'. They can be agreeable or disagreeable; they can be for or against; but they are like de Tocqueville's smiling maid . . . There is no longer the possibility of theorizing unicity because the other thing has been affirmed and asserted ontologically: it is a new and irreducible desire for freedom and solidarity.

What is citizenship today? How can it be defined, if not precisely in this complete and continuous opening? And how can law be defined if not – here too – in the terms of these irreducible instances, these claims that the new ontological fabric of the singularities continually reopens? This is the new political fabric on which a new political dictionary must be organized. The great founder of modern political thought, Thomas Hobbes, passed precisely from a mechanicist conception of man to a conception of citizenship, to a conception of the Leviathan state, within a clear and continuous line: the line of possessive individualism. We have overturned this mechanism, because our critique has passed from the definition of the capitalist subsumption of the world – what we call Empire – to the recognition of an irresistible, singular, multiple, multitudinarian resistance. In other words we have recognized the impossibility of fixing resistance on the philosophy of individualism and sovereignty, because at its base we find an opening, the proliferation of singularity and difference, and new determinations of production and liberty.

Today we have a natural need for this entirely excedent force. In Hobbes's *Leviathan* individuality was constructed in a way which was complete and monolithic. We, on the other hand, find ourselves facing Empire. It, too, is corrupt and incapable of representing itself as justice. But we have recognized the central excedence of labour and solidarity: a singular, excedent and differing element which is at the basis of today's world. And perhaps herein lies the possibility of its transformation.

Recently I was in Madrid, just after 11 March and the fall of Aznar. The singularities had come together in that crisis and had recognized themselves as an enormous multitude, in which movement, the relationship between singularities, and the discovery of reality had become an expression of *potenza* – in two days, or rather one day and a night. There the world was in part transformed, by means of a real and actual uprising of difference.

33

The Actor and the Spectator: Immaterial Labour, Public Service, Intellectual Cooperation and the Construction of the Common*

When I received the invitation to take part in *Theaterformen*, I was writing a theatre piece myself. I was doing it as a bit of fun, with the idea of trying to give a more bodily form to various concepts that I was developing in philosophical, theoretical and abstract terms. I told myself, why not take these concepts – which I am constantly debating with myself, which sometimes I manage to master, but which sometimes leave me dazed and full of bruises – why not try to turn this clash of ideas into an art event? I wondered how a head like mine, which is forever thinking about ideas and studying collective material forces – how such a head might succeed in personifying the diagrams of suffering and of life, in rendering them concretely symbolic and immediately expressive. In the days when I was beginning to write my theatre piece I happened on Flaubert's *Temptation of Saint Anthony*. A remarkable text, in which the baroque of his imagination makes itself subjectivity and literature becomes theatre. Here something new was opening up: a theatrical construction could only be an adventure of subjectivity that invented the real. Theatrical representation is a material, objective excavation which produces reality from the subjective point of view. There is an ontological function of the author: this means that the theatrical text – if it wants to exist in its singular consistency – needs to succeed in constructing a new reality and in pulling together, in common, the minds of many people, within this new dimension.

---

* Talk given at the Theaterformen Festival, Hanover, 13 June 2004.

Now, this ontological function is taken up by the actor. If there was not this transmission of ontological power from the author to the actor, there would be no theatre, because the actor is the centre of the theatre and the intersection of all the transitions. It is the actor who – as a motor – effectively transforms the thought into action, the plot into something real. The further I progressed in the writing, the more I realized that, in order to write, I had to put myself in the position of the performer, to pretend to be the actor. Of course theatre can live without authors, but it can never live without actors. In the Commedia dell'arte and in all the Atellan comedies written and yet to be written, the author is subsumed, without problem and without uncertainties, in the actor; the decision of the actor understands the imagination of the author; every actor is a Paganini.

At this point, in this tangle of questions that I was setting myself, the piece was taken on by a theatre with a view to staging it. I was very happy. However, far from arriving at a resolution, the theoretical problems only began to multiply. Indeed, after having discovered that you can't write unless you yourself become the actor, and now finding myself to have the opportunity to represent my piece concretely, in a theatre, and having struck up with my actor a good fraternal relationship, I began to reason that the actor could not realize himself without making himself the public. Although you can have actors without authors, you cannot have actors without a public. So playwrights are really clever: when they write, they write as at least two people. But how remarkable is the actor! When he performs, he is acting for at least three sets of people: himself, the author, but above all the public – he is multitude. This is something new that is happening, something really sacred (that is how the Greeks saw it), or perhaps something comical (laughing, public laughter, possibly have some immediacy; certainly they represent the arcane heart of the sacred). This is also how the Romans and the giants of the Renaissance saw it. Yet we have to say again that there is an open relationship between vocation and destiny in the action of the actor, in his relationship with the author, but above all in this contact with the public – here the theatrical relationship is able to create itself as story, a representation (whether realistic, symbolic, fantastic or utopian) of ways of life, a tendency to a definition of the times, to the appropriation and expression of its spirit. From Romanticism to socialist realism, we have lived this becoming-destiny of drama.

1   What I have said thus far is intended simply to emphasize that the theatrical machine does not have an outside. It is a machine that

has only a centre, a 'Middle Empire' – just like China! By this I mean that theatre has to be seen as a temple of immanence: it creates every value and tells every story and determines every pronouncement within a magic circle which links the actor (or actor–author – Ruzante, Shakespeare and Molière, for instance) to the public. Whether sacred or comic, theatre is a ritual or game: 'the game of reality', as it has been called. In his analysis of theatrical language, Bakhtin, a student of Dostoyevsky, emphasized that language was (paradigmatically, as far as literature is concerned) carnivalesque ritual, and thus essentially a dual event. Theatrical dialogue pulls reality back (as does Carnival), towards a centre which has no outside, in a kind of voracity of dialogue, expressing an attempt to flatten and to draw every linguistic transcendental within the exclusive, complex, pregnant clarity of human praxis. Theatre is a practice of immanence. But what is a practice of immanence? It is simply the conviction that this world does not have an outside, that its construction and its necessity are entirely in the range of our experience. Finally, it is the concrete laboratory in which, in this condition, language, anthropology and ontology mix and merge, and in which imagination, history and labour, joined as one, are given full rein.

Now, you don't need to be a revolutionary or a materialist ideologue to recognize that this world does not have an outside. Postmodernism has generalized this awareness and has shown the truth of this statement. It has recognized in the world a unity in which the relationship between society and expressive phenomena has become circular: a unity where production and reproduction overlap, and circulation and reifications get confused. This world has become a vortex that sweeps everything into its logic, absorbing it. Capital has in real terms subsumed labour, society and life itself. What interests us is to define the passages – better, the geometric places and the algebraic tensions – within this vortex, which also is a space which seeks to be homogeneous. That theatre has always been a space is obvious to all. Perhaps the construction of this space has been the very prefiguration, the genealogy, of the growing awareness of the dimension of immanence. However, when one realizes that this immanence not only extends towards the edge of totality, but also presents itself as a lived fabric, one sees this space configuring itself as an open environment and as a dramatic structure of language: a network which is not only homogeneous but also multiple. A multiple intersection of singularities and nodes. You take the Bakhtinian dialogic flour and stir in the multiplicity of the voices of the world. This gives you a dough to which you will add the season's flavourings and the spices of the imagination. You put it all to cook and set it on the table with the requisite musics, scenery and visual effects – and there you have the construction of an event of dialogue, an ongoing and never-ending debate between subjects, the structure of one life or many lives, a machine which will continue to produce. A multitude.

So, when we speak of immanence, we are not speaking only of a space without an outside; we also find ourselves within the motor of movement. What does 'motor' mean for theatre? It means that this space without transcendence which theatre defines is a space of rupture and mobility; not a compacted reality but continuous cracks and splits, antagonisms, insoluble crises which have a direct effect on language and on the human, and show all this both as concept and as form of theatre.

So here we are, back again with the relationship between author, actor and public. Here it becomes a conflict. And an antagonism which passes not only between author, actor and spectator but also through each one of them. This multiple and proliferating conflict does not arrive at synthesis or mediations; it does not know gradualness, nor does it know conclusions. As Heiner Müller said, for there to be theatre, 'all that is human must become alien' – and this is what it becomes, always becomes. But when, on this basis, everything is alien, then everything is also common; and this common is not here because there exists a possible synthesis, or the proposal of a constructive dialectics; it is here because there continues to be a deepening and articulation of critiques and disjunctures. It is this absoluteness of antagonism that makes theatre the great logical and passion-involving dialogue it is. If the performance you have experienced is real, you will know it from the emotion or the disenchantment, the painful reasoning or those moments of resistance that you take with you as you leave the theatre. Just like when you read the great theatrical text which is Spinoza's *Ethics* – between theorems and footnotes you never get to heaven, but you do reconstruct the world in an inexhaustible interplay of passions.

2   Thus far (apart from the odd reference to postmodernity) I have been discussing theatre as something which forms an eternal practice of the human spirit. But epochs change, labour is transformed, the organization of society becomes revolutionized and

the construction of language assumes different functions and degrees of importance. When we use the term 'postmodern' we are referring to the cultural epiphenomenon of a transformation which, in our present time, has had a profound effect on reality itself, modifying labour, public space and forms of participation in it, and productive cooperation, and which has therefore redefined the common.

Let us start with the changes in the nature of labour. Today labour is above all immaterial, in other words intellectual, affective, relational and linguistic. When we speak of immaterial labour in all the richness of its meanings, we are speaking of a biopolitical reality: intellectuality and emotions, communication and passions, reason and body can here no longer be separated. This is the ensemble of things that labour mobilizes, turning intellectual innovation into (at the same time) the basis for the valorization of commodities and bodies (of bodily labour), and the physical fabric of the capacity for intellectual valorization of commodities. Life – all of life – has been set to labour, has become productive. What will it be, the theatre of these new subjectivities constructed by intellectual labour and by the biopolitics of affects and passions? What does theatre mean when, in postmodernity, that process – or rather that ensemble of relationships in move-ment which we have seen to exist in the theatre, as they exist between actor and public – becomes the very form of production? At this point, to speak of public space is to speak of these huge processes which put heads and bodies into a common relation, which spread and extend over all the relations of life. Public space (which is no longer civil society, which is no longer the outcome of individual actions, and which can no longer be market or con-tractual relationships either) – public space is rather this theatre of life. Everyone is an actor in it; the cooperation between the actors and the public, like invention-power and intellectual coop-eration, has become an ontological *potenza* in the fabrication of life. If there is no longer an outside, you no longer know where to turn except towards the within: you do it the way a swimmer does it, by diving into the water, or as a bird does it in the air which supports it. Public space is the precondition of our life, not the measure of its becoming or its expressive complement: it is the preliminary condition of common existing. So could theatre be thus defined as the consistent, ontological, productive and no longer ritual index of the new public space, and of this condition of existence?

3   Merleau-Ponty: 'In a general way, expressive gestures, where
    physiognomy sought vainly the sufficient signs of an emotional
    state, only have a univocal meaning when they are related to the
    situation they underline or punctuate. But, like the phonemes,
    without yet having meaning by themselves, they already have a
    diacritical value, they anounce the constitution of a symbolic
    system capable of redrawing an infinite number of situations.
    They are a first language. And, reciprocally, language can be
    treated as a gesticulation, which is so varied, precise, systematic
    and capable of so many duplications and conjunctions, that the
    internal structure of what is enunciated [*l'énoncé*] in the end can
    only pertain to the mental situation to which it corresponds and
    becomes the unequivocal sign of it. The meaning of language, like
    that of gestures, thus does not reside in the elements of which it is
    made; it is rather their common intention, and the spoken phrase
    is not understood unless the listener, following the "verbal chain",
    moves along each of the links in the direction in which, as a whole,
    they are pointing. From this derives the fact that our thought, even
    when solitary, never ceases from using language, which supports
    it, snatches it from the transitory, re-launches it – and is, as
    Cassirer, put it, its "flywheel"; however, language, considered
    part by part, does not contain its meaning, and all communication
    presupposes, in those who are the listeners, a creative taking up of
    what is heard. From this it also follows that language takes us
    towards a thought which is no longer simply ours, which is pre-
    sumptively universal, without this universality ever being that of a
    concept that is pure, identical in all minds. It is, rather, the appeal
    which a situated thought addresses to other equally situated
    thoughts, and to which each person responds with their own
    resources' (*Parcours deux*, 1951–61).
        Is this excerpt from Merleau-Ponty, this phenomenological
    rediscovery of language in theatrical form, sufficient to tell us what
    language is and to explain how the theatrical function has become,
    in postmodernity, implicit in the very figure of language? Perhaps
    Merleau-Ponty's statement is merely a paraphrase of the essays
    and theatrical work of the great Diderot. But it is a paraphrase of
    great amplitude, with a great hold on the future. Perhaps it is
    an anticipation. Certainly it is the indication of a model that
    does not seek to be exemplary and which will never be so;
    however, it is a track that crosses desert and forests and requires
    always to be redesigned or reconstructed. Through theatrical
    structure language becomes dramatic; in other words it finds that

of-the-moment intensity and that dialogic extension which is proper to the logical and passional *kairos*. Theatrical language invents the word, purveys it via the public performer, throws it into the space where the real ends and the future begins as a great bridge, which it extends over the void of what-is-to-come [*a-venire*]. The theatrical word is constructed in the same moment in which the common of life reveals itself as a proposal for the conquest of the future. In postmodernity, faced as we are with the end of every ideology and locked into the capitalist subsumption of society, this is the situation we have to address. (Furthermore, if we remain on the terrain of anticipation, is this not a clear intuition of Walter Benjamin's, when he writes: 'Revelation too must be heard, in other words resides in the metaphysically acoustic sphere'? For Benjamin, as Hannah Arendt points out, language was not at all primarily the gift of speech which distinguishes man from other living beings, but, on the contrary, 'the essence of the worlds from which speech is born'.)

4   So we are acting in common. Theatre? Theatre again? Certainly – theatre in its highest ontological and creative representation. The actor and the spectator stand there, in the reciprocal agitation of a moment of being. Hence agitation – in a sense which is historic and active. Actor and spectator are here two agit-props of a world to come, in which the relationship between the singularities, in the multitude, becomes ever closer in the search for the common, or, to put it better, in the unveiling of the common, because the common is the basis of the linguistic cooperation between subjects. The image which today can best describe the relationship between actor and spectator is that of the swarm, of a continuous coming and going of the figure of the person who is speaking: he is also the one who acts and transforms the world of the one and the other, carries it from one event to the other. The location in the swarm and the location in life are each time different, but the difference is what constitutes the network of alterity. What invests this kind of context is diagrams, transversal figures which are as rich and diverse as, for example, the patterns that the frost leaves on the windows of our houses in winter, or the wind leaves on the expanses of sand in deserts. However, it is neither cold nor aridity that characterizes those conditions as common, but rather the events which depict them. The relationship between actor and public is therefore immaterial labour, it is public space, it is intellectual cooperation, and above all it is the

construction of the common. Reactionaries have always thought that this relationship between actor and public, and also the one between author and actor (think of the frequent defence of the organic unity that a musical orchestra is supposed to represent), can only be defined in terms of harmony (in reality: discipline, subjection and repression, not to mention property rights, author's copyright in respect of the actors). From this point of view all reactionaries are Confucians (Hegel too is probably a Confucian), and dialectics is Confucian because it exalts synthesis and harmony through overcoming [*superamento*]. Now, dialectics resolves nothing. The public is not dialectical but creative. The common is discovered by the actor and by his public. But to the same extent that they create something of the common, the actor and the public clash and remain other: difference. There is no identification in the theatre. The footlights and the applause produce the same *dispositif* of difference: the former have the result of establishing continually the difference between the actor and the public; the latter, the difference between singularities in the theatrical common. Theatre will never have a figuration which is mystical and unitarian; it does not presuppose unities that are preconceived, or prefigured, or pre-existent. Theatre is a negative ascetics which, in the common, determines separation. Irreducible separation. And yet, a separation which is overflowing and productive. Every spectator can become actor, in the theatre even more so than in music; the common is repeated singularly in the experience of the spectator. The richness of expressive nuances on the actor's part is the basis of a communication that is always different, worthy of the swarm, and irreducible to that which the single subjects of the swarm construct or reproduce or express. Theatre becomes increasingly theatre in the degree to which it identifies, with great sincerity, the comic relationship (or tragic, and so on, but anyway dual) constituted by the public in its relationship with the actor. This is the richness of theatre, and this is its extreme fascination. Postmodernity exalts all this as the condition of common life. Theatre has a biopolitical function.

5   Theatre is a public service. Not only the little provincial theatres, not only the big metropolitan theatres, but also the multitude of actors and performing arts workers are a public service. The major experience of the struggles of the performing arts workers in France [*intermittenti dello spettacolo*] has also raised, beside the workers' needs of reproduction, the problem of the profession's

biopolitical function. What lies in store is a struggle which is long and tiring: the public will have to be not only the ally of the author and actor, but also their support; it will have to identify with the theatrical profession.

On the other hand, the performing arts worker [*lavoratore dello spettacolo*] is a person who has prefigured, and now fully enacts, the figure of the intellectual worker. In other words, the theatre worker has to be set alongside the scientific researchers, and teachers in schools, and workers in electronics, and with those who operate in the area of personal services. All this makes a lot of sense. But I would add that – compared with all the rest of immaterial labour which is today hegemonic in the production of goods and services, in other words in the setting to work of society – the theatre worker has a primary dignity. The performing arts worker has anticipated – in the comic translation of pleasure and in the tragic allegory of life, in epic tragedy and in the drama of realism – a model of knowledge management of the world and of cooperative construction of its concept. This anticipation, this prefiguration of the world hegemonized by immaterial labour honours this profession. Today, in the era of mass communication, in the face of the fetishistic homogenization of language, the theatrical niche is still the temple to which we go in order to seek and verify our desire for public. Woe betide anyone who seeks to attack, or deny, or simply weaken this function of truth – whose sacrality is immanent – this materialistic witnessing which the theatre always represents, because this centuries-long expressive experience has become a model for all the labour that produces wealth today. The actor makes himself public through the act of producing, and the the public multitude discovers itself as a network of actors. Singularity and difference play with the common under the same cover.

The struggles of the performing arts workers in France have shown us that theatre work is a public service; it should be supported, paid and reproduced, because it constitutes the very basis of the reproduction of this world of ours.

6   Now, to conclude, I would like to pursue some thoughts regarding the concept of the people, which in our discussions has often been deliberately confused or metaphorically taken as tantamount to the concept of public. Here I would venture to offer the critique of the concept of people and the definition of the concept of multitude, as they were outlined in Empire. 'People' is considered as

a construction of a unitary population on the part of the sovereign. In the people, in the age of modernity, the citizen is subjected [*suddito*], not a subject [*soggetto*]. 'Multitude', on the other
hand, is a concept born from below, as a multiplicity of singularities, as an ensemble which has no need for a sovereign mediation
in order to exist. Rather it is given as a *potenza*, as constituent
power, and, beyond the (individualist) private and/or the (statist)
public, the multitude produces the common. In the multitude,
citizens are not subjected but subjects.

It is clear that this concept of multitude develops a critique of
'democracy', when this is considered (along with monarchy and
aristocracy) as a 'form of government'. Machiavelli, Spinoza and
Marx, on the other hand, saw democracy as an alternative to the
modern conception of sovereignty – hence a theory no longer of
the one but of the many, not of the management of the one on the
part of the many, but of the self-management of the many against
the one. If you like, within this framework, democracy becomes
an always open relationship, a *dispositif* which is always in the
process of transformation, and an environment in which subjects
present themselves as militants.

It is clear that, in the tradition of modernity, in the theatre (and
in all the arts of communication), the public has been considered
in terms of the metaphor of the people. Not even the avant-garde
succeeded in modifying the formal relationship with the public:
they have broken the opacity of the public with extreme and revolutionary contents, but they have not resolved the problem of
a pre-constituted communicative duality. In the light of the
positions that have been advanced at this conference, the public
presents itself in a tight relationship with the author and the actor.
The public is not a people of subjected persons, but begins to be
a multitude of subjects. We must make a common in action out of
the public. From the theatrical point of view, we have to consider
the public as democratic militancy in action. Once again, the
theory of theatre presents itself as a paradigm which is critical of
the concepts of politics. Democracy cannot be representative, the
elected person cannot alienate the subject . . . here the actor is in
contact with his public, and the public with its actor, within a
community of differences, of actions, of militancy and of constitution. Theatre can teach us a democracy which is born from
below. In democracy, as in theatre, the spectator is a political
subject.

34
Real Time and the Time of Exploitation*

I am here to discuss the two essays contained in my *Time for Revolution* (published in English in 2003). The first essay was originally the introduction (written in 1981) to a series of texts which I had collected in the book *Macchina tempo*; the second was a piece written during 1997 and 1998 and published under the title *Kairos, Alma Venus, Multitudo*. Only chance – or perhaps providence – has brought together these two works, written more than fifteen years apart. As luck has it, this has come about thanks to Matteo Mandarini, who decided to create an editorial composite which even I consider entirely appropriate today. However, these are two pieces of research which developed each in its own way and with results which are not immediately compatible with each other.

The first essay, that of 1981, was an extreme attempt by me to go beyond the Marxist labour law of value. This was intended as a refinement of the studies conducted some year previously and published in my *Marx beyond Marx* (1979). What was the concept, or rather the thread, that ran through this study? It was as follows. Bearing in mind the hypothesis of the completion of the real subsumption of society by capital (this was the phenomenological statement which I took as my starting point), it seemed to me obvious that capital invested the world of production, but also and above all the world of social reproduction, in a totalitarian way. In asserting and developing this phenomenological perception, I was clearly relying on

* Talk given at the Faculty of Sociology, Goldsmiths College, University of London, 25 June 2004.

the work done by the Frankfurt School. Amplifying – but being in agreement with – the conclusions of the Frankfurt writers, I reached the conclusion that the 'real subsumption of society by capital' meant that temporality was the substance of productive existence. Therefore I added: at the same time, however, capital was forced to deny any possibility of determining measure to that temporality which was defined by the law of value – and in this I was going a long way beyond Frankfurt. A paradox and a formidable hypothesis: if social temporality constitutes the substance of production (the Heideggerian resonance of this statement are obvious), it is clear that the time-measure of exploitation loses any accurate capacity of dealing with reality: and this was a conclusion that anticipated postmodernity! But (such was the conceptual forcing which I allowed myself in that essay) at this point a completely different question needed to be posed: namely whether this transformation of temporality from measure of exploitation into weft or global fabric of society did not produce the generalization (over the whole social fabric) of the antagonism between command and production, dead labour and living labour. In the 1981 essay my answer to this question was in the affirmative.

The basis of this research, or rather its result, was soon transferred to the level of political activity, both as regards the periodization of the transformations of capitalism and as regards analysis of the technical and political composition of the working class. The consequences were extremely important; in particular, the prevailing (and tendentially hegemonic) historical subject was defined as the *operaio sociale* [socialized worker], understood to be different from the mass worker by being mobile, flexible and generic. There was a very clear break here in the continuity of the processes of transformation of the working class (theoretically justifiable given the ambivalence of the practices of the time).

However, the position developed in that first essay was very ambiguous. The intuition of the contradiction (antagonism) between dead labour and living labour, as extended to the entire reality of the world subsumed within capital, was developed around two axes of inquiry. The first was to emphasize, within the processes of transformation of the working class, the emergence of a new figure of living labour, which was different and increasingly powerful. This was therefore a process which involved the biopolitical ontologization of resistance. It was a big step forward in relation to existing Marxist theories, and also in relation to the critique which militant Marxism had developed up to that point. As a consequence of the fact that the resistance of labour power began to define itself at the level of both production and social reproduction, there emerged, in counter-position, a biopolitical horizon and a horizon of bio-power. A vast and solid terrain of resistance to bio-power was delineated.

Nevertheless, this first line of research was somewhat unsatisfactory. In fact it was conjugated with a second line, in which the new, ontological, inner, endogenous subjectivity ended up being, despite everything, defined in negative terms. As a result, this new and emergent subjectivity, rather than presenting itself as autonomous, independent and creative, ended up being locked into a kind of negative parallelism with the structure of bio-power. Although – on the abstract terrain of real subsumption – I had deepened the event of the division of the working-class productive force by capitalist bio-power, and had in some way anchored refusal and resistance in an endogenous way, I had still not grasped (in that first text of 1981) the ontological dislocation that the new definition of the subject and that of exploitation had determined in this transition. My reflections were hovering around an intuition that I was having difficulty putting into words. The fact is that it had to go beyond the terrain on which there was still the homology between power and *potenza*, on which – since we still had the powerful ideology of 'the seizure of power' – new, ambiguous relations and analogies were formed: between resistance and repression, between different conceptions of power, and, in the final analysis, between peace and war. It was necessary to redefine living labour as the creation of being. We had to rediscover the concept of labour: no longer simply as a force of production, but as general activity (intellectual, immaterial, relational, affective, linguistic), external to – and irreducible to – any dialectical dimension. If the only politics is ontology, the only temporality of this politics is the radical revolution of the relations of power: this seems to have been the conclusion of my own self-criticism.

It was in the second essay (written in 1997–8) that I tried to resolve this transition. I pursued various lines of thought. The first was an attempt to understand the relationship between the name and the event, between the concept and the history. In other words the problem is put at the ontological level, when one asks how, within reality, a concept, a common name, are borne – and why and where. This essay answered that the only valid epistemological terrain is that of a temporality rooted in resistance. In order to break the homology of domination and resistance, of power and *potenza*, it was necessary to root the concept outside of the mirroring which, in the classical tradition, the definition of these concepts presents, and in which they are characterized in universal terms. On the contrary, if the concept is implanted in reality, it defines itself as the common name of a series of events which intersect in resistant temporality: this is what concept is, this its life and its freedom.

But this was not enough. I therefore had to go further, to give continuity and articulation to the relation of the event (determined at the existential level) with the construction (the epistemology) of the common name. What was the inner key to these processes, what was the motor, the dynamics of the construction of the concept? If the event of the construction of the common name (which we call *kairos*) extends in a constructive historical process, how is its *telos* constructed, its purpose, its indefinite tension?

The answer to such questions has to be sought at the level of the biopolitics of general intellect, that is, on an ethical–cognitive terrain of which the figure of the network is the emblem. Now, if we take up this question with precision (I shall come to the question of networks shortly) and place ourselves on the ethical terrain, we will recognize that the dynamics of the teleological process determined by the *kairos* traverse dimensions and determinations that are quite concrete. These are poverty and love, the former as the motive cause and the latter as the final cause, forces which keep always open, and always reopen, the political process driving towards the common. When I speak of an ethical terrain I mean that the body is directly involved in the cognitive processes and, obviously, in the common tension of action. It is the body which becomes here the fundamental ethical element, the foundation of the dynamics of every historical process: and it is precisely the body that is traversed by poverty and love, wherein the former determines movement – the flight from poverty and the desire for a rich life – while the latter determines the ability to connect with others, to recognize these groupings as cooperative ensembles and thus to construct common dimensions of knowledge and of acting.

But here a further problem emerges, still in the effort to break the homology of power and *potenza*. Now, as a third stage, I had to take into consideration the tension established in the effort of the singularity to become common, in other words in the lines of articulation of the common, or, better still, in the perspectives of the constitutive process. Within these dimensions and articulations, what does the decision to be multitude represent? What is it that breaks definitively, not only from the epistemological point of view, and not even only from the ethical point of view, any homology between *potenza* and power? At the ontological level this decision could only be recognized by identifying the conditions in which a new world emerges. It is clear that this discourse maintains a fundamental materialist tension, not only immanentist, but corporeal. We have here a kind of summary of every battle against transcendentalism that has been conducted in modernity and in our era of postmodern anticipation of new revolutionary processes.

I can add that in this essay some fundamental concepts are articulated, or rather some methodological presuppositions which had emerged in my previous writings and were later to be developed in *Empire* and *Multitude*. These presuppositions can be summarized in three statements. The first is that this world has no outside; the second is that resistance is the motor of every historical development; the third is that the common goes beyond, destroys and reformulates both the private and the public. A fourth could be added: namely that the body and the common name have no basis except in acting, in the event determined by the action.

As you can see, during that fifteen-year period that I referred to, my various considerations of time had taken many and deeply divergent forms. But there was also a deep continuity in this process: a continuity which was rooted in the ontological autonomy of resistance.

35

A New Foucault*

QUESTION   Is the analytical work carried out by Foucault useful today in helping us to understand social movements and institutions? In the view of yourself and Hardt, in what respects might it need to be reviewed, adjusted or extended?

ANSWER   Foucault's writings are a strange machine. They make it possible to think of history only as present history. As Deleuze has already said, probably everything that Foucault ever wrote needs to be rewritten. Foucault is continuously seeking, describing and deconstructing, and he hypothesizes and imagines, constructs analogies and tells stories . . . But that is not his most important aspect. The important thing is his method, because it allows him to study and to describe the movement between past and present and between the present and the future. This is the method of a transition whose present is the centre. He is right in there, not between the past and future, but in that present which distinguishes between them. That is where the questioning process locates itself. With Foucault historical analysis becomes an action, knowledge of the past becomes a genealogy, perspective becomes a *dispositif*. For those who come from the militant Marxism of the 1960s (and I don't mean the dogmatic caricature traditions of the Second and Third Internationals), Foucault's point of view is correct, and in fact normal – it corresponds to the perception of the event, of struggle, and to the joy of taking risks outside of all necessity and of all pre-established teleology. In Foucault's thought,

---

* Talk given at the Research Institute of the Fédération Syndicale Unitaire (FSU), Paris, 11 June 2004.

yes, Marxism is dismantled – both as regards the analysis of power relationships and as regards historical teleology – as also are historicism and positivism; but at the same time it is reinvented and remodelled from the point of view of movements and struggles. To know is to produce subjectivity.

People have identified three Foucaults: in 1960s, the study of the formation of human sciences, that is, the archaeology of knowledge and the deconstruction of the concept of *episteme*; in the 1970s, the studies on the relationship between knowledge and power, on disciplinary forms and on the development of the concept of sovereignty in modernity; finally, in the 1980s, his analyses of the processes of subjectivation. Myself, I do not know if one can distinguish three Foucaults (or rather two – people often referred to two prior to the publication of his last courses); to me it seems rather that the three questions to which Foucault's attention was applied are continuous and coherent – coherent in the sense of a unitary and continuous theoretical production. What changes is probably only the specificity of the historical conditions and political necessities which Foucault has to confront. From this point of view, to assume a Foucauldian perspective is thus also something else: it is – in my language (and perhaps in that of Foucault) – to put a style of thought (what we recognize in the genealogy and production of subjectivity) into contact with a given historical situation, into contact with a specific dimension of domination, with the development of its relationships, in other words with that figure of capitalist development which sees command investing life and the relationships which reproduce life fully. Power has become biopower. In Foucault's discussion of capitalist development you will search in vain for the determination of the transitions from the welfare state to its crisis, from the Fordist to the post-Fordist organization of labour, or from Keynesian macro-economics to neo-liberalism; but in his pared-down definition of the transition from disciplinary regimes to regimes of control you will discover that postmodernity does not represent a withdrawal of the state from domination over social labour, but a further perfectioning of control over life.

In Foucault's writings this intuition is developed everywhere, as if the analysis of the post-industrial transition constituted the central element of his thought. The methodological determination, the theory of genealogy and finally the *dispositifs* of the production of subjectivity are unthinkable outside of the material determination of this present and outside of this horizon of transition. It is the transition from the definition of modern politics to that of postmodern biopolitics that Foucault implicitly theorizes here. The concept of politics – and that of action, from the biopolitical context – separates itself radically in Foucault from the conclusions of Max Weber and the twentieth-century epigones of the conceptions of power of modernity (Kelsen, Schmitt and others). One should also note that Foucault had probably flirted with them – but after 1968 the picture changes radically and Foucault himself unveils what was implicit in its thought.

Thus there is nothing that needs to be updated or adjusted: we need only to extend Foucault's intuitions in relation to the construction of subjectivity. The struggles of minorities that Foucault, Guattari and Deleuze supported around the 1970s, for instance the struggles in the prisons, construct a new relationship between knowledge and power. And this means not only prison relations, but the entire framework of the development of subversive powers. As for the *dispositif* of the production of subjectivity, it can probably be understood in the perspective of a process which is constitutive of a new order, in which individuals are replaced by networks and constellations of singularity and multitudes.

Foucault is not only great for the work of deconstruction he did or for the work of reconstruction he undertook. He created a new framework of theoretical possibilities arising out of new material determinations of reality, out of the transformation of the productive and revolutionary context.

QUESTION   Would you agree that in France there has been a certain setting-aside of Foucault's analyses by currents which are intent on renewing social and political critique, and that this is also happening in the rest of Europe (in particular in Italy) and in the United States?

ANSWER   Academia hates Foucault. First they shunned him, then they promoted him to the Collège de France in order better to isolate him. When Foucault was not hated he was isolated. Sociological positivism *à la* Bourdieu, which of course is much more generous in its political inclinations, proves incapable of intersecting with Foucault's thought and its exponents prefer to denounce what they see as the latter's subjectivism. This, however, is a false accusation: there is no subjectivism in Foucault. Indeed transcendentalism is precisely what Foucault always refuses, in every aspect of his work – in other words, philosophies of history which do not accept locating determinations of reality within the network and within the clash of subjective powers. By transcendentalism I mean, in short, all conceptions of society which believe that they can evaluate or manipulate society from an external, transcendental and authoritarian point of view. This is not permissible. There is only one method which allows us access to the social: it is that of absolute immanence, of the continuous invention of signifying constellations and *dispositifs* of action. Like other important writers of his generation, Foucault is here definitively settling his accounts with the last remnants of structuralism – that is, with the transcendental fixation of epistemic categories which structuralism prescribed (today this error is being renewed in the revival of naturalism . . .). But, beyond the clash at the level of method, Foucault is also rejected (particularly in France) because he does not allow his critique to be subjected to the mythologies of the republican tradition. There is nothing more remote and inimical to him than sovereignism, even where it is Jacobin in nature; than unilateral secularism, even where it is egalitarian; than traditionalism in the conception of the family and patriotic demography, even where it is integrationist, and so on. But then, people object, when all is said and done, Foucault's methodology is nothing more than a reproposition of that historicist, relativist, sceptical point of view which we have seen all too often, as a degeneration of an idealistic conception of history. No, and no again. Foucault's thinking, asserting the ideological point of view, reconquers the rich revolutionary contents of that European and American thought which had freed itself from the modern tradition of the nation–state and socialism. A proposition which was far from being sceptical or relativist, but which was constructed instead on the exaltation of the *Aufklärung*, of the reconstruction of man and his democratic *potenza*, after every illusion of progress and common reconstruction had been betrayed by the totalitarian dialectics of modernity. Each of us is guilty of this: national socialism is a pure product of the dialectics of modernity. Freeing ourselves from it is a step forward. The *Aufklärung* – Foucault reminds us – is not a utopian exaltation of the lights of reason. On the contrary, it is dystopia, it is daily struggle around the event, around the 'this here', around questions of emancipation and freedom. Would you see Foucault's battle around the issue of the prisons, conducted with prison groups such as the GIP (Groupe d'Information sur les Prisons) in the early 1970s, as relativist or sceptical? Or his battle to affirm the right to revolution of the Iranian people, against the USA and the international oil companies? Or the position he took in support of the Italian autonomy movement during the most difficult moment of the repression and of the 'Historical Compromise' in Italy?

In France Foucault has often been the victim of a mystification by his students. Anti-communism has played a key role here. The methodological rupture with materialism and collectivism has been presented as support for neo-liberal individualism. Foucault was OK as long as he was deconstructing the categories of dialectical materialism, but he was not OK when he was reconstructing the categories of historical materialism. When the system of Foucauldian genealogies and *dispositifs* then opened into the freedom of the multitudes, the construction of common goods, and a deprecation of and contempt for neo-liberalism, lo and behold, his students took their leave. Perhaps for them Foucault died at just the right time.

In Italy, the USA, Germany, Spain, Latin America and Britain, we do not have this perverse Parisian game, geared at eliminating Foucault from the intellectual scene. Foucault has not been subjected to the deadly ideological *querelles* so common among the French intelligentsia, but is simply valued on the basis of what he says. The analogy with the tendencies engaged in the renewal of Marxist thought from the 1960s onwards can therefore be taken as fundamental. However, this is more than just a coincidence of epochs: we have seen rather that Foucault's thinking lies midway along the road between the experience of emancipation and that of liberation, in the interconnection between ethical–political and epistemological concerns. European workerists and American feminists in particular have found in Foucault an orientation for research and, above all, an encouragement to transform their particular jargons into a common and perhaps universal language for the twenty-first century.

QUESTION   In *Empire* you and Michael Hardt wrote that 'the biopolitical context of the new paradigm is completely central to our analysis'. Can you explain to us the relation (which in our view is not immediately obvious) between the new imperial forms of power and bio-power? Is it fair to say that, despite your debt to Michel Foucault (a debt which you often acknowledge), you are also critical of him? You write that Foucault failed to understand the 'real dynamics of production in biopolitical society'. What do you mean by that? Are we to deduce that Foucauldian analyses lead into a kind of political impasse?

ANSWER   Regarding *Empire*, I shall try to clarify what Michael Hardt and I have taken from Foucault and where we express criticism. In speaking of Empire we have not tried just to identify a new form of global sovereignty beyond the nation–state. In addition to examining this tendency, we have tried to grasp the material causes – both political and economic – of this development, and at the same time to define the new fabric of contradictions which has necessarily been brought into being. For us, in Marxian terms, capitalist development (including the extremely developed forms of the world market) is based on transformations in, as well as in contradictions of, the exploitation of labour. What transforms the political institutions and forms of capitalist command is the struggles of workers. The process which led to the hegemonic affirmation of imperial rule is no exception: after 1968, with the great revolt of waged labour in the central countries and the revolt of the colonial peoples, capital finds that (on the economic, monetary, military and cultural terrain) the movements of labour power can no longer be controlled within the framework of the nation–state. The new global order is a response to the need to order a new world of labour. The capitalist response takes shape at many levels: the fundamental terrain, however, is that of the technological organization of labour processes. These become automated in industry and informaticized in society: the political economy of capital and the organization of exploitation come to be developed increasingly around immaterial labour; accumulation comes to be based on the intellectual dimensions of labour, and on its spatial mobility and temporal flexibility. Power thus comes to invest the whole of society and the lives of people (and also, above all, intellectual activity). Marx (in both the *Grundrisse* and *Capital*) had perfectly foreseen this development, which he called the 'real subsumption of society within capital'. Foucault, for his part, also documented this historical transition when he described the genealogy of the way power extended its grip over life – both individual life and social life. But the subsumption of society in capital (as also the totalitarian vocation of bio-power) is far more fragile than we are allowed to see (by capitalism, but also by the objectivism of the heirs of Marxism – the Frankfurt School for instance). In reality, the real subsumption of society (that is, of social labour) in capital generalizes the contradiction of exploitation over every level of society; in the same way as the totalitarian self-assertion of bio-power opens the biopolitical context of society to rebellion and to the proliferation of freedom, and therefore to the production of subjectivity. When capital invests the entirety of life, life itself is revealed as resistance.

So this is where Foucault's thematics of bio-power and our analysis of the genesis of Empire intersect: namely at the point where the new forms of labour and struggle (produced by the multitudes of immaterial labour) are discovered as a production of subjectivity. Note that, for Michael Hardt and myself (I do not know if Foucault would agree here), the production of subjectivity means moving within a biopolitical metamorphosis which opens towards communism. In other words

I think that the new imperial condition in which we live (and the socio-political conditions in which we construct our labour, our languages and therefore ourselves) places the common at the heart of the biopolitical context. Not the private or the public, not the individual or the social, but the common – that is to say, the whole of what all of us, together, construct for the reproduction of man. So there are a thousand roads that link the creative review of Marxism (of which we are a part) to the revolutionary conception of biopolitics and to the production of subjectivity elaborated by Foucault. One thing is clear, however: in Foucault the interest in the economic factors of development and in the critique of political economy is much less deep than his interest in the study of all the other conditions and activities of development. A suspicion arises: is it possible that, following the tradition of the old French clerics, Foucault (measuring himself against Marx) said to himself: '*Larvatus prodeo*'?

QUESTION   Foucault's two late works on the modes of subjectivization seem to have attracted your attention to a lesser degree. Could one say that the construction of styles of life and ethics that are different from, or resistant to, bio-power is a road far too removed from what you are proposing (namely the figure of the communist militant)? Or are there deeper possibilities of coincidence which we have not perceived?

ANSWER   From what I have said thus far, it should be clear that Foucault's last works have been as influential on me as his earlier works. If you will permit me a slightly curious recollection: in the mid-1970s I was waiting to see which way Foucault would turn. At that time I was in Italy, writing an article on him (on those works which someone was later to call the 'first' Foucault). I had noted the structuralist limitations, and I was hoping for a step forward, a stronger stress on the production of subjectivity. For my part, in that period I was trying to move out of a Marxism which, although it was deeply innovative at a theoretical level (was a Marx beyond Marx possible?), was risking lethal errors at the level of militant practice. By this I mean that in that period, the years of passionate and extreme struggle that followed 1968, and in the situation of ferocious repression that right-wing governments were exercising against the movements, many of us ran the danger of taking a terrorist turn. Now, what underpins extremism is always the conviction that there is only one power, that that power is singular, that bio-power is homologous and homologates both Right and Left – the present power and that of the future, even if it were to be revolutionary: this is what led to the desperate terrorist reaction. Foucault, together with Deleuze and Guattari, put us on guard against this kind of view. They were revolutionaries. When they criticized Stalinism and the practices of 'real socialism' they were not doing so in hypocritical and pharisaic ways, like the 'new philosophers' of liberalism; rather, they were asserting that it was possible to express a new 'power' of the proletariat against capitalist 'bio-power'. So resistance to bio-power and the construction of new styles of life were not so far removed from the figure of communist militancy. As in Empire, the figure of the communist militant was not based on old models – on the contrary, the communist militant was seen as the production (ontological and subjective) of struggles for liberation from labour and for a fairer society.

Foucault's last writings are of exceptional importance. They outline a 'strong' figure of political intervention in life (and therefore a radical experience of being itself) and a laboratory of transformative praxis. Genealogy here loses every weak feature; epistemology becomes 'constitutive', ethics assumes 'transformative' dimensions. After the death of God we were seeing the rebirth of the human; on the ruins of the teleology of modernity we are rediscovering a materialistic *telos*.

36
Postmodernity or Contemporaneity?*

Thank you for your question. In replying I shall perhaps be slightly contentious, but it is worth it. The contemporaneity of which you speak raises the question: what does it mean to be contemporary between modern and postmodernity?

If we survey the cultural history of recent years, we find that we have been immersed (in general terms) in a construction of the concept and of an experience of postmodernity that saw itself as being in direct line of descent from modernity, in other words as a heightened form and sublimation of the characteristics of modernity. The Frankfurt School in particular has been the source of many misunderstandings and gross mystifications in the construction of this linear configuration – 'hyper-modern' (as it has sometimes been defined), and sometimes catastrophic – of modernity, which has developed a despairing sense of our destiny and a deep pessimism, albeit always self-critical, derived from a certain 1920s brand of Marxism. These conceptions, with their characteristic similarities, have led to the ideological construction of a notion of 'hyper-modernity' rather than to a realistic vision of the emergence of postmodernity and a recognition of the 'radical break' that this has entailed.

As has often happened with heretical positions in Marxism, the concept of 'tendency' [*tendenza*] has come to be used in teleological terms, as if it referred to some necessity. In fact the opposite is the case. The concept of tendency, already as it appears in Marx, is a concept of rupture, division and discontinuity. The tendency is never dialectical, let alone reconciliative. It reveals objective contradictions

* Videoconference at the Mellon Foundation, Pittsburgh (Penn.), 15 November 2004.

of development which combine and interweave with the subjective *dispositifs* of the class struggle, through a complex interplay of transformations of the material conditions of consciousness.

This line of thinking is paradoxical and tragic: it has created a situation in which the critico-catastrophic lines (from Lukács to Adorno, passing through Benjamin) and the critic–reactionary lines in defining notions of capitalist development and the imperialist state (from Max Weber to Carl Schmitt) end up by coinciding. The Heideggerian synthesis has an easy time of it.

The fact is that postmodernity, when defined as a theory of the real subsumption of society within capital, shows how this subsumption is not linear in relation to modernity, but antagonistic. Antagonistic in relation to modernity and contradictory within itself. Contemporaneity (as the two of you understand it) is within postmodernity, where postmodernity is understood as a context of forces which are not only new and attracted within global circulation, but also innovative and antagonistic. To be contemporary – and hence to take on board the historical upheavals which have marked the course of the twentieth century and the counter-reformation which is under way today (if the comparison were not too flattering, we could describe Bush as a 'hyper-modern' Cardinal Bellarmino) – will therefore mean defining postmodernity as a break with modernity, a break within which the antagonism between the old and the new, between reaction and innovation, is expressed in radical terms.

In more recent debates (and especially in the debate which has developed in cultural studies and in the countries of so-called underdevelopment), the categories of modernity have often been strongly counter-balanced by anti-modernity. In this case too, modernity, in its construction and in the step forward it represents, went hand in hand with a definition which was linear, rigid and technological: the development model, whether capitalist or socialist (we should never forget that socialism always had the skeleton of capitalism in its cupboard), prevailed.

But might 'another' modernity exist? A modernity that did not seek to be – or, better, that was not constructed as – either a return to archaic methods of accumulation or a reproduction of static definitions of (eurocentric and western) values, but which created alternatives in the development and materiality of existing social and political forms? A modernity which did not hark back to paradigmatic and utopian 'use-values' but raised the problem of living different kinds of lives and of transforming the world starting from the maturity of its productive dimensions and from the firmly established modes of commodification of this society of ours? This debate has been particularly lively in a number of developing nations (China, India, Latin America). However, the weight of a postmodernity which was rigid and fixated on eurocentric or western models of continuity with modernity has often neutralized efforts to construct 'other' ways of being – or, better still, to find within development alternatives which might not be determined, constrictive and pretextually held to be necessary but might instead be free, inventive and original. (Permit me here to cite as an example the great debate in China between the end of the Cultural Revolution in 1976 and the Tiananmen Square massacre of 1989, when those who were being repressed were not the defenders of western civilization but those who were seeking an alternative, an original mode of development within underdevelopment and beyond it.)

We need to remember that similar debates developed in the classical age of the genesis of modernity, between the 1500s and the 1700s. The terrain of antagonism was at that time identified as a terrain of the expression of the ontological *potenza* of the multitude. In that case too, against the logic of the capitalist centralization of power expressed by Hobbes, we had the logic of liberation expressed by Spinoza and by many other antagonistic tendencies in modernity. This alternative often repeats itself within the debates and struggles of developing societies. No equilibrium and no new hope can be found if one does not break with the teleology of modernity, in other words with the command imposed by Hobbes and capitalist transcendentalism.

When people argue for the concept of 'contemporaneity', I wonder whether what they are really trying to do is find a shorthand for the breaking of the teleological paradigm of modernity. If that is what is happening, then theories of 'contemporaneity' are very welcome, but they will have to take as their basis the breaking of the paradigm of modernity, the opening of a bundle of new possibilities which are founded on a different potential of resistance and difference.

In other words, when we speak of contemporaneity, we have to address it as a terrain of antagonism. But why is this antagonism powerful? Here we need to stress, first, that this antagonism has nothing to do with that described in modernity in the old days, because it implants itself on a new social, economic and political fabric: on a fabric which is biopolitical.

When I use the phrase 'biopolitical fabric', I mean on the one hand that capitalist power has invested social relations in their entirety; at the same time, this fabric is considered as a historical reality

inhabited by new subjects and by new social and political configurations. The Empire is a biopolitical reality; in other words it
is not simply a new capitalist organization of labour but an ensemble
of forces which inhabit it and express the *potenza* of life. An all-impor-
tant ensemble of bodies, a surface of passions.

Contemporaneity is a concept which one will be able to construct
and to propose usefully only if one addresses it within the transition
from modernity to postmodernity, and thus within the 'contemporary' transition from the bio-power of modernity to the biopolitical of
postmodernity, from the invasion and colonization of existence by
power to the antagonistic dimensions and powerful contradictions of
the biopolitical fabric.

Several consequences follow from this.

1   The biopolitical fabric is that on which the antagonisms (between
    invention and exploitation) of labour have been made social.
    When we say social, we mean that the paradigm of labour (or,
    better, of productive activity) in becoming immaterial and coop-
    erative, invests the entirety of society. Now, the capitalist invasion
    of society, society's subsumption within capital, is accompanied
    by and contradicted by the transformation of the paradigm of
    labour. Modern bio-power was disciplinary, postmodern bio-
    power is a power of control.

      Our deconstruction of modernity thus invests the material con-
    ditions of the totality of existence (in the modern period) in order
    to reveal postmodern contemporaneity as a fabric of new contra-
    dictions.

      When we say that the social composition of contemporaneity no
    longer has anything to do with that of modernity, this innovative
    transformation has to be identified at the level of labour. Thus the
    decisive elements are the transition from the mass worker to the
    socialized worker, from material labour to cognitive labour, and
    the transformation of the processes of construction of value from
    the time-measure of labour to the construction of new, innovative,
    excedent figures of value. Here new technologies (new technologi-
    cal structures and new machines) and new social composition inter-
    weave. This is a decisive leap. As we said above, the description of
    postmodern contemporaneity brings into being a new periodization
    of historical development. The change in the nature of labour and
    of technologies involves anthropological mutations. But at the same
    time – and this is the true meaning of the new historical periodiza-
    tion – such processes are not simply technical, and they are not

simply anthropological (if anthropology refers to the individual): they are 'social transitions' which bind together the transformation of the human being with that of social cooperation. Labour becomes linguistic in its very mode of expression; it is cooperative, not simply inasmuch as it implies cooperation but inasmuch as it expresses cooperation. In other words, it brings about cooperating innovation and produces continuous excedence of significations.

2   In the philosophy of postmodernity we have witnessed a long and laborious philosophical path, which has tried to approach the event of the rupture of continuity and of the teleologies of modernity. It is perhaps worth recalling three broad lines of this development.

The first is that inaugurated by the French theorists of post-modernity when they insisted on the complete circularity of the process of production of goods and subjectivity: weak thought [*il pensiero debole*], aesthetic conceptions of life, Marxist heresies of a mode of production which is by now completely dominated by capital and therefore uncontrollable and beyond measure, heading for catastrophe – all of this reshaped the terrain of analysis. But at the same time it neutralized it. (Between Lyotard and Baudrillard it is hard to say who has done most in this direction.)

A second line is the one which has tried to deconstruct this context (because it recognized it exactly as neutralized and insignificant), so as to locate a breaking-point: the 'marginal' point of a real rupture which might allude to another form of existence, or at least to an ability to renew its significations. This line developed its potentiality with force and intelligence from Derrida to Agamben. But the breaking-point was and remains marginal, the fields and horizons within which this attempt of overturning took place are extreme and become difficult to traverse, because they are fragile and open to passages which cannot be experimented and which have tendencies to extremism. Here theoretical critique wins against practical reconstruction: the problem is recognized, but a solution is lacking.

The third line is that of Foucault and Deleuze: a line of strong production of subjectivity, at the centre of the process of constitution of the real, rooted in a resistance to absorption into the world of the production of commodities. This conquest of a creative ontological point (or, if you prefer, of a 'point of difference') is fundamental: this difference, this resistance, this production of subjectivity, located at the heart of the metropolis, at the centre of culture, at the heart of intellectual and affective exchanges, at the centre of linguistic and communicative networks – in short, this centre which is everywhere – well, it is from this point on that an ontological alternative, not desperate but constructive, can develop.

3   When we shift to the biopolitical terrain, labour becomes social activity and vice versa. Social activity is a part of general intellect. But in the biopolitical context general intellect is also eros: this means, obviously, that in contemporaneity becoming-anthropological is a process of pragmatic and intellectual, affective and somatic singularization. The production of subjectivity is accompanied by an affective and somatic singularization. Thus, when we say general intellect, we are referring to that set of relational and cooperative, affective and ethical activities which metaphysically have been called eros. To take just one example: the processes of artistic innovation (from Cézanne to Beuys) can point the way for the reconstruction of this new ontological compact of matter and spirit. Spinoza spoke of it as a synthesis of complexity and ingenuity. Between material labour and immaterial labour, between production of goods and production of services, labour power invests the totality of life experience and discovers itself as social activity. Living labour, and thus the construction of value, presents itself as excedence. Let us now look at what this means.

4   The control over technological development by capital and by the state, in answer to the struggles and resistance of workers and citizens (of worker–citizens), is developed essentially through the attempt at the reappropriation of social cooperation, and thus of the dissolution of the common of life, and thus in a colonization of affects and passions, in a continuous commodification and financialization of the ambits of resistance and antagonistic cooperation.
    However, increasingly manifest *dispositifs* of resistance exist and are expressed. Today the expression of living labour is, as I said, directly 'productive excedence': hence it is (on the anthropological terrain) a production of subjectivity and (on the political terrain) a production of democracy.

We are coming close to the end . . . We cannot entirely jettison the category of postmodernity: it has allowed us to identify – beyond those conceptions which saw postmodernity as purely and simply a capitalist invasion of life – a terrain of power, antagonism and struggle. Postmodernity has given us the possibility to imagine contemporaneity as an environment of the production of subjectivity; it has allowed us to discover, within the totality of subsumption, the continued existence of antagonism. An ethical *potenza* which is entirely immanent.

Thus we have the concept of multitude taking us back to contemporaneity. It is true that, when we speak today of multitude, we sometimes find ourselves in an ambiguous situation: we define it as a multiplicity of singularities, but this multitudinarian reality is inserted within the antagonistic context of postmodernity. We say that the multitude is capable of a recomposition of the sensible; we further assert that the figure of imagination is capable of innovation and, vice versa, that innovation is able to constitute a fabric capable of imagination. However, the multitude is presented to us within a frame which is catastrophic. There is nothing terroristic in this statement, nothing to be scared of: but neither is there anything messianic in it. I only want to stress that the emptying of meaning of the capitalist development finds as its alternative (as the alternative to catastrophe) the *potenza* of the multitude. For this reason, the multitude presents itself today as a figure of the eventual recomposition of the contemporary sensible in the catastrophe. It poses itself as a liminal figure between bio-power and biopolitics; better, between *pouvoir* and *puissance*. Might one at this point re-propose, as did the English in the 1600s, a violent figure of antagonism between power and multitude?

I would define contemporaneity in Spinozan terms – as a path which extends between the natural *conatus* towards cooperation and the *amor* which constructs sensible dimensions of social, institutional and democratic process; as a cooperative opening of living labour and of every movement of renewal. The 'contemporary' has to be related back to the antinomy of postmodernity, that is, to the new figure of the contradiction which is configured in postmodernity, between capital and labour, between power and life: living in postmodernity, not as utopia but as 'dys-utopia' (a pragmatic tension which traverses the real contradictions, able to review its contradictory content, not to go beyond it, not to dream beyond this, but to transform the existing state of things), can be understood as a struggle to reconquer the meaning of contemporaneity – dystopia is the contemporary *dispositif* of the collective will to resolve (in revolutionary ways) the contradictions of postmodernity, in other words to have done, for ever, with the capitalists and all bosses. In Spinozan terms, one might say that contemporaneity is the only way to express humanity's eternal desire for resistance and liberty.

Lightning Source UK Ltd.
Milton Keynes UK
UKHW022016180522
403195UK00011B/2060